International Political Economy Series

Series Editor: **Timothy M. Shaw,** Visiting Professor, University of Massachusetts Boston, USA and Emeritus Professor, University of London, UK

The global political economy is in flux as a series of cumulative crises impacts its organization and governance. The IPE series has tracked its development in both analysis and structure over the last three decades. It has always had a concentration on the global South. Now the South increasingly challenges the North as the centre of development, also reflected in a growing number of submissions and publications on indebted Eurozone economies in Southern Europe.

An indispensable resource for scholars and researchers, the series examines a variety of capitalisms and connections by focusing on emerging economies, companies and sectors, debates and policies. It informs diverse policy communities as the established trans-Atlantic North declines and 'the rest', especially the BRICS, rise.

Titles include:

Ernesto Vivares, Cheryl Martens, Robert W. McChesney (*editors*)
THE INTERNATIONAL POLITICAL ECONOMY OF COMMUNICATION
Media and Power in South America

Leslie Elliott Armijo and Saori N. Katada (*editors*)
THE FINANCIAL STATECRAFT OF EMERGING POWERS
Shield and Sword in Asia and Latin America

Md Mizanur Rahman, Tan Tai Yong, Ahsan Ullah (*editors*)
MIGRANT REMITTANCES IN SOUTH ASIA
Social, Economic and Political Implications

Bartholomew Paudyn
CREDIT RATINGS AND SOVEREIGN DEBT
The Political Economy of Creditworthiness through Risk and Uncertainty

Lourdes Casanova and Julian Kassum
THE POLITICAL ECONOMY OF AN EMERGING GLOBAL POWER
In Search of the Brazil Dream

Toni Haastrup, and Yong-Soo Eun (*editors*)
REGIONALISING GLOB AL CRISES
The Financial Crisis and New Frontiers in Regional Governance

Kobena T. Hanson, Cristina D'Alessandro and Francis Owusu (*editors*)
MANAGING AFRICA'S NATURAL RESOURCES
Capacities for Development

Daniel Daianu, Carlo D'Adda, Giorgio Basevi and Rajeesh Kumar (*editors*)
THE EUROZONE CRISIS AND THE FUTURE OF EUROPE
The Political Economy of Further Integration and Governance

Karen E. Young
THE POLITICAL ECONOMY OF ENERGY, FINANCE AND SECURITY IN THE UNITED ARAB EMIRATES
Between the Majilis and the Market

Monique Taylor
THE CHINESE STATE, OIL AND ENERGY SECURITY

Benedicte Bull, Fulvio Castellacci and Yuri Kasahara
BUSINESS GROUPS AND TRANSNATIONAL CAPITALISM IN CENTRAL AMERICA
Economic and Political Strategies

Leila Simona Talani
THE ARAB SPRING IN THE GLOBAL POLITICAL ECONOMY

Andreas Nölke (*editor*)
MULTINATIONAL CORPORATIONS FROM EMERGING MARKETS
State Capitalism 3.0

Roshen Hendrickson
PROMOTING U.S. INVESTMENT IN SUB-SAHARAN AFRICA

Bhumitra Chakma
SOUTH ASIA IN TRANSITION
Democracy, Political Economy and Security

Greig Charnock, Thomas Purcell and Ramon Ribera-Fumaz
THE LIMITS TO CAPITAL IN SPAIN
Crisis and Revolt in the European South

Felipe Amin Filomeno
MONSANTO AND INTELLECTUAL PROPERTY IN SOUTH AMERICA

Eirikur Bergmann
ICELAND AND THE INTERNATIONAL FINANCIAL CRISIS
Boom, Bust and Recovery

Yildiz Atasoy (*editor*)
GLOBAL ECONOMIC CRISIS AND THE POLITICS OF DIVERSITY

Gabriel Siles-Brügge
CONSTRUCTING EUROPEAN UNION TRADE POLICY
A Global Idea of Europe

Jewellord Singh and France Bourgouin (*editors*)
RESOURCE GOVERNANCE AND DEVELOPMENTAL STATES IN THE GLOBAL SOUTH
Critical International Political Economy Perspectives

Tan Tai Yong and Md Mizanur Rahman (*editors*)
DIASPORA ENGAGEMENT AND DEVELOPMENT IN SOUTH ASIA

Leila Simona Talani, Alexander Clarkson and Ramon Pachedo Pardo (*editors*)
DIRTY CITIES
Towards a Political Economy of the Underground in Global Cities

Matthew Louis Bishop
THE POLITICAL ECONOMY OF CARIBBEAN DEVELOPMENT

Xiaoming Huang (*editor*)
MODERN ECONOMIC DEVELOPMENT IN JAPAN AND CHINA
Developmentalism, Capitalism and the World Economic System

Bonnie K. Campbell (*editor*)
MODES OF GOVERNANCE AND REVENUE FLOWS IN AFRICAN MINING

Gopinath Pillai (*editor*)
THE POLITICAL ECONOMY OF SOUTH ASIAN DIASPORA
Patterns of Socio-Economic Influence

Rachel K. Brickner (*editor*)
MIGRATION, GLOBALIZATION AND THE STATE

Juanita Elias and Samanthi Gunawardana (*editors*)
THE GLOBAL POLITICAL ECONOMY OF THE HOUSEHOLD IN ASIA

Tony Heron
PATHWAYS FROM PREFERENTIAL TRADE
The Politics of Trade Adjustment in Africa, the Caribbean and Pacific

David J. Hornsby
RISK REGULATION, SCIENCE AND INTERESTS IN TRANSATLANTIC TRADE CONFLICTS

Yang Jiang
CHINA'S POLICYMAKING FOR REGIONAL ECONOMIC COOPERATION

Martin Geiger, Antoine Pécoud (*editors*)
DISCIPLINING THE TRANSNATIONAL MOBILITY OF PEOPLE

Michael Breen
THE POLITICS OF IMF LENDING

Laura Carsten Mahrenbach
THE TRADE POLICY OF EMERGING POWERS
Strategic Choices of Brazil and India

Vassilis K. Fouskas and Constantine Dimoulas
GREECE, FINANCIALIZATION AND THE EU
The Political Economy of Debt and Destruction

Hany Besada and Shannon Kindornay (*editors*)
MULTILATERAL DEVELOPMENT COOPERATION IN A CHANGING GLOBAL ORDER

International Political Economy Series
Series Standing Order ISBN 978–0–333–71708–0 hardcover
Series Standing Order ISBN 978–0–333–71110–1 paperback
(*outside North America only*)

You can receive future titles in this series as they are published by placing a standing order. Please contact your bookseller or, in case of difficulty, write to us at the address below with your name and address, the title of the series and one of the ISBNs quoted above.

Customer Services Department, Macmillan Distribution Ltd, Houndmills, Basingstoke, Hampshire RG21 6XS, England

---

The International Political Economy of Communication

Media and Power in South America

Edited by

Cheryl Martens
Head of Research, Universidad de las Américas, Ecuador and *Senior Lecturer, Bournemouth University, UK*

Ernesto Vivares
Research Professor, Facultad Latinoamericana de Ciencias Sociales (FLACSO), Ecuador

Robert W. McChesney
Gutgsell Endowed Professor, University of Illinois, USA

Foreword by

Ernesto Laclau

palgrave
macmillan

First published 2014 by
PALGRAVE MACMILLAN

Palgrave Macmillan in the UK is an imprint of Macmillan Publishers Limited, registered in England, company number 785998, of Houndmills, Basingstoke, Hampshire RG21 6XS.

Palgrave Macmillan in the US is a division of St Martin's Press LLC, 175 Fifth Avenue, New York, NY 10010.

Palgrave Macmillan is the global academic imprint of the above companies and has companies and representatives throughout the world.

Palgrave® and Macmillan® are registered trademarks in the United States, the United Kingdom, Europe and other countries.

ISBN 978–1–137–43467–8

This book is printed on paper suitable for recycling and made from fully managed and sustained forest sources. Logging, pulping and manufacturing processes are expected to conform to the environmental regulations of the country of origin.

A catalogue record for this book is available from the British Library.

A catalog record for this book is available from the Library of Congress.

In memory of Ernesto Laclau

Contents

Foreword

Gabriel Tarde (1843–1904) provides a subtle but important twist on the analysis of mass society found in the work of Gustave Le Bon (1841–1931). For Le Bon (1896), the constitution of *masses* as historical agents, presupposes a process of homogenization of the actors intervening in it. The differentiation and individualization of the social roles and demands had to be replaced by a non-differentiation of those roles and demands: In becoming part of a mass, the agent experiences a loss of individuality and can be replaced by any other similar actor. Tarde (1903) questions the possibility of giving universal validity to the mass phenomena as described by Le Bon. In his analysis, the notion of 'masses' is replaced by that of *publics*, which entails a more complex articulation between differentiation and homogeneity. 'Publics' – as different from crowds – are not gathered in a single space; public opinion is more diffuse and does not exclude diversity. In this transformation, for Tarde, there are two decisive changes: The development of new means of transportation – especially railways – and the diffusion of the press, which in the second half of the nineteenth century becomes a massive feature of the new society. Needless to say, in our digital era, those features have become a universal phenomenon of our civilization and the locus of a political confrontation, which has acquired increased relevance in defining the social antagonisms of our time.

It is to this aspect that the essays collected in this volume are devoted. I would like in this Foreword to concentrate on two dimensions, which, I think, have particular importance for our understanding of politics. The first concerns the complexity of the interaction between homogenizing and differentiating logics, which Tarde started visualizing in his pioneering work. In our analysis, this has become the distinction between *equivalence* and *difference*, which points to two radically diverse ways of constructing the social. The first involves an essential substitutability of social positions, all of which converge around a paradigmatic pole. The second, on the contrary, presupposes a proliferation of syntagmatically differential points, and moves in the direction of institutionalism. Le Bon's picture of modern society was a pessimistic description in which social differentiation is radically eroded by a homogenizing movement in the direction of a mass society. Tarde's vision was more sophisticated, and his conception of 'publics' combined equivalential and differential logics in ways that announces many aspects of the societies in which we are still living.

Many of the chapters in this volume refer to 'populism', and I want to say a few words concerning this notion in connection with the general issue that we are discussing. 'Populism' is not an ideology but a way of constructing the political, consisting in dividing society into two camps and interpellating those at the bottom of the social pyramid, the underdog, against the existing power. As such, the populist dimension can be present in discourses of the more diverse ideology, from the Right or from the Left. In terms of the distinction that we were establishing before, populism would put emphasis on the logic of equivalence over the logic of difference, which, on the contrary, would dominate in more institutionalist types of discourse.

There is here, however, a difference between populism and the analysis in terms of mass phenomena *a la* Le Bon. In terms of the masses as described by Le Bon, all differentiation disappears, and we have a totally homogeneous group, only responding to the charismatic appeal of the leader. In the case of populism, on the contrary, there is equivalence between a plurality of demands, so that the internal differentiation of the group is maintained. What happens, however, is that differentiation is weakened through the inscription of the actors' demands in the equivalential chain. We have thus a continuum: At one pole of it we would have, reduction ad absurdum, the purely undifferentiated mass described by Le Bon; at the other extreme, we would have a totally institutionalized system in which the different actors and demands are entirely heterogeneous with each other – which is also, of course, an impossible extreme. In the actual world, political systems always oscillate between both extremes, combining in different proportions equivalential and differential logics – that is, fluctuating between populism and institutionalism.

This stress in the internal differential moment within equivalential chains is important for political analysis for a variety of reasons. Firstly, it shows that the unity of the popular camp is always a *constructed* unity, with nothing natural or spontaneous about it. The operation through which a 'people' emerges is a hegemonic operation. But, secondly, this hegemonic operation always takes place in a terrain in which the duality equivalence/difference is already cutting across identities and institutions. With regard to institutions, it is crucial to understand that they are never neutral, but represent the crystallization of relations of force between groups. That is, institutions express moments in 'war of position' to use Gramsci's (1971) words. It is not that groups are previous to institutions but, rather, that the building up of institutions is the way in which the unity of a group is achieved. So constituting the identity of a group and bringing about new institutional frameworks are dimensions of the same hegemonic operation. That is the reason why, when new social forces try to bring about fundamental social changes, they necessarily clash with the existing institutional arrangements. Corporate power will defend *à outrance* a purely institutionalist outlook, which represents the existing status quo.

The constructed unity of the group – of a 'people' in the case that we are discussing– means that plurality of social and political demands has to be brought to some kind of unity. In an era in which there is a proliferation of points of social ruptures and antagonisms, this articulating/hegemonic moment acquires an increased centrality. This is why the debates concerning the democratic control of the media have become so crucial. As several essays in this volume make clear, it is impossible to ensure a democratic functioning of society if the monopoly of information is in the hands of a small number of corporate groups that own most of the press and radio and TV channels. Laws passed recently in Argentina and Ecuador try to limit this monopolistic power. It is necessary not only to call for the promulgation of similar laws in other Latin American countries but also to stimulate a wider discussion and information about the way in which corporate power in the media operates and how biased information contributes to give a systematically distorted version of what is happening in various national contexts and, more generally, in the international scene. This is what makes the publication of this present book so timely.

Ernesto Laclau
London, April 2014

References

Gramsci, A. 1971. *Selections from the Prison Notebooks*, edited and translated by Q. Hoare & G. Nowell Smith. New York: International Publishers.

Le Bon, G. 1896. *The Crowd: A Study of the Popular Mind*. New York: The MacMillan Co.

Tarde, G. 1903. *The Laws of Imitation*. New York: Henry Holt & Company.

Acknowledgements

This volume began as a result of collaborations which took place at the International Conference 'Media, Power and Citizenship', organized at FLACSO Ecuador in May 2012. We thank Adrian Bonilla of FLACSO for his unwavering support for research in this area from the outset and Timothy Shaw, IPE series editor for his enthusiasm and encouragement in bringing the ideas presented here to a wider audience.

We are very grateful to each of our contributors whose reflections demonstrate the richness of using multiple approaches in the analysis of media and power in the international political economy. We are especially indebted to Ernesto Laclau, whose support and reconceputalization of populism has been fundamental to this project. His posthumous contribution included here is his last piece of writing on populism. We would like to thank Chantal Mouffe for her approval of the final version of the Foreword in Ernesto's absence.

We thank our colleagues and students at FLACSO Ecuador, Universidad de las Americas in Quito and Bournemouth University for their encouragement and engagement with many of the ideas presented here. We would especially like to thank Liosday Landaburo Sánchez and Liudmila Morales Alfonso.

In addition we would like to acknowledge the high level of professionalism of Christina Brian, Ambra Finotella and Flora Kenson at Palgrave Macmillan.

Finally, we would like to extend our thanks to our children, and families for putting up with this and the many projects related to this book.

Contributors

Mauro Cerbino coordinates the Department of International Studies and Communication in FLACSO-Ecuador. He has lectured in Ecuadorian, Latin American and European universities. He has a PhD in Urban Anthropology. He has written books and academic articles on media and power, political communication and youth studies.

Diana Coryat is a communications scholar and media practitioner. She is an associate researcher in the Department of International Studies and Communication in FLACSO-Ecuador. She is currently pursuing a doctoral degree in Communications at the University of Massachusetts Amherst. Her fieldwork is on the reconfiguration of media power in Ecuador.

Roberto Follari is Professor of Epistemology and Social Sciences at the National University of Cuyo, Mendoza, Argentina. He holds a BA and PhD in Psychology from the National University of San Luis, Argentina. He has lectured to postgraduates at a majority of universities in Argentina and has also lectured in Chile, Uruguay, Ecuador, Venezuela, Spain, Costa Rica and Mexico. His work has been translated into English, German, Galecian, Italian and Portuguese. He has authored 18 books in Social Sciences and Philosophy. His most recent work includes *La selva académica* (2008) and *La alternativa neopopulista* (2010).

Pablo Gasloli is Professor of Arts in the Faculty of Philosophy and Arts, University of Buenos Aires, Argentina, and Professor of Communication and Media in the Department of Visual Arts, Instituto Universitario Nacional de Arte, Buenos Aires. He is also a researcher in the University of Buenos Aires Science and Technology Project (UBACYT) project entitled 'Cinematographic Practice and Audiovisual Communication in the Digital Era', funded by the Secretariat of Science and Technology in the Institute of Research, Gino Germani, Faculty of Social Sciences, University of Buenos Aires. He is also a founding member of the editorial board of the journal *Mancilla*.

Ximena Gonzalez Broquen is Researcher and Coordinator of the Center for the Study of the Social Transformations, Sciences and Knowledge at the Instituto Venezolano de Investigaciones Científicas (IVIC), Venezuela.

She holds a PhD in Philosophy and Political Studies from the Ecole des Hautes Etudes en Sciences Sociales (EHESS), Paris, France. Her work focuses on communication, power and participative democracy.

Arne Hintz is Lecturer at the School of Journalism, Media and Cultural Studies at Cardiff University, UK. He previously worked at McGill University in Montreal and the Central European University in Budapest. His research connects communication policy, media activism, citizen media and technological change. He is Chair of the Community Communication Section, and Vice-Chair of the Global Media Policy Working Group, of the International Association for Media and Communication Research (IAMCR). He has a practical background as journalist, media activist and communication rights advocate. His publications include *Civil Society, Media and Global Governance* (2009) and the co-edited volume *Beyond WikiLeaks: Implications for the Future of Communications, Journalism and Society* (2013).

Marcia Maluf is a Visiting Research Professor at FLACSO-Ecuador. She is currently completing her doctoral thesis at the National University of San Martin in Argentina. She has a BA in Psychology and a Master's in Social Sciences from FLACSO-Mexico. She has researched the impact of communication and new technologies on education and examined the conflict between President Rafael Correa and media groups in Ecuador.

Cheryl Martens is Head of Research at the Universidad de las Américas, Quito, Ecuador and Senior Lecturer in the Media School at Bournemouth University, UK. She holds a PhD in Sociology from the University of Manchester, UK and has lectured at universities in Argentina, Ecuador, Slovakia, Japan and the United Kingdom. Her research and publications concentrate on the sociology and political economy of communication and media policy. She is co-editor of *Strategies for Media Reform: International Perspectives* (forthcoming).

Robert W. McChesney is the Gutgsell Endowed Professor in the Department of Communication at the University of Illinois at Urbana-Champaign. He is the co-founder of Free Press, a national media reform organization (www.freepress.net). His work concentrates on the history and political economy of communication, emphasizing the role media play in democratic and capitalist societies. McChesney has written or edited 27 books, which have been translated into 31 languages. He co-edits, with John Nerone, the *History of Communication Series*.

David McQueen is Lecturer and Programme Director for the Media and Politics Degree in the Media School at Bournemouth University, UK. He has been teaching on media courses since 1991. His PhD research focused on the BBC TV *Panorama* programme's conflict coverage and the Westminster Consensus.

Carolina Matos is Lecturer in Media and Communications at the Department of Sociology, City University London. She was previously a part-time lecturer in the Government Department at Essex University, UK. Former Fellow in Political Communications at the London School of Economics (LSE), Matos obtained her PhD in Media and Communications at Goldsmiths College and has taught and researched in the United Kingdom in political communications, Brazilian media and politics at the University of East London (UEL), St. Mary's College, Goldsmiths and the LSE. With 20 years of professional experience both as a journalist and academic, Matos has many articles in journals and has worked as a full-time journalist in Brazil for *Reuters, UNESCO, Folha de Sao Paulo, Tribuna da Imprensa* and *Globo.com*. Matos is the author of *Journalism and Political Democracy in Brazil* (2008) and *Media and Politics in Latin America: Globalization, Democracy and Identity* (2012).

Isabel Ramos is Professor of Communications in the Department of International Studies and Communication, FLACSO-Ecuador, where she coordinates the master's program. She has published academic articles on the relations between communication, collective action and mass media. She is currently working on a research project entitled 'Communication and Collective Action at the Ecuador-Colombia Border'.

Susana Sel has a PhD in Anthropology from the University of Buenos Aires, Argentina, where she is a Professor in the Department of Communication and directs a number of research projects. She is a researcher and lectures in Communications at the Instituto Universitario Nacional de Arte in Buenos Aires. She was the coordinator of the working group on Media and Communication in Consejo Latinoamericano de Ciencias Sociales (CLACSO) (2004–2010) and member (2011–2013) since the debate on media regulation in Latin America. She has also been involved in the Coalition for a Democratic Communication since 2004, and was a member of Coordinating Committee during the debates concerning the creation of the Audiovisual Communications Law number 26.522.

Katherine M.A. Reilley is Assistant Professor of Global Communications and Social Justice in the School of Communication at Simon Fraser University in Vancouver, Canada. She is the co-editor of *Open Development: Networked Innovations in International Development* (2013) and publishes in the areas of international and development communication with a focus on Latin America. She is currently working on two projects: a digital textbook on the history of community media in Canada and a research project that examines Latin American media reform from a regional and international point of view.

Ernesto Vivares is Research Professor in the International Relations and Communications Department, FLACSO-Ecuador. He has a PhD in International Political Economy from the University of Sheffield, UK. His work focuses on the political economy of South American regionalism and development. Recent books include *Financing Regional Growth and the Inter-American Development Bank* (2012) and *Exploring the New South American Regionalism* (2013).

Abbreviations

AAPEBCAP	American Association of Bolivarian Journalists, Chapter of Panama
ADEPA	Association of Argentine Journalism Entities
AFTA	American Task Force Argentina
AGD	Deposit Guarantee Agency
ALAI	Agencia Latinoamerica de Información (Latin American Information Agency)
ALBA	Bolivarian Alliance for the Americas
AMARC	World Association of Community Broadcasters
ANMCLA	National Association of Free and Alternative Community Media
ARPA	Argentine Private Broadcasters Association
ARPAS	Association of Participatory Radios and Programs
ATA	Argentine Broadcasting Association
ATVC	Argentine Cable Television Association
BANDES	Bank of Economic and Social Development of Venezuela
CADAL	The Center for the Opening and Development of Latin America
CAFTA	Central American Free Trade Agreement
CEO	chief executive officer
CLACSO	Consejo Latinoamencano de Ciencias Sociales (Latin American Sociales Sciences Board)
CLOC	Latin American Coordination of Rural Organizations
CMFE	Community Media Forum Europe
COMFER	Federal Broadcasting Committee
CONADE	Consejo Nacional de Desarrollo (National Development Council)
CONARTEL	*Consejo Nacional de Radio y Televisión* (National Council of Radio and Television)
CONATEL	National Telecommunications Commission
COSECCTI	Working Group on Culture within the South American Council on Education, Culture, Science, Technology and Innovation
COSIPLAN	South American Infrastructure and Planning Council
COSUCTI	South American Council on Science, Technology and Innovation
CPJ	Committee to Protect Journalists
CRD	*Coalition for a Democratic Broadcasting*
CSC	South American Council on Culture

CTV	Confederation of Workers of Venezuela
ECTV	Ecuador TV
EU	European Union
FA	Frente Amplio
FC	Federal Communications Commission
FLACSO-Ecuador	Facultad Latinoamericana de Ciencias Sociales Sede Ecuador (Latin American Faculty for Social Sciences – Ecuator)
FM	modular frequency
FTAA	Free Trade Area of the Americas
GDP	gross domestic product
GESAC	*Governo Eletronico Servico de Atendimento ao Cidadao* (Electronic Government Service to Assist Citizens)
IACHR	Inter-American Commission on Human Rights
IAPA	Inter American Press Association
IFF	International Freedom Foundation
IGF	Internet Governance Forum
IMF	International Monetary Fund
IMMI	Icelandic Modern Media Initiative
IPE	international political economy
ISDB	digital television standard
IT	information technology
ITC	International Telecommunications Union
JUNAPLA	*Junta Nacional de Planificación y Coordinación Económica* (National Board of Planning and Economic Development)
LED	Liberty of Expression and Democracy
LOC	*La Ley Orgánica de Comunicación* (the Organic Communication Law)
LSE	London School of Economics
MAS	Movement Toward Socialism
NAFTA	North American Free Trade Agreement
NGO	non-governmental organizations
NIEO	New International Economic Order
NWICO	New World Information and Communication Order
PPP	Plan Puebla Panama
PSDB	*Partido da Social Democracia Brasileira* (Social-Democratic Party)
RMR	Radio Mundo Real
RPE	*Radio Pública Ecuador* Public (Radio of Ecuador)
RWB	Reporters Without Borders
SENPLADES	*La Secretaria Nacional de Planificacion y Desarrollo* (National Secretary of Planning and Development)
SMEs	small radio and television entrepreneurs

RESORTE law	Law on Social Responsibility on Radio and Television
MINCI	Ministry of People's Power for Communication and Information
OECD	Organisation for Economic Co-operation and Development
PR	Public Relations
PT	Worker's Party
TSE	Supreme Electoral Court of Justice
TV	Television
TWFD	Television Without Frontiers Directive
UBACYT	University of Buenos Aires Science and Technology project
UK	United Kingdom
UN	United Nations
US	United States
UNASUR	Union of South American Nations
UNESCO	United Nations Educational, Scientific and Cultural Organization
WEF	World Economic Forum
WSF	World Social Forum
WSIS	World Summit on the Information Society
WTO	World Trade Organization

Introduction

Cheryl Martens and Ernesto Vivares

Over the past decade, the rise of populist democracies in South America has taken place against a backdrop of growing corporate media opposition and the polarization of views concerning media power in the region. The battle between governments and private media, state and corporate power, is a question, however, which goes well beyond the borders of South America. At the heart of this debate is the public's right to balanced sources of information. For some, the debate revolves around the freedom of speech (IAPA 2011), whilst for others, this struggle is a result of civic movements (Waisbord 2009a) and a quest for new development strategies, impacting on the political economy of the region (Martens and Vivares 2013).

The dynamics of media across Latin America are complex and closely related to questions of international political economy (IPE) and the global politics of unequal development (Payne 2005). The current volume focuses on the case of South America in relation to IPE, where media corporations, in many cases, have come to play the role of political opponents (Follari, this volume). The legitimacy of the governments of Bolivia, Venezuela, Argentina, Ecuador and, to a certain extent, Brazil, Paraguay and Uruguay has been questioned, not by elected oppositional political parties, but by media conglomerates, which share the economic interests of many of the most powerful economic sectors. Defending limited notions of the concept of the freedom of speech, promoting neoliberal paradigms of development, mainstream media corporations in the post-dictatorship years of the 1980s and 1990s grew accustomed to influencing public opinion in effort to set national and regional agendas, with large sectors, producing heavily biased information, favouring particular groups (Matos 2008).

As Fox and Waisbord (2002) point out, both local politics and globalization have impacted on the development of media systems in Latin America. In South America, in particular, civil society actors and developmentalist governments have come into direct conflict with mainstream media. In contrast to free market views that democracy is best served by unlimited media ownership, governments across the region argue that the freedom of speech should not equate with the freedom for corporate power to define the development agenda of the country. For the media corporations that oppose media reform, the return of state, in one of the most socio-economically unequal regions of the world, is contaminated by left-wing neopopulism and out-of-date and failed politics. This conflict, as this edited collection highlights, revolves around debates concerning freedom of speech and new democracies in South America and intertwined with the dimensions of media, power and regionalism in a changing world order.

Following social demands and calls for reform from civic movements, states across South America have confronted, to varying degrees, corporate media power. This has sometimes further entrenched existing divides and played out in the debates and the revision of legislation on media ownership and communication services. This includes Argentina's adoption of a law on Audiovisual Communication Services in 2009; Ecuador's recently passed Communication Law in 2013; Bolivia's promotion of the General Telecommunications, Technology and Communications Law in 2011; and debates concerning community media law and the widening of the law for the social responsibility of television and radio in Venezuela in 2004.

This book is the result of discussions held at an international conference on media, power and citizenship held at FLACSO-Ecuador (Facultad Latinoamericana de Ciencias Sociales Sede Ecuador [Latin American Faculty of Social Sciences – Ecuador]) in 2012 between academics, journalists and media reform activists. The contributions here, however, seek to reflect on media and power beyond the conflict between neopopulist–developmentalist governments and private media corporations. Considering a range of debates and case studies, looking beyond the politics of freedom of expression, it is important to ask to what extent this conflict involves more substantial change? For this reason, it is particularly important to consider the issues within a new political economy of media and development, examining the way in which new democracies are fighting to solve decades of market crises and political instability through substantive democracies.

This collective project set off with pluralist and critical aims, the main purpose being to highlight some of the valuable lessons that have come out of the media reforms taking place in South America over the past ten years and to begin to connect these lessons to wider media reform issues and other regions. The chapters and the case studies presented here consider how South America is facing this challenge, demonstrating the possibilities as well as the complexities involved in creating a more diverse and democratic media landscape and the strengthening of civil society.

A secondary aim of this collection is to broaden methodological and theoretical approaches to media and power, bringing IPE and media activists and scholars based in South America into discussion with scholars and activists in other regions. Given the current global concern with questions of media and democracy (Charles 2013), the book seeks to draw out theoretical discussions concerning the connections and parallels between regions, to demonstrate how the efforts to reshape the media landscape in South America can inform media reform discussions internationally.

The book considers three main dimensions of the political economy of media and development in South America: Part I – Media Power and Democracy in the International Political Economy; Part II – The Politics and Cultural Practices of Media and Power in South America; and Part III – Regionalism and the International Political Economy of Communication.

The first part focuses on the analysis of media, power and democracy in IPE and seeks to relate the current media–government conflict in South America to the cases of the United States and Europe, exploring the core relation of media–government conflicts, including debates concerning democracy and media power. In Chapter 1, Robert W. McChesney considers current media battles in relation to traditional democratic theory and the role of news media in advanced capitalist nations. Drawing on examples from the field of US journalism, McChesney highlights the flaws of US-style professional journalism under capitalist management, pointing out the need for nations to construct a credible popular independent news media for the digital age.

McChesney argues that at the heart of the battle over media reform are the media corporations, which have traditionally advocated a politics representing their own interests, becoming hostile to popular reforms and democratization, impeding the effective functioning of a democratic political system. McChesney argues that this is the case of the US-style media–government relations, where 'free press' theory stipulates that freedom of the press means letting the rich dominate the news if they can buy it up, and dominate the politics of a nation, over and beyond public legitimacy. In the United States, argues McChesney, 'the solution is often to ask monopoly owners to introduce a more professional journalism'. The author points out that the alternative of implementing censorship or monitor the news media content closely and shutting down the discontents does not provide a better solution.

Drawing on the history of US media, McChesney's chapter highlights how, for example, public subsidies for news media have been useful in broadening political participation. McChesney argues, 'The future of news media is to be nonprofit, noncommercial and decentralized, in any number of forms, with public funding but no government control'. McChesney views that this is a difficult path for South America progressives to follow, given the power of reactionary forces, and concludes that the state must also demonstrate a toleration for dissent.

In Chapter 2, bringing South American media reform debates into conversation with current calls for media reform in the United Kingdom, David McQueen argues that the case of media reform in South America provides significant lessons for ongoing media policy debates in Europe, particularly in the areas of corporate control of the mass media, public service broadcasting and debates concerning 'deregulation'. McQueen's chapter presents a broad survey of the reform laws from a range of South American countries and considers their policy relevance for Europe in general and the United Kingdom in particular.

McQueen argues that the international struggle for democratic media reform consists of corporate oligopolies on the one hand and political power games on the other. The author highlights how media reform efforts in Argentina and Ecuador have been fiercely opposed and beset by allegations of violation of 'freedom of press'. However, the author also points out that media laws, many of which have been in place since the military dictatorships of the 1970s, require reform to overcome obstacles that have historically undermined democratic journalism and opportunities for civic expression and engagement. Drawing on recent UK media reform debates, the chapter argues that efforts to reform the press in the United Kingdom have also met with fierce resistance in the name of freedom of the press, echoing many of the concerns surrounding the concentration of media power and political control in South America.

For McQueen, the complex and heterogeneous media reform process in South America is of policy relevance for Europe as the different laws in the region have dealt with obstacles that have historically undermined democratic journalism and opportunities for civic engagement. According to the author, the lessons from these efforts help us to understand the value of supporting the diversification of media ownership, strengthening the participation of civic organizations, the promotion of community radio and other small media and freedom of information and transparency in the use of public and private services, all of which strengthen the dynamics of democracy in Europe. In McQueen's view, a more democratic and plural media requires engagement by media reformers with a broad range of stakeholders against the narrow interests of corporate or political elites.

In Chapter 3, Arne Hintz argues that community and non-profit media are increasingly significant components of the political struggles taking place in South America. Drawing on case studies from South America and Europe, Hintz's chapter considers the role of community media in the media environment globally, as well as international trends towards legislation and third-sector involvement.

According to the Hintz, the focus on community broadcasting has been particularly significant in South American media reforms. Hintz discusses the role that civil society groups and citizen networks have played in policy reforms, the role of citizen-based policy change and the importance of international connections and policy diffusion. This chapter also problematizes the concept of policy hacking and considers the overlaps and limitations facing community media in relation to policy reform movements in South America and internationally.

Part II brings together a range of empirical case studies by South American scholars, journalists and activists, which focus not only on power struggles over media, but also on their role as transformative forces for public engagement. Beginning with a case study of the conflict between corporate media and the government in Ecuador, Mauro Cerbino, Isabel Ramos, Marcia Maluf and Diana Coryat historicize the relationship between the Ecuadorian government and the media in Chapter 4, examining how this has been reflected in the state's policies and institutional framework. The chapter also establishes how, in a mediatized society, political governability is conditioned by the corporate media and shaped government actions. Using Ernesto Laclau's conceptual framework of populist rupture, which is characterized by the dichotomization of social and political space, the chapter analyses the relationship between the Correa government and the private media in Ecuador. The authors argue that these entities are at odds with each other and engaged in a fight for public opinion. For the government, the main objective of this dispute has been to consolidate its hegemonic project. The politicization of the media has been indispensable to this project, to which end the government has taken up using the same devices used by corporate media.

The authors argue that such confrontation has served to erect a platform upon which the government and the private media wage a battle for public opinion. This has significant consequences for governability, and particularly for shaping public opinion. Cerbino et al. examine to what extent that mediated action is constitutive of a populist rupture, via the mediatization of politics. Moreover, the authors argue that the Ecuadorian government is using a mediatized approach to politics in its confrontation with private media and how such confrontation is making use of populism in the dispute for public opinion.

In the following empirical chapter, Susana Sel and Pablo Gasloli examine the long battle by social movements for the regulation of the services of audio-visual communication in Argentina, which culminated in Law no. 26.522 in October 2009. Based on a long-standing social project, the law was passed by the government in the middle of a confrontation of social forces shaped by a wide range of civic alliances. Despite the imposition of informational monopolies, acting in complicity of a part of the judicial power, which continues to impede the full application of the law, the democratization policies proposed by the legislation are now being implemented. For the first time, university media and indigenous media are taking part as leaders of public services, whereas community media is recognized as leaders of non-profit services. Through diversity and the plurality of voices, this new social configuration is breaking with the hegemony of concentrated capital interests. The authors point out, however, that long-lasting changes are limited, due to the economic concentration of power of corporate media, and disparate ways in which mediatized communication is being integrated into a social practices and values. Drawing on Williams (1980), Sel and Gasloli argue that, as a result, the new media law is implicated in the creation of culture, whereby residual, dominant and emergent forms converge.

Focusing on the case of Venezuela in Chapter 6, Ximena Gonzalez Broquen analyses public policies concerning the media implemented by the Venezuelan government to promote and consolidate participatory democracy. The chapter begins by examining the social re-appropriation of the radio-electric spectrum, the participation of the third sector and the construction of the national media as a platform for democratic empowerment. Gonzalez Broquen argues that the creation of a participatory media is based on the idea of media's potential for social empowerment. Venezuela, as she highlights, is facing this challenge on a trial-and-error basis while contending with a global media offensive against the reforms. Gonzalez insists, however, that it is important to think beyond human rights based communications models to consider how we can create genuine spaces for collective action.

Engaging with the participatory potential of the Internet in Brazil, Carolina Matos argues in Chapter 7 that the re-democratization of Latin America's social and political institutions since the 1990s has seen various changes affecting the region since the collapse of military dictatorships, from economic reforms and demands for social inclusion to wider equality, which has resulted in significant social changes, such the election of female leaders throughout the continent. Against this backdrop, according to Carolina Matos, the Internet has slowly emerged in Brazil as a counter-public sphere that is invigorating debate, challenging the status quo and creating avenues for wider political pluralism and engagement.

Matos argues that the lack of access of less privileged sectors of the population to the Internet poses problems to its use for political mobilization, its capacity to offer counter discourses and general use as a vehicle for the public interest. Matos, however, also argues that despite the ongoing lack of widespread Internet access in Brazil, the potential of the Internet for democratization is strong and, especially during election periods, it can have a powerful role not only in mobilization but also to challenging taken-for-granted discourses.

Roberto Follari draws Part II to a close through a theoretical discussion of the ongoing battle between corporate media and South American governments. Drawing on Laclau's approach to populism and Bourdieu's notion of field, Follari considers the populist regimes in relation to corporate media power. According to Follari, the study of this conflictive relation provides a good opportunity to debate the political nature of populist regimes and their relation to media power in politics, highlighting the tense relations between corporate media and substantive democracies and their heterodox development strategies in South America.

Follari not only focuses on the empirical case of Argentina but also includes the cases of Ecuador and Venezuela. This is not of minor importance, as many discussions in the area of media and politics have tended to draw on Anglo-Saxon political views on liberal democracy. Follari states that media conglomerates have been acting as political actors engaged to a great extent in bringing about return of neoliberal economic and political strategies. However, in doing so, the author argues that media powers have yet to present viable instruments or alternatives to neopopulist forms of governance.

The chapters of Part III offer an IPE analysis of the regional dimensions of media power. From a macro IPE perspective, which considers the multilateral and international dimensions of media reform, to the specific cases of community media and citizen-based policy change, this part draws out the international implications of media reform efforts in South America.

Katherine Reilly's chapter on South America's ongoing processes of media reform from a critical political economy perspective identifies patterns of global capitalist insertion and processes of media reform. Reilly suggests three different models: interdependence, cordial power and limited media reform (e.g. Brazil); strategic autonomy and counter hegemonic network power (e.g. Venezuela or Bolivia); and network economy dependent development (e.g. the Plan Puebla Panama corridor). The author argues that the existence of these different models provides evidence of the importance of the relationship between capitalist insertion and media reform. Reilly thus discusses the implications of this global political economy reading of South American media reform. These implications include:

(1) The plurality of voices, resting on successful distribution of resources and requiring a wider analysis of post-neoliberal developmental policies within global trade and production networks.
(2) The need for strategic alignment of media reform with development processes at the national, regional and international levels.
(3) Impact on work of social movements in terms of medium, strategy, message and target.

Reilly urges communications scholars to pay greater attention to new institutional arrangements driven by social forces. Reminding us of key questions such as how private, public and citizen media are impacting media publics in the region, her work suggests that it is necessary to re-think the concept of media environments as 'the products of uneven capitalist processes', seeking new approaches to address the shifts between post-democratic processes directed at localized processes of media reform and new regionalized processes of convergence.

In Chapter 10, Martens and Vivares reflect on the potential directions for IPE research in the area of media power and development. This closing chapter argues that IPE allows us to view the issue of media power in South America as a complex and dialectical process of conflict associated with a structural change at regional and national levels, in response to a changing world order in the aftermath of neoliberal development.

The chapters in this collection purposefully present a wide range of theoretical and methodological approaches, which, read together, by no means paint an exhaustive picture of South American approaches to media and power. The varied responses presented here do, however, highlight the rich range of new possibilities for media engagement beyond corporate models, which have dominated global understandings of media to present. Many of the similar questions raised and addressed by the media debates taking place across South America are gaining momentum internationally, challenging current understandings of the complex interactions between media and politics.

Part I

Media, Power and Democracy in the International Political Economy

1
The Struggle for Democratic Media: Lessons from the North and from the Left[1]

Robert W. McChesney

Over the past decade, the eyes of the world have been on Ecuador, Venezuela, Bolivia and other Latin American nations as their elected governments attempt to achieve fundamental social reform through their respective constitutional systems. In every nation with an elected government that traditional elites regard as dangerous to their interests, the core battle has turned to questions of media. The news media in these nations are generally owned, sometimes effectively monopolized, by a handful of the wealthiest families. These news media have traditionally advocated a politics that represents their interests, and are not known for being especially sympathetic to the plight of the poor and working class. In some cases, they have been singularly hostile to popular reforms and democratization. This has created a problem for the effective functioning of a democratic political system – one based on political equality – which is predicated upon there being a wide range of effective and credible sources of information.

'Lies had destroyed Latin America. People lie too much, from the press, the politicians, and on the street,' Ecuadoran president Rafael Correa said in 2013 (Real News Network). 'I think one of the main problems around the world is that there are private networks in the communication business, for-profit business providing public information, which is very important for society. It is a fundamental contradiction.' Consequently, the battle to establish a media system that serves democratic values has been a defining issue in each of these nations. As nations in other parts of the world turn to similarly popular governments, the issue of media is likely to emerge there as well. To Correa, one solution is clear: 'I think there should be more public and community media, organizations that don't have that conflict between profits and social communication' (ibid).

In certain respects, the nations of Latin America are taking media debates and prospective policies to places they have never gone before. The outcome will go a long way towards determining the nature of these societies; this is an existential issue for popular governance. Western observers who showed little interest in the state of Latin American democracy or press issues when those governments were popular with Washington suddenly regard any challenge to the dominance of the wealthy over Latin American news media as a grave threat to human freedom demanding the world's attention. In its vulgar adaption, this argument boils down to 'freedom of the press means rich people should be allowed to own all the media, and they should be able to do whatever the hell they want to do with their private property. That's quintessential freedom and democracy'.

At the same time, this is not purely a black-and-white, good guys–bad guys issue. Constructing a free and democratic media system – especially in a dynamic and explosive political environment – is a complex undertaking. The elected governments have their own agendas and their own relationships with their voting base, and there are serious issues of censorship that need to be addressed.

In this chapter, I put these contemporary media battles in context. I look at traditional democratic theory and how news media has been regarded in the advanced capitalist nations, especially the United States. Professional journalism was the North American solution 100 years ago to the problem posed by having the news media concentrated in the hands of mostly right-wing millionaires. As the US model of professional journalism is often held up as the democratic ideal, it is imperative to have a sense of its history, and its weaknesses. In my view, the evidence suggests that US-style professional journalism under capitalist management offers no hope for the people of the United States, let alone anywhere else on the planet.

More important, I provide an accounting of the current free-fall of commercially based journalism in the United States, which is happening simultaneously to varying degrees worldwide. Every nation faces the same existential dilemma: whether to allocate resources to journalism as commercial interests abandon the field. This is an issue that will only grow more severe until it is addressed. It is time for nations to be thinking big about how to construct a credible popular independent news media for the digital age. The old system, whatever its merits, is dying.

In the second part of the chapter, I argue that media democratization has been a neglected area on the left, and that the legacy of the Communist era has retarded progress in this area. At the same time, and more important, there is a radical democratic media tradition on the left from which the people of Latin America and worldwide can profitably draw. In the end, I argue that creating a genuinely independent and competitive non-profit and non-commercial media system is the foundation not just for democracy, but for any system worthy of the name socialism. As the Latin American experience demonstrates, it is an idea whose time has come.

Journalism and democracy

There is considerable consensus in democratic theory and among journalism scholars about what a healthy journalism should entail (e.g. Christians et al. 2009):

1. It must provide a rigorous accounting of people who are in power, or who wish to be in power, in the government, corporate and non-profit sectors.
2. It must have a plausible method to separate truth from lies, or at least to prevent liars from being unaccountable and leading nations into catastrophes.
3. It must regard the information needs of all people as legitimate; if there is a bias in the amount and tenor of coverage, it should be towards those with the least amount of economic and political power, as they are the ones who most need information to participate effectively. Those atop the system generally get the information they need to maintain control.
4. It must produce a wide range of informed opinions on the most important issues of our times – both the transitory concerns of the moment and the challenges that loom on the horizon. It also must accurately translate important scientific issues into lay language. These issues cannot be determined primarily by what people in power are talking about. Journalism must provide the nation's early warning system, so problems can be anticipated, studied, debated and addressed before they develop into crises.

Not every media outlet can or should provide all these services; that would be impractical. It is necessary, however, for the media system as a whole to make such journalism a realistic expectation for the citizenry. There should be a basic understanding of the commons – the social world – that all people share, so that all people can effectively participate in the political and electoral processes of self-governance. The measure of a free press is how well it gives citizens the information they need to keep their freedoms and rights.

There is more. Great journalism, as Ben Bagdikian put it, requires great institutions. As with any complex undertaking, a division of labour is required to achieve success. Copyeditors, fact-checkers and proofreaders are needed, in addition to reporters and assigning editors. There must be institutional muscle that can stand up to governments and corporate power – institutions that people in power not only respect, but fear. Effective journalism requires competition, so that if a story is missed by one newsroom, it is exposed by another. It requires people covering stories that they would not cover if they were doing journalism on a voluntary basis. In short, in order to have democratic journalism, material resources must come from somewhere, and they need to be organized on an institutional basis. It also must be an open system, allowing anyone to engage in the practice without needing a licence, credentials or approval from someone high.

Of course, journalism is not the sole provider of political information or the only stimulant for informed debate and participation. Political information can also come from schools, art, academic research, entertainment media and conversations with friends and family. But such avenues are much more effective and valuable when they rest atop, and inform, a strong journalism.

In the United States, it has long been assumed that democratic journalism will naturally emerge from a market system where the news media is owned by profit-maximizing firms in largely semi-monopolistic markets. As long as any person has the formal right to launch a news medium without government interference, the society has a free press. At worst, the conventional wisdom goes, the commercial system may have flaws, but it will always be superior to any possible alternative, so there is no point in even thinking about an alternative. But professional journalism is a recent invention in the United States and, under close inspection, has severe limitations, at least as it has been practised.

In the first century of the republic, US journalism was marked by a ubiquitous and highly partisan press that represented a wide range of viewpoints, including a crucial abolitionist press. A little-known fact is that this system was based on extraordinarily large public subsidies, primarily through the post office, which delivered most newspapers at a fraction of the real cost; it was anything but a testament to the free market. As advertising increased and publishing became a source of growing profitability, the subsidies decreased in importance. For much of the final third of the nineteenth century, the news media system tended to be quite competitive in economic terms. Large cities often had over a dozen daily newspapers; papers came and went, and nearly all newspapers were owned by a single publisher who also was the editor, or had a strong say in the editorial direction.[2]

But capitalism proceeded apace. In some cases, profit-hungry publishers found that sensationalism, what came to be called 'yellow journalism', was a lucrative course. Bribery of journalists, showing favouritism towards advertisers, and assorted unethical practices were common. Most important, by the 1890s, newspaper markets were becoming more oligopolistic, even monopolistic. Although revenues and population continued to increase sharply, the overall number of newspapers began to stagnate and then fall. 'The stronger papers are becoming stronger and the weaker papers are having a hard time to exist,' one newspaper executive observed in 1902 (Kaplan

2002: 123–124). Newspapers began to serve a larger and larger portion of their community's population – with much less fear of new competition than had been the case – and had considerable power as a result.

The great national chains of Pulitzer, Hearst and Scripps were formed almost overnight. The new publishing giants no longer needed to be closely tied to political parties; in fact, as local newspapers grew more monopolistic, partisanship could antagonize part of the market and undermine their commercial prospects. Yet, many publishers continued to use their now-monopolistic power to advocate for their political viewpoints, which were generally conservative, pro-business and anti-labour.[3] In this sense, a century ago, US news media was not unlike Latin American news media of recent years. The great progressive Robert La Follette (1920) devoted a chapter of his book on political philosophy to the crisis of the press. 'Money power ... ', he wrote, 'controls the newspaper press.... wherever news items bear in any way upon the control of government by business, the news is colored' (345).

By the first two decades of the twentieth century, this had become a major crisis for US journalism. The news was under constant attack for venality and duplicity. As even the publisher of the Scripps-owned *Detroit News* privately acknowledged in 1913, the corrosive influence of commercial ownership and the pursuit of profit were such that the rational democratic solution would be to have municipal ownership of newspapers, with popular election of the editors (Kaplan 2002: 166). In view of the explicitly political nature of newspapers in US history, this was not as absurd a notion as it may appear today. Scripps, always the most working class oriented of the major chains, even launched an ad-less daily newspaper in the 1910s, because it saw how commercialism undermined the integrity of the news (see Stoltzfus 2007).

Is professional journalism under commercial control the solution?

Reconciling a monopolistic commercial news media with the journalism requirements of a political democracy is a difficult challenge. In some wealthier European nations, the solution, such as it has been, has taken the form of strong partisan and occasionally public subsidies to support journalism oriented to working-class and labour interests, and the creation of independent public broadcasting. In the United States, the problem was solved through self-regulation by the newspaper industry, in the form of professional journalism. This was a revolutionary idea: The owner and the editor could now be separated, and the owner's (and advertisers') political views would not be reflected in the nature of the journalism, except on the editorial page. It was a 180-degree shift from the earlier history of US journalism, which was founded on the notion of an explicitly partisan and highly competitive press.

Under professionalism, trained journalists would determine and produce the news, and it would be objective, non-partisan, factually accurate and unbiased. Whether there were ten newspapers in a community or only one or two would be mostly irrelevant, because professional journalists – like mathematicians addressing an algebra problem – would all come up with the same reports. As press magnate Edward Scripps explained, at one time readers 'did not care what the editor's views were; ... when it came to news one paper was as good as a dozen' (Kaplan 2002: 126). There were no schools of journalism in the United States (or the world, for that matter) in 1900. By the 1920s, all the major journalism schools had been established, and by 1923, the American Society of Newspaper Editors had formalized a professional code for editors and reporters to follow.

There is nothing inevitable or 'natural' about the *type* of professional journalism that emerged in the United States in the last century. The values that came to dominate it were contested; the journalists' union, the Newspaper Guild, in the 1930s, unsuccessfully attempted to have a non-partisan journalism that was far more critical of everyone in power, and viewed itself as the agent of people outside of power – to 'afflict the comfortable and comfort the afflicted', as the saying goes. It regarded journalism as a third force independent of both government and big business, and wanted to prohibit publishers from having any control over the content of the news. According to the leading history of the association, 'The idea that the Guild could rebalance the power struggle between public and publisher through a new kind of stewardship of the freedom of the press became a core tenet of their mission as an organization' (Scott 2009: 260). This remains a compelling vision, worthy of being part of a good news system, and is still practised today by some of our best journalists.

This practice of journalism was anathema to most publishers, who wanted no part of aggressive reporting on their fellow business owners or the politicians they routinely worked with and relied upon for their businesses to be successful. They were also never going to relinquish direct control over the newsroom; editors and reporters had their autonomy strictly at the owners' discretion. The resulting professionalism was to the owners' liking, for the most part, and more conducive to their commercial and political needs. It was also porous, such that commercial factors could influence the values that led to story selection, and advertising could still influence the nature and content of news coverage (see Collins 1992).

The core problem with professional journalism as it crystallized was that it relied far too heavily upon official sources – people in power – as the appropriate agenda setters for news and as the 'deciders' with regard to the range of legitimate debate in US political culture. There is considerable irony in this development. In two brilliant essays written in 1919 and 1920, Walter Lippmann – generally regarded as the leading advocate of professionalism and a ferocious critic of the bankrupt quality of journalism in 1910s' United

States – argued that the main justification for professionalism in journalism was that a trained group of independent non-partisan reporters would systematically and rigorously debunk government (and, implicitly, corporate) spin, and not regurgitate it (Lippmann 2008; Lippmann and Merz 1920).

This reliance upon official sources removed some of the controversy from the news, and it made it less expensive to produce. It didn't cost as much to put reporters where people in political power congregate. This gave the news an 'establishment' tone. It made reporters careful about antagonizing those upon whom they depended for 'access' to their stories (see Nichols and McChesney 2005). 'It is a dirty quid pro quo', wrote Chris Hedges (2009), the former *New York Times* Pulitzer Prize-winning reporter. 'The media get access to the elite as long as the media faithfully report what the elite wants reported. The moment that quid pro quo breaks down, reporters – real reporters – are cast into the wilderness and denied access' (170).

This fundamental limitation of professional journalism does not manifest itself in coverage of those issues where there is rich and pronounced debate between or within leading elements of the dominant political parties. Then journalists have a good deal of room to maneuver, and professional standards can ensure a measure of factual accuracy, balance and credibility. There tend to be slightly fewer problems in robust political eras, like the 1960s, when mass movements demand the attention, respect and fear of the powerful.

The real problem becomes evident when political elites march in virtual lockstep. Then professional journalism is at best ineffectual, and at worst propagandistic. This has often been the case in US foreign policy, where both parties are beholden to an enormous global military complex, and accept the right of the United States, and the United States alone, to invade countries when it suits US interests (Friel and Falk 2004; Herman and Chomsky 1989; Mermin 1999). In matters of war and foreign policy, journalists who question the basic assumptions and policy objectives and who attempt to raise issues that no one in the leadership of either party wishes to debate are considered 'ideological' and 'unprofessional'. This has a powerful disciplinary effect.[4]

So it was that even in the glory days of 1960s' journalism, the news media helped lead the United States into the Vietnam war, despite the fact that dubious claims from the government – for example, the Gulf of Tonkin hoax – could in many cases have easily been challenged and exposed. 'The process of brain-washing the public starts with off-the-record briefings for newspapermen', I. F. Stone (1964: 4) wrote at the time. Two great dissident Democratic senators, Alaska's Ernest Gruening and Oregon's Wayne Morse, broke with both their own party and the Republicans to warn against imperial endeavours in places such as Vietnam. Their perspective, which history has shown to be accurate, was marginalized in the mainstream media. The press, Stone observed, had 'dropped an Iron Curtain ... on the anti-war speeches of Morse and Gruening' (2). Morse recognized that the lack of critical coverage and debate in the news media was undermining popular participation in foreign policy: 'The American people need to be warned before it is too late about the threat which is arising as a result of the monopolistic practices [in newspaper ownership]' (U.S. Congress 1960: 18331).

Journalism schools lament these lapses in retrospect, but the situation never improves; such is the gravitational pull of the professional code towards the consensus of those in power in matters of war and peace. The 2003 invasion of Iraq – based upon entirely fictitious 'weapons of mass destruction' – was one of the darkest episodes in US journalism history. It had astronomical, almost unimaginable, human and economic costs. Foreign correspondent Michael Hastings (2012), who spent considerable time in the company of General Stanley McChrystal and his staff, described military officials gloating in private at 'how massively they were manipulating the press', including the most prestigious correspondents (90–91). Glenn Greenwald (2012) critiqued National Public Radio's hallowed coverage, in particular a report on Iran in which the correspondent

> gathers a couple of current and former government officials (with an agreeable establishment think-tank expert thrown in the mix), uncritically airs what they say, and then repeats it herself. This is what establishment-serving journalists in Washington mean when they boast that they, but not their critics, engage in so-called real reporting; it means: *calling up Serious People in Washington and uncritically repeating what they say.*

It seems the only time elite journalists exhibit rage is when their practices are exposed. 'The unwritten rule' for journalists is a simple one, Hastings (2012) wrote: 'You really weren't supposed to write honestly about people in power. Especially those the media deemed untouchable' (329).

Coverage of the elected governments in Venezuela, Bolivia and Ecuador follows this pattern to a tee. Despite their popularity and accomplishments, and their commitment to constitutional rule, these governments are treated in the mainstream US news media – across the political spectrum – with breathtaking hostility. News media that directed almost no critical attention to corrupt Latin American governments or dictatorships in the past became obsessed with the immense threat to the free world posed by these democratically elected governments. The reason was simple: The elite sources that set the range of debate in the United States unanimously agreed that these governments are extremely dangerous because they are not sufficiently deferential to US corporate and military interests. Journalists received no countervailing input from a 'legitimate' source.

Another weakness built into professional journalism as it developed in the United States was that it opened the door to an enormous public relations industry that was eager to provide reporters with material on their clients. Press releases and packets came packaged to meet the requirements of professional journalism, often produced by former journalists. The point of public relations (PR) is to get the client's message in the news so that it looks legitimate: The best PR is never recognized for what it is. Although reporters generally understood the dubious nature of PR, and never embraced it, they had to work with it to get their job done. Publishers tended to appreciate PR because it lowered the costs of production. The dirty secret of journalism is that even at the most prestigious newspapers in the glory days of the 1970s, some 40–50 per cent of news stories were based upon press releases – and surprisingly, often, those press releases were only loosely investigated before publication (Morris and Goldsworthy 2008; Smith 2004: 191; Solomon 1992: 66; see also Turney 2002). Thus, powerful interests could subtly determine what was covered in the news and how it was covered.

The high-water mark for professionalism was the late 1960s and 1970s. Even at its best, however, professional journalism tended to take the context and excitement out of politics, turning it into a dry and sometimes incoherent spectator sport. Unlike the partisan journalism of the nation's first century, it tended to promote depoliticization and apathy as much as participation. Christopher Lasch (1995) characterized one of the limitations of US-style professional journalism:

> What democracy requires is vigorous public debate, not information. Of course, it needs information too, but the kind of information it needs can be generated only by debate. We do not know what we need to know until we ask the right questions, and we can identify the right questions only by subjecting our own ideas about the world to the test of public controversy.
>
> (162–163)

Farewell to journalism?

Since the early 1980s, commercial pressure has eroded much of the autonomy that professional journalism afforded newsrooms, and that provided the basis for the best work done over the past 50 years. It has led to a softening of standards such that stories about sex scandals and celebrities have become more legitimate, because they make commercial sense: They are inexpensive to cover, attract audiences and give the illusion of controversy without threatening anyone in power.

The Internet has accelerated the demise of commercial journalism and made it irreversible. The existential threat it posed to the commercial news media system soon became clear: Now digital content can be spread instantly, at no charge, all over the world with the push of a button. The marginal cost of reproducing material is zero, nothing, nada. By free market economics, that is its legitimate price. To make matters worse from the capitalist perspective, advertising, which has provided the vast majority of revenues for commercial news media for over a century, has been radically transformed by the Internet. No longer supporting specific news media websites, digital advertising increasingly is deployed through networks that locate target consumers wherever they might be online. Content-producing websites are not privileged over other sites and get virtually no support for their activities. That is not going to change.

In 2012, the President's Council of Economic Advisors described newspaper publishing as 'the nation's fastest-shrinking industry' (Editors 2012). A survey of 200 possible careers by CareerCast.com (Sieff 2012) listed 'newspaper reporter' as the fifth worst way to make a living. (The worst job? Lumberjack.) Broadcast journalism hardly fared better, finishing ninth worst. To convey some sense of the collapse, in 2012 Philadelphia's legendary *Inquirer* and its sister properties sold for just 10 per cent of their sales price only six years earlier (Newsosaur 2012).

In 2010–12, I visited a good two dozen US cities to discuss the state of journalism. In virtually every city, I asked veteran newspeople how many paid working journalists there were in their community – in newspapers, broadcast, the Internet, *the works* – compared to the 1980s. The general response, after serious contemplation, was in the 40–50 per cent range, and in a few cities considerably less than that. In 2011, a former *Seattle Times* reporter said, 'I don't know anybody from my profession who isn't heartbroken, devastated, terrified, scared, enraged, despondent, bereft. I just don't know anybody' (Fancher 2011).

In a comprehensive analysis of the sources for original news stories in a 2009 study of Baltimore, the Pew Center ('How News Happens') determined that fully 86 per cent originated with official sources and press releases. (A generation earlier, PR accounted for more like 40–50 per cent of news content.) These stories were presented as news based on the labour and judgement of professional journalists, but they generally presented the PR position without any alteration. As the study concluded, 'the official version of events is becoming more important. We found official press releases often appear word for word in first accounts of events, though often not noted as such'.

On the surface, it may seem that we are inundated with endless news. Increasingly, however, it is unfiltered public relations generated surreptitiously by corporations and governments, in a manner that might make Walter Lippmann turn in his grave. In 1960, there was less than one PR agent for every working journalist, a ratio of 0.75-to-1. By 1990, the ratio was just over 2-to-1. In 2013, there were *four* PR people for every working journalist. At the current rate, the ratio may soon be 6-to-1 (McChesney and Nichols

2002: ix–xv, 256). Because there are far fewer reporters to interrogate the spin, the likelihood that press releases will be presented as legitimate 'news' has become much greater.[5] 'As a direct result of changing media platforms', one 2011 media industry assessment of the future of journalism put it, 'PR pros are now a part of the media in a way they never have been before' (Vocus 2011).

And in an environment where doing actual reporting is less likely, what passes for news has increasingly embraced pre-professional explicit partisanship, as if offering a political perspective can be a substitute for journalism. In the United States, the partisanship tends to run to the right, as the right has the money to shape the news and buy the media.

It is hard to avoid what seems like the obvious conclusion: Corporations and investors no longer consider journalism a profitable investment (O'Shea 2011). If anything, they are stripping what remains for parts, and milking monopoly franchises until they run dry. That leads to an immediate problem for a society that has entrusted its news media to the private sector: 'The independent watchdog function that the Founding Fathers envisioned for journalism – going so far as to call it crucial to a healthy democracy – is... at risk', concluded a Federal Communications Commission (FCC) study on the crisis in journalism (Waldman and Working Group 2011: 5). The pattern is the same to varying degrees worldwide.

Journalism is something society requires but that the market cannot generate in sufficient quantity or quality, no matter how fantastic the technologies. The solution to the problem is to recognize it as a public good. For all nations, devising polices to create and support competitive viable news media is a central political issue going forward. There is no doubt that the commercial system is dying, as it has few resources and less protection for genuine independent reporting. Hence, the peculiar kind of professional system that grew out of the commercial system, for all its flaws, no longer has a basis for existence. The way forward must be in a different direction.

There must be some way out of here

But what alternatives are there? Certainly the political left has nothing of value to contribute, right?

Wrong.

It is true that the Communist regimes' approach to communication featured censorship, party monopoly and propaganda. In many respects it was the antithesis of what one wants from a genuine democratic press system. Without meaning to provide an apologia, I would argue that those propaganda systems had far less to do with socialist theory than they did with expediency and the logical consequence of implementing socialist systems in poor countries with an increasingly unenthusiastic general population and in a generally hostile world environment. Such environments quickly produce stagnation, cynicism, banality and corruption. More than anything, these deplorable media systems exposed the Communist countries for the antidemocratic nations they were, despite their routine proclamations to the contrary. And to my knowledge, no one became a socialist because they were attracted to Communist news media. Quite the opposite.

Prior to the emergence of Communist regimes, however, the socialist left was always at the forefront of the movement to expand and protect civil liberties, and stood in sharp opposition to censorship. The left historically focused on creating its own media and, as far as policy was concerned, preventing the government from censoring them. Socialist and left groups were *defined* by their newspapers and periodicals until the age of the Internet. To the extent that socialists pondered what a post-capitalist press system might look like, it certainly did not entail the banning of dissident publications and viewpoints. Socialism was the extension of democracy, well beyond the limits that capitalism placed on self-government, to include, most importantly, the economy and economic organizations. A post-capitalist press system would be one of freedom and plenty. But well into the twentieth century, to most of the left the media system was a dependent variable that would work itself out once control over the economy had been settled.

By the mid-twentieth century, with the emergence of film, recorded music and especially radio and television broadcasting, it became obvious that media was a lot more than a dependent variable. People had more leisure time, and they were devoting it to the products of the culture industries. As culture and journalism became a significant new source of profitability, often fueled by corporate advertising, the industries became far less open and competitive and found themselves under the thumb of major corporations. This has led since the 1970s to significant academic examinations of media industries, and much critical work, but the research has been 'academic', in that it offers superb critique but little sense that reform is possible.

What has regrettably been underappreciated is how in the middle of the twentieth century in Western Europe and North America, socialist and Marxist scholars took a fresh look at media and culture and the role they played in society. These scholars shared a revulsion at what passed for media systems in the then-Communist Eastern European nations, as well as a growing concern that corporate-controlled commercial media was becoming a significant barrier to progressive reform in the West. On the one hand, this work demonstrated a creative and open-minded Marxism or radical social criticism that embraced the issue of communication and plunged into the problems it posed for social theory. It animated much of what would be most impressive about the New Left that was about to explode into prominence. On the other hand, the examination of communication gravitated from criticism of the deleterious effects of capitalist culture to being concerned with the politics of culture, and how control of communication systems was becoming a necessary political battlefield for the democratic left.

This line of inquiry developed in the late 1950s and 1960s and was a key part of the New Left. With the demise of the social movements of the 1960s and early 1970s and the emergence of neoliberalism, this tradition has largely been forgotten. I believe it holds valuable insights and lessons for Latin America, and for people everywhere who aspire to a more just and democratic society, be it socialist or otherwise.

Who are the scholars I am talking about? The key figures include Paul A. Baran, Paul M. Sweezy, Herbert Marcuse, Leo Marx, E. P. Thompson, Ralph Miliband and Eric Hobsbawm. The two most important, by a wide margin, were C. Wright Mills of the United States and Raymond Williams of Britain. All of these people were in regular communication with each other.

Beginning in the late 1950s, Mills commenced writing a book to be entitled *The Cultural Apparatus*. The historically specific context of his entry into this sphere is powerfully described by Stanley Aronowitz (2012):

> Mills had come to the conclusion that it was not the economy or even self-interest in general that drove contemporary social agents to action or inaction. Mills concluded that in the epoch of what he termed 'overdeveloped' capitalism, the masses were moved more broadly by 'culture' than by reason. He had become convinced that the cultural apparatus played a central role in reproducing the entire 'set-up'. But it is not the anthropological conception of culture – a whole way of life – that he believed determined politics or secured the domination by the leading institutional actors. Mills's invocation of the cultural apparatus... signaled that culture was no longer the spontaneous creation of the people but instead was an aspect of the organization and reproduction of social and political domination. If social transformation was at all possible, its protagonists were obliged to understand the process of the production and distribution of the key cultural forms, especially the mass media. Clearly, the implication of his projected study was to argue for a new counterhegemonic strategy of the Left that matched the force of the culture industry.
>
> (241–242)

Mills delivered three university lectures at the London School of Economics (LSE) in January 1959, utilizing a manuscript entitled 'The Cultural Apparatus, or the American Intellectual'. The lectures were later published as 'Culture and Politics: The Fourth Epoch', 'The Cultural Apparatus', and 'The Decline of the Left'. Together they constitute the main extant materials of *The Cultural Apparatus* – left behind unfinished when Mills died in 1962 of a heart attack at age 45.

Mills did not get very far in defining what he actually meant by the cultural apparatus. His approach was broader and more obscure than the way the concept was being used in Marxist theory, where it was essentially equivalent to the cultural means of production, including the technical means themselves. In contrast, Mills (2008) used the notion of cultural apparatus somewhat ambiguously in terms of 'the observation posts, the interpretation centres, the presentation depots', and went on to say that it was 'composed of all the organizations and milieux in which artistic, intellectual, and scientific work goes on' (204). His emphasis was more on processes than on structures, allowing him to emphasize agency, namely the intellectual – to the point that he could say, 'I have been studying, for several years now, the cultural apparatus, the intellectuals – as a possible, immediate, radical agency of change' (263). This tended to downplay the power dimension, reducing the question of the cultural apparatus itself to the question of the intellectual, of agency – rather than emphasizing the dialectical relation between cultural producer and the capitalist cultural apparatus as in Brecht and the Frankfurt School. Nevertheless, he went on to make a critical point:

> What intellectuals now confront is the expropriation of their cultural apparatus itself. We do not have access to the means of effective communication, but more than that, many of us are losing control of the very means of cultural production itself. The situation of the serious moviemaker – is not this the prototype for all cultural workmen? We are cut off from possible publics and such publics as remain are being turned into masses by those businessmen or commissars who do control and manage the effective means of communication. In their hands, these are often less means of communication than means of mass distraction.... What we ought now to do is repossess our cultural apparatus, and use it for our own purposes.
>
> (ibid: 217–218, 221)

Mills's approach had a big impact on the New Left Marxists in Britain. E. P. Thompson attended the last of the three LSE lectures on the cultural apparatus, and called it 'absolutely splendid' (ibid: 213). But there was friendly criticism from a Marxist standpoint. In a long letter to Mills, Thompson wrote: 'You argue intellectual workers must repossess their own cultural apparatus and use it for their own purposes. In what sense have they ever possessed it?' (qtd in Geary 2009: 196). For Thompson, it was a question not of repossession of the cultural apparatus, but of the construction of a left cultural apparatus. 'The problem', he wrote, 'presents itself as one of constructing (however painfully slow the process may seem – though steady progress is being made) an *alternative* "cultural apparatus" which by-passes the mass media and the party machinery, and which opens up direct channels between significant socialist groupings inside and outside the labour movement' (Thompson 1959).

Williams shared with Mills a concern to translate the critique of commercial media as a regressive force into a political strategy and program for the left. The starting point for his analysis was 'the subordination of a general communications process to an increasingly powerful system of advertising and public relations' (Williams 1976: 180). 'The central problem, as I see it, is cultural. The society of individual consumers which is now being propagandized by all the weight of mass advertising and mass publications, needs a new kind of socialist analysis and alternative' (Williams 1960: 333). He went on to argue that

> Instead of the ritual indignation and despair at the cultural condition of 'the masses' (now increasingly uttered even by their supposed friends) it is necessary to break through to the central fact that most of our cultural institutions are in the hands of speculators, interested not in the health and growth of the society, but in the quick profits that can be made by exploiting inexperience. True, under attack, these speculators, or some of them, will concede limited policies of a different kind, which they significantly call 'prestige'; that is to say, enough to preserve a limited public respectability so that they will be allowed to continue to operate. But the real question is whether a society can afford to leave its cultural apparatus in such irresponsible hands.... We should be much clearer about these cultural questions if we saw them as a consequence of a basically capitalist organization, and I at least know no better reason for capitalism to be ended.
>
> (Williams 1961: 338–339)

In a series of three pieces published in 1961 and 1962, Williams laid out the foundations of a radical socialist platform for democratic media reform. One was a pamphlet published by the Fabian Society, *The Existing Alternatives in Communications* (Williams 1962b). This almost entirely unknown piece drew from his two well-known books from that period: *The Long Revolution* (1961) and the first edition of *Britain in the Sixties: Communications* (1962a), generally called *Communications*.

In the latter work, Williams defined communications as 'the institutions and forms in which ideas, information, and attitudes are transmitted and received', and communication (without an 's') as 'the process of transmission and reception'. He argued that the spectacular growth of communications in modern times had 'created social problems which seem to be of a quite new kind'. Communication had joined economics and politics as 'equally fundamental' to understanding society. 'We have been wrong in taking communication as secondary,' he wrote. 'The struggle to learn, to describe, to understand, to educate, is a central and necessary part of our humanity. This struggle is not begun, at second hand, after reality has occurred. It is, in itself, a major way in which reality is continually formed and changed.' This emphasis, he argued, 'is exceptionally important in the long crisis of twentieth-century society' (Williams 1962a: 17–19).

Accordingly, Williams argued that control over communication was of paramount importance, with commercial control of media constituting a disaster for humanity, not to mention democracy. 'The only alternative to a control by a few irresponsible men, who treat our cultural means as simple commodities, is a public system.' He insisted that there was an important place for consumer information and advice in a communication system, 'but advertising is a very primitive way of supplying it'. He recognized the 'genuine difficulties' of establishing a public cultural system, but that did not alter his belief in its central and immediate importance as a political project. What was required was 'no direct control by government' over content, along with public debate and deliberation over the 'actual allocation of resources'. He was emphatic that the Old Left model of state monopoly and censorship was not a legitimate or attractive alternative. Indeed, the bankruptcy of the Soviet-style system was demonstrated most decisively in its hideous communications structure and policies. Until socialists 'can show a convincing alternative, which is free of these dangers', people would have no rational reason to change. 'The idea of public service must be detached from the idea of public monopoly, yet remain public service in the true sense. The only way of achieving this is to create new kinds of institution' (Williams 1962a: 129–130, 166–173).

In *The Existing Alternatives in Communications*, Williams sums up these points and argues that the Labour Party needs to make reconstruction of the media and communication system a central part of its political program going forward. Implicit in his argument is that the very nature of a socialist regime can be gleaned by assessing its communication system, for that is where the rubber meets the road and the commitment to genuine democracy moves from words to practice. The new developments in culture and the media demanded 'a new kind of socialist analysis and alternative' (1960: 333). In Williams's view, a well-funded public system was essential, with true independence and legitimate access for ordinary citizens, not just for socialism but also for democracy itself. The point was to create a system where the means of production were held in trust by the public and leased out to individuals without control from the top, in ways that would create a dynamic, popular, decentralized and democratic media system. Unless the Labour Party – and by extension, the left everywhere – made restructuring communications a high priority, it risked irrelevance and ultimate failure.

The fact that there was in the 1960s a historical moment for reform in broadcasting, after which change would become far more difficult (and British broadcasting would begin to move in the direction of the US system, with its commercialism and cultural degradation), was made clear in Williams's comments in the second edition of *Communications*. 'It is now more than ever certain', he wrote, 'that we shall have to get rid of a commercial television structure, and especially of this one, with its close connexions in ownership with our already concentrated commercial press'. If another commercial channel were established, he predicted, 'we shall have lost for a generation any chance of making a genuinely public system'. The real goal, he insisted, should be 'to start dismantling both the present commercial structure of ITV and the present centralization of BBC', replacing them with a system of public control over the technical and transmission apparatus, holding it in trust, coupled with 'genuinely independent programme companies' that would lease the technical facilities and take responsibility for policy and content (Williams 1966: 156–158; see also Garnham 1990: 128–132).

In many respects, Williams captured the core arguments of all the other writers from this period. He used this not as a gateway to despair over the duping of the masses, but, to the contrary, as a crucial new political battleground where the political left could rejuvenate itself and create a truly democratic socialism. It was no small accomplishment. At the same time this work was being done, Jürgen Habermas had just completed his dissertation in Germany. In reading what was later translated into English as *The Structural Transformation of the Public Sphere* (Habermas 1989) today, one is struck by the manner in which the analysis and arguments are complementary with those of Baran, Sweezy, Miliband and especially Williams and Mills. Indeed, Habermas closes the book by invoking Mills approvingly (249–250).

By the early 1970s, accompanying the global upsurge in political activism, considerable attention was devoted to communication issues on the left. In the global South, the newly liberated nations organized for a New World Information and Communication Order (NWICO) in conjunction with a New International Economic Order (NIEO) to redress imbalances in control over communication networks and media resulting from centuries of imperialism. It was the first time in global politics that communication was put on the same level as the economy, or better yet, seen as integral to the political economy.

It was a defining concern for the New Left. In Britain, Nicholas Garnham, who would go on to become a central figure in the political economy of communication, wrote a manifesto for media activism in 1972 that drew directly from Marcuse and Williams. 'The media of mass-communication', Garnham (1980) wrote, 'clearly play a vital role and the control of those media is a matter of central political concern' (14). 'The media are not neutral in the struggle for democracy. In the Long Revolution the pen may indeed turn out to be mightier than the sword. The outcome of that battle will therefore depend upon which side gains control of the pen.' In Garnham's view, a problem with much of the 'counterculture' media activism of the times was the belief that 'alternative cultures, life styles and the institutional forms to go with them could be constructed within the existing social formation and alongside the more traditional social forms' (14). Williams shared this concern, noting that the commercial system had succeeded in 'incorporating large areas' of alternative popular culture into its own domain (1976: 184).

In this retrospective look at the preceding 15 years in British (and, to a certain extent, western) communication, Williams found some hope that the counterculture that had developed in that period might have lasting progressive value. But he was also skeptical.

> The idea of an alternative culture is radical but limited. It can very easily become a marginal culture; even, at worst, a tolerated play area. It is certainly always insufficient unless it is linked with effective opposition to the dominant system, under which the majority of people are living.
>
> (Williams 1976: 186–187)

He was especially heartened by the emergence of cooperatives to generate communication and culture, but here, too, direct political confrontation with the powers-that-be was unavoidable: 'One of the key developments, that of workers' or producers' or contributors' cooperative, depends, in the high-capital areas, on active support by a reforming government, and that takes us back to one of the central areas of conflict' (ibid: 187).

In the United States, there was an explosion of such 'alternative' media in the form of community theatre and, especially, alternative newspapers and periodicals. But policy activism also emerged. In the early 1970s, African American groups and other community and civil rights groups participated in hundreds of license challenges to existing commercial radio and TV broadcasters before the FCC in a failed effort to claim those channels for community use. By the mid-1970s, this activism had helped to create scores of new community FM radio stations and public-access TV. It was a testament to the vision Williams and the others had laid out a decade earlier.

By the end of the 1970s, the political projects associated with the vision of Williams, Mills and the other writers were disappearing with the collapse of the left and the rise of neoliberalism. As Garnham (1980) acknowledged, the 'need' for radical media reform was growing 'more acute' at the same time that the prospects for such reform were much further away (9). The fields of political economy of communication and cultural studies downsized their immediate political ambitions and crystallized as academic undertakings, finding a toehold at a handful of universities where they provided a muscular critique while maintaining a tenuous institutional existence thereafter. Williams (1976) regarded the emergence of academic media studies as 'significant', though he added that it was 'ironic that this work should have developed in the same period in which the general situation was so sharply deteriorating' (183). Much of critical communication research subsequently turned away from the structural issues that were central to the work of the

1960s, as institutional reform, not to mention socialism, appeared impossible. At its most extreme, this devolution ended up in the varieties of post-structuralist, postmodernist and postcolonial schools. In such an environment, it was easy for this tradition to be forgotten, even by some of those associated with it.

In the past decade, with the growth of global corporate media empires and the Internet, not to mention economic stagnation, media reform has returned as a major political issue in countless nations. At times the reform efforts can be marginal, especially when they are not associated with popular movements and a political left that can provide vision and courage. But what is more important is how the left has embraced the central importance of structural media reform and communication issues as never before, much as the writers mentioned above desired. Nowhere is this more apparent than in Latin America today, where many of the great struggles concern how progressive forces can get elected left governments to create truly independent media systems, free of the traditional domination of a few capitalist clans, in every nation, as well as the state. The capitalist forces are determined to use their media power to maintain their class privileges. The fate of these governments and socialist politics writ large may well ride on the outcome. (Notions about the creation of a public media system that would be 'accountable to the public rather than the state' [or the market], similar to the general approach advocated by Williams, as part of a broader turn towards a decentralized democratic socialism, have been informally broached in the current period of experimentation and debate in Cuba [Burbach 2013]).

It has been said that Beethoven's late string quartets were so far ahead of their time that we have not yet caught up to them. So it is with this work by Williams and the other writers from this period that has been all but lost to history until now. Activists today still have much to learn from this visionary work about how to think about communication. All of these writers, for example, were aware of the radical changes that new communication technologies were going to create in the decades to come, but none of them thought those technologies would magically solve fundamental political problems on their own. The future of news media is to be non-profit, non-commercial and decentralized, in any number of forms, with public funding but no government control. It will have to be open and uncensored. Even sympathetic governments must be forced to tolerate dissent, and truly progressive governments embrace it. If anything, the left has been too timid with regard to communication politics; it is time to be realistic, as the 1960s saying goes, and demand the impossible.

Notes

1. This chapter draws in part from Robert W. McChesney, *Digital Disconnect: How Capitalism Is Turning the Internet against Democracy* (New York: New Press, 2013); and

also from John Bellamy Foster and Robert W. McChesney, 'The Cultural Apparatus of Monopoly Capital – An Introduction,' *Monthly Review*, July–August 2013. The author thanks co-author Foster for his assistance and insight.

2. For hard data on newspaper markets in the late nineteenth and early twentieth centuries, see McChesney and Nichols 2010: ch. 3.
3. For the classic treatment, see Sinclair 2003.
4. For a superb treatment of this issue, see Bennett, Lawrence and Livingston 2007.
5. This is a fruitful scenario for those who wish to have their press releases published as 'news'. The head of an environmental organization in Wisconsin told me in 2012 that his group has never had as much success getting the remaining newspapers in his state to carry their unadulterated press releases. His group gets little coverage otherwise. It is even better for those that can afford high-quality and slick press releases, and video material for television and online.

2
Media Democracy and Reform in South America: Lessons for Europe

David McQueen

Introduction

> Official news management ensures that government newsmakers and sources are dominant. The public relations machinery of large corporations exerts significant power in newsmaking. Routine practices and the professional norms of journalism reinforce the power of official sources and newsmakers. Thus, the encroachment of states and markets poses major obstacles for the existence of plural and diversified press. Strengthening the presence of civic issues and voices in the news is a crucial challenge for democracy.
>
> (Waisbord 2009a: 106)

A string of well-publicized revelations in Britain from the Leveson Inquiry into the culture, practices and ethics of the media set up following the phone hacking scandal of 2011 has exposed in remarkable detail the tightly interconnected world of politics and media power. While criticism of the influence of media moguls such as Rupert Murdoch over British political life has gone on for decades, the degree of complicity between News International and senior politicians revealed by the Parliamentary Inquiry has led to renewed and urgent calls for tighter restrictions on media ownership laws and press standards (Miliband 2012; Major 2012). The focus of this chapter is on the political and policy lessons of recent media reform efforts in South America for Europe generally and for the United Kingdom in particular, where the issue of concentrated media power has now moved centre stage (Curran 2012). Primarily, this chapter presents a broad survey, rather than a theoretically grounded inquiry, into legislative and policy initiatives over the past decade across a number of South American countries and their effects on the media environment.

There are, clearly, dangers in trying to generalize about media developments in any continent and substantially different approaches to, and levels of progress in, media reform can be found from nation to nation in South and Central America. For Lugo-Ocando, national contexts still provide by far the most crucial explanatory frameworks for media systems throughout Latin America – a point he is at pains to stress when criticizing politicians, academics and the general public alike for treating Latin America as 'a single region with a common culture' (2008: 211). Nevertheless, he argues that that once such national specificities have been taken into account certain general characteristics in relation to media systems can be observed. These include the influence of intellectual trends and policy debates in the West (see also Waisbord 2000).

However, it would be fair to say that the trade in ideas about media legislation and reform has, until now, been imbalanced with North American and European nations presuming to instruct South America in the need for the kinds of reforms (often neoliberal in character) that it believes the continent requires (Vialey et al. 2008). This assumption of 'unidirectional policy change' (Hintz 2011: 149) and lack of interest in lessons that the region might teach 'the west' has persisted, and not least because of limited and often biased academic and media coverage of Latin America in the United States and in Europe, particularly beyond the Iberian peninsula (see Porto and Hallin 2009).

This is certainly true of the United Kingdom, where Anglocentric views of media and politics persist. Despite the end of Empire and our fall in the league table of world economies behind so-called emerging nations such as Brazil, the British media manage to retain an inflated sense of the nation's international importance. The consequence of this Anglocentricism, for non-specialists at least, is the conspicuous absence of reporting of South America issues. Until relatively recently then, it has been very difficult to learn any policy lessons from the continent simply because it has been virtually ignored by the British media (Coffey 2004).

It is not just South America, however, that has been poorly covered. While elite politics in the United States does gain attention, the British media is guilty of systematic under-representation of Africa, Latin America and parts of Asia, except at times of crisis (see Institute of Development Studies 2012). This structured absence in media coverage also applies to entertainment culture – film, television productions, music, the arts and so on.

However, there are encouraging signs that this is beginning to change with a modest increase in the United Kingdom's media coverage of nations in the Global South as their growing economic power becomes apparent. This is especially true of China, which now receives considerable media interest and, to a lesser extent, Brazil, which has risen to become the world's sixth largest economy – overtaking the United Kingdom in the process (Financial Times 2012). Other countries have gained more attention since the economic crisis of 2007 began because the parallels between earlier IMF 'restructuring' of economies in South America and 'austerity measures' in

Europe have been too stark to ignore (Sheinin 2006; Santiso 2006). In particular, observers have noted how the economic and social outcomes of the failed 'structural adjustments' imposed on Greece, Spain and other European nations echo the traumatic results of Argentina's neoliberal shock therapy at the beginning of the millennium (Fiorentini 2012a; Biglieri 2012).

For many western observers, crushing austerity has also made it more difficult to ignore South America's economic progress and rising self-confidence as Europe and the United States have struggled to control or find solutions to a series of damaging political, economic and military crises. Furthermore, the political lessons of the continent's popular 'pink revolution' (Sheinin 2006: 218) have been picked up, with some success, by political parties in Europe. The newly formed *Front de Gauche* (Left Front) in France attracted rallies far beyond the expectations of its organizers and was at one point threatening to outperform the powerful National Front. In the end, the *Front Gauche* polled 11 per cent and helped propel Francois Hollande to power in the second round of voting on the May 6th.

What is interesting is where this French political movement came from. In an interview with Al Jazeera, a Front de Gauche activist and long-time ally of Melenchon, Raquel Garrido, claimed that the origins of the Left Front lay in the Latin American experience. She says:

> We first started questioning our strategy when we started seeing Latin America left-wing governments coming into power, but not with your traditional Social Democrat party. To the contrary, most of those experiences – in Argentina, Brazil, Venezuela, Ecuador, Bolivia – were being triggered by new parties. New political instruments that were organised outside of Social Democratic, left-wing, traditional parties.
>
> And the methods they were employing were radical, whether it be in their fight against the IMF, or whether it be in the means of remobilising their societies through constitutional assemblies.
>
> (cited Al Jazeera 2012: 1)

Similarly, Alexis Tsipras the leader of Greece's newly-formed anti-austerity party, Syriza, which came second in the June 2012 elections, has pointed to nations in South America for successful models of challenging a crippling national debt burden. Tsipras cites Ecuador's debt audit commission, which found much of the country's debt was illegal and illegitimate. This finding was used by the country's President Correa to justify a default that ultimately reduced debts by 65 per cent (Jones 2012).

European ignorance of Latin America therefore is slowly changing, bringing a new interest in political developments across the continent. There was, for instance, extensive coverage in the United Kingdom of the 2012 Summit of the Americas in which Latin American leaders, across the political spectrum, unified in outspoken opposition to the United States' refusal to meet with the Cuban government. While President Kirchner's anger over the issue of the Malvinas/Falkland islands gave the item a special interest to the British media, it was the continent's rebuff to President Obama that propelled the story into the headlines. The isolation of the United States and Canada on Cuban relations and disagreement over strategies for dealing with drugs revealed shifting power relations and underscored increasingly assertive acts of independence by South American nations that are of 'historical importance' (Chomsky 2012).

Through such films as John Pilger's film *The War on Democracy* (2007), *The Revolution Will Not be Televised* (2008) and Oliver Stone's 2009 documentary *South of the Border*, there has been wider public awareness of how hostile media coverage both within and beyond the region has posed a threat to democratically elected governments, in some cases actively contributing to political instability and coups attempts. The problem of media monopoly power is emerging as a key issue in both continents with one study claiming that more than 82 per cent of communication and information markets in Latin America and the Iberian peninsula are controlled by just four media groups (Becerra and Mastrini 2009, cited Cohen 2011: 1).

The struggle to reign in media monopolies by leftist governments in South America has not gone unnoticed, particularly amongst those active in the media reform movement in Europe. However, reactions to the reform efforts has often been shaped by hostile media coverage (Stoneman 2008; Salter and Weltman 2012), and elements of the challenge to private media are undoubtedly controversial and contested. For while the Left turn in Latin American politics has propelled the region into the news headlines, reactions to elected leftist presidents in Europe has been mixed. As Porto and Hallin have remarked, for some, 'these new leaders are revolutionaries or reformists who have contributed to deepening democracy. For others, they are neopopulist demagogues who seek to impose authoritarian regimes' (2009: 291). Yet, whatever the view of these individuals, the remarkable political efforts to address the region's social inequality and poverty have helped transform the context for addressing questions about the political role of the media (Ibid).

These questions include the following: how to challenge media monopoly, how to promote citizen engagement, how to fund and promote community media, how to license and regulate the media and how to ensure freedom of expression and encourage a diverse and pluralistic media. They are the same questions Europeans and people around the world are wrestling with, and in many ways South America is setting a progressive example in answering these questions.

But unfortunately the example is not always positive. The media in many areas of South America remains held back by sophisticated mechanisms of control, with repressive elements of the dictatorship periods still in place. Media owners and political elites continue to use the media's increasingly prominent role in politics to pursue their own agendas and interests, sometimes forming alliances to protect their own markets and interests (Lugo-Ocando 2008: 2). Organized crime, drug trafficking and violence still blight large areas of South America, corrupting politics and the public sphere and muzzling the media through fear, or by force, with ten journalists and media staff killed in 2013 alone (International Federation of Journalists 2014).

The *Economist Intelligence Unit's* Democracy Index for 2010 indicates that, following Latin America's period of rapid democratisation in the 1980s and 1990s, the advance of democracy in the region as a whole has 'deteriorated slightly' since 2008. The report points to a steady advance in democracy in the region offset by deterioration in basic security and the curbing of media freedoms in some countries.

Although the deterioration in the average score for the region between 2008 and 2010 was minimal, there was more significant erosion in democracy in a number of countries in the index with three countries in the region Bolivia, Honduras and Nicaragua being downgraded from 'flawed democracy' to 'hybrid regime'.[1] Evidence of fragile democratic institutions in the region have been reinforced by the 'institutional coup' that removed President Fernando Lugo from power in Paraguay in June 2012 with evidence of US agribusiness involvement linked to Grupo Zuciollio, owner of one of the major Paraguayan newspapers, *ABC Color* (Fiorentini 2012b).

The *Economist Intelligence Unit* report identifies a deterioration of media freedoms in some Latin American nations, resulting largely from the increased conflict between government and the private media in some countries, such as Venezuela and Bolivia. While assessment from a monitoring group with clear neoliberal sympathies must be regarded with suspicion, their findings are echoed by The Inter American Press Association (IAPA) and The Committee to Protect Journalists (CPJ) amongst other groups. The IAPA (2011) picks up the concern around authoritarian tendencies in some nations, pointing to government moves against the work of the press, often legal and constitutional, which have worried observers. These concerns have been echoed in interviews and private discussions with academics, journalists, media workers and activists from Ecuador, Argentina, Peru and Colombia.

Nevertheless, it is important to put some of these concerns in a wider context. The Reporters without Borders Press Freedom Index (2012) places several Latin American countries above many European countries. Belarus languishes near the bottom of the list at 168th. Following a wave of arrests of journalists, Turkey fell ten places to 148th. Within the European Union there remain huge gaps between countries such as Finland and the Netherlands at the top of the list, and countries such as Bulgaria (80th), Greece (70th) and Italy (61st) that 'fail to address the issue of their media freedom violations, above all because of a lack of political will'. As the report makes clear, media freedom cannot be assumed because a country has a certain reputation. Britain has fallen to 28th place way behind Costa Rica and Namibia, while the United States (47th and tied with Argentina) lies ten places behind El Salvador.

These rankings leave no room for complacency, either for Europe or the Americas. And as Lugo-Ocando remarks, after less than two decades of democracy, some Latin American nations still struggle to cope with an inescapable characteristic of free speech, which is 'the persistent clash of elites' interests' (2008: 3). Meanwhile, weak institutions, political confrontation and extreme poverty create a volatile environment in which the requirement for rational and peaceful debate is regarded by some as a political inconvenience or even as a threat to democracy itself. Hence:

> Explicit censorship and strict media-state control are still the norm in many cases, even in those nations where democratic values such as freedom of speech are constitutionally guaranteed. In reality the institutions entrusted to safeguard these rights are still too frail, or are unwilling to do so. Faced with this scenario, newly elected governments have opted to perpetuate the censorship mechanisms created by the former military regimes, a phenomenon that still defines the normative and legal framework of the media in many places. (3)

Developments in Ecuador illustrate some of these questions around censorship mechanisms and state efforts to control the media.

Ecuador

Following Rafael Correa's election as president in 2007 on a popular platform of rejecting parties dominated by traditional elites and their discredited 'Washington-consensus' ideology, voter approval was given for a special assembly to rewrite the constitution. Many of the provisions in this constitution are amongst the most progressive in the world – including advancing the rights of indigenous people, civil unions for gay couples, increased state regulation and involvement in the economy, recognition of the rights of nature and the human right to an education and health care (see Becker 2011). Article 19 introduced the concept of government intervention in news media, with the aim of regulating 'the prevalence of informational, educational, and cultural content in the media's programming' (CPJ 2011: 5) as well as promoting 'the creation of spaces for national and independent producers' (ibid).

The recently passed Communications Law also includes positive measures, such as improving transparency for those organizations administering public money (Human Rights Watch 2009). The law explicitly prohibits monopolies and oligopolies in media ownership, which remains a serious problem for freedom of expression in the country with just eight groups[2] dominating Ecuador's media landscape (UNESCO 2011). The draft legislation also promotes use of subtitles or sign language to facilitate more equal access for those with hearing disabilities, an important step towards ensuring equality under the law and ending discrimination (Human Rights Watch 2011). Crucially, Ecuador, taking heed of a UNESCO report recommendation and following Uruguay and Argentina's lead, will devote one-third of broadcast spectrum to community and non-profit media that is independent of the state (2011: 89). As Reilly argues, dividing spectrum resources between the public, private and community serves to repair the relationship between state and citizen in four significant ways:

> First, they reduce the power of private media, forcing it to abandon its role as a powerful interlocutor between state and citizen. Second, they help enable the state to assume a more powerful role in directing the development of the national economy. In particular, access to media allows developmental states to advance agendas that may be unpopular with entrenched elites. Third, new media laws give citizens access to the media so that they are better able to inform government about their needs and desires. Finally, new media laws wrest control from international media interests, which often work in tandem with elite owners of domestic media.
>
> (Reilly 2012: 2)

The Communications Law (2013) was passed in a context in which Ecuador's media environment has already changed significantly since 2007. Historically, Ecuadoran broadcast media was controlled by powerful banking groups with close ties to politicians and political power bases (Correa 2012). Some broadcasters were criticized, even within the profession, for not vigorously investigating the banking crisis that caused the collapse of several financial institutions in 2000 and which cost taxpayers hundreds of millions of dollars (CPJ 2011). In 2007, several public media outlets were created including Ecuador TV (ECTV), Public Radio of Ecuador (RPE) and *El Telégrafo* newspaper. These last two were renamed following their confiscation by the Deposit Guarantee Agency (AGD) from its owner, a former banker.

In 2008, further media assets of ex-bankers were seized, and, according to the Radio and Television Frequency Audit Commission, confiscated media includes three television channels (Gama TV, TC and Cablenoticias), two magazines (*El Agro* and *La Onda*) and two radio stations (Carrusel and Súper K). A new constitutional provision prohibiting bankers from owning stock in media forced some organizations to sell their stocks (UNESCO 2011: 14–16).

Those sympathetic to the government reforms note that the majority of Ecuador's mass media, to varying degrees, have shared the opposition's agenda and in many cases appears willing to present an overly pessimistic or even catastrophic scenario in order to help advance their cause (Weisbrot 2009). There are also real grounds for alarm about the role of powerful media groups in the region following the coup attempt against Chavez in 2002, the overthrow of elected President Manuel Zelaya in 2009 (Weisbrot 2011) and an apparent coup attempt against Rafael Correa in 2010 (Reuters 2010).

However, there are other observers who note authoritarian elements in the government's media reform program that have polarized Ecuadorian society against a backdrop of sporadic attacks on journalists (Human Rights Watch 2011). A recent Inter American Press Association (IAPA 2011) report points to a number of measures in the proposed Communication Law that would enable strict controls and effective censorship of news media so they would be unable to play their role as watchdogs over the government. The IAPA is concerned that there has been an attempt to reinstate obligatory membership by journalists in a guild in Ecuador (and also Brazil and Panama), a practice that was being reversed in Latin America since the Inter-American Human Rights Court recommended its elimination in a 1985 advisory opinion. The Committee to Protect Journalists (CPJ) is also highly critical of Rafael Correa's administration, accusing it of 'widespread repression by pre-empting private news broadcasts, enacting restrictive legal measures, smearing critics and filing debilitating defamation lawsuits' (2011: 1).

Article 18 of the new constitution states that all individuals have the right to 'find, receive, exchange, produce, and release truthful, verified, timely, contextualized, and plural information without censorship'. The text's emphasis on 'truthful, verified' information opens the door to official restrictions on information that the government disputes (5). The independence of a regulatory council charged with controlling radio, television and print content in relation to violence, sex and discrimination is also called into question as five of its seven members would either be appointed by the executive branch or be chosen from groups with close ties to the executive (4).

In 2010, this battle over regulation of the media reached the front pages of the Ecuadorian press with a leading daily, *El Comercio*, referring to the fight as one for 'defence of human rights and the free practice of journalism'. This was in response to the government's closing down of a major TV station, *Teleamazonas*, for three days beginning December 22 (Weisbrot 2010). There is some dispute over the details of why broadcasting of *Teleamazonas* was suspended. The government found that it had, for the second time in a year, violated a rule that prohibits the broadcast of false information that can lead to social disturbances. In the first offence of this type, for which the station was fined $40, it questioned the legality of a vote-counting facility in the coastal city of Guayaquil (CPJ 2009). The second offence, committed in May, was a report claiming that proposed exploration for natural gas on the island of Puná would have devastated fish stocks. Since many on the island make their living from fishing, the report led to social unrest (Weibrot 2010).

While the facts over this case are disputed, Correa's hostility to some environmental groups, such as Acción Ecológica, which are opposed to the government's oil and mining policies, is not (see Dangl 2010). The president has used state media to call those who oppose his mining law 'childish,' 'nobodies' and 'allies of the right'. These attacks have deepened the rift between Correa and the social movements that supported the Ecuadoran constitution and which are now concerned that aspects of Ecuador's economic policy represent a continuation of neoliberalism (Dosh and Kligerman 2010). The failure of the international community to back Correa's Yasuni-ITT Initiative, which would compensate the Ecuadorian government for ending oil prospecting in the Yasuni National Park (a UNESCO biosphere reserve), has not helped break the country's dependency on its fossil fuel resources (Bernier 2012: 12).

The most high-profile and controversial case of media intimidation was the sentencing of three newspaper executives of the news daily *El Universo* and its former opinion editor to three years' imprisonment in 2011 (interview with Diego Cornejo 2012). The judgement given on July 20th by District Criminal Court of Guayaquil also ordered them to pay US $40 million in damages as the result of a personal libel suit filed by President Rafael Correa in response to a February 6th opinion column, which called Correa a 'dictator' (World Movement for Democracy 2011).

Set against the positive and progressive media reform moves, these incidents demonstrate a lack of respect for diversity of opinion in Ecuador, threatening to set back media freedoms and legitimate challenges to corporate media that are slowly being won across the region. However, if those framing the new Communication Law could follow the recommendations of the 2011 UNESCO report, which followed detailed consultations with a wide range of actors, Ecuador's media and civil society could flourish and a genuinely free press encourage the democratic exchange of ideas, enshrined and protected in law, which would help reduce the tensions that have been building in recent years.

Argentina

Some of the same challenges and questions exist in Argentina, whereby privatization was imposed on the national communications system in the 1990s and on all information media enterprises previously controlled by the state. Lack of media diversity was entrenched by a dictatorship-era law, which put the Federal Broadcasting Committee (COMFER) under the control of the State Intelligence Agency. The law essentially allowed only private media conglomerates, the Intelligence Agency, and the military to control and regulate the media. As Trigona (2009) points out, non-profit groups, universities, cooperatives or community associations did not have the right to apply for a broadcast licence. For community radio and television stations, this law was a holdover from the days of authoritarian rule that 'literally blocked any possibility of gaining legal permission to broadcast' (2).

The rise, in particular, of two media conglomerates, Clarín and CEI-Telefónica, meant that those who already dominated the print market also had access to the biggest share in cable and satellite television while also controlling a large part of Internet provision in Argentina (Vialey et al. 2008). By the end of the decade, 70 per cent of the communications networks in the country were controlled by just four telecommunications holdings. In many cases, these groups acted as partners as well as competitors, and through the dominance of news provision were capable of shaping and defining the topics for public debate, 'not so much telling people what to think, but what to think about' (Lugo-Ocando 2008: 26).

Generally good relations between President Néstor Kirchner's leftist government (2003–07), the Clarín Group and the handful of other media conglomerates were bolstered by a Resolution in 2005 extending their domination of the airwaves and effectively eliminating any vestiges of media diversity, especially in TV programming (Trigona 2009). However, following Grupo Clarín's opposition to a farm exports tax increase by Néstor's successor Cristina Fernández de Kirchner in 2008, the relationship between state and the Clarín Group, in particular, soured dramatically. In October 2009, President Kirchner's government passed a new media law '26.522' (described as 'Ley K' by the Grupo Clarín), which overturned military dictatorship-era laws and stipulated that broadcasting cables be apportioned equally between the private sector, the government and community organizations. The law also established limits on the number of broadcasting cables any one company could hold and the number of cities where they can operate (Cohen 2011). The world of Argentine journalism has subsequently polarized between 'journalists K' (for the Kirchners) and 'journalists anti-K' (Waisbord 2010a).

The law has its vocal supporters, who regard such a move against the 'towering presence' of the Clarín Group as long overdue, and equally vocal opponents who see a 'thinly veiled attempt by Kirchner to silence her critics and gain more control over the media for the government' (Cohen 2011: 1). Congress also passed a law that declared newsprint to be of 'public interest,' implying, according to an Inter American Press Association (IAPA) report (2011), that the production and sale of this commodity for newspapers will be regulated by the government and 'who will be able to be use it as a means of applying pressure'. There have also been expressions of unease about the Argentine government's use of advertising revenues to curry favour and promote uncritical community media outlets.

One result of these steps is a highly polarized media climate that is harmful for professional, balanced journalism (Waisbord 2010a), although, ironically, the very public row may force readers and viewers to be more 'mindful of the forces influencing their news' (Cohen 2011: 1). Who can say how much the tensions between Clarín Group and the Kirchner administration have created the context for media reform, which its opponents say has been used to reduce the power of the government's critics? However, positive outcomes for media diversity have emerged in the Audiovisual Communication Services law passed in 2009, setting limits to media **concentration** (Biglieri 2012). Two-thirds of the Radio and TV spectrum have been reserved for non-commercial stations and it require TV companies to carry channels operated by universities, union, indigenous groups and other non-governmental organizations. Furthermore, 70 per cent of radio and 60 per cent of TV content must be produced in Argentina, thus protecting local media industries and restricting the flow of US and European programming, which is dumped at low prices to achieve economies of scale. Political interference in the licensing process is theoretically protected by a seven-member commission to oversee licensing made up of two designated by the executive branch, three by congress and two by a Federal body representing provincial governments. According to Hintz, the law was initially drafted by a communications professor and World Association of Community Radio Broadcasters (AMARC) policy consultant, followed by extensive consultations with civil society and other sectors, and the final text was physically brought to parliament for adoption by a procession of 20,000 citizens, making it a 'law of the people' (2011: 154).

What other positive developments in media reform have occurred across the continent? The last decade has seen significant social and political change, leading to radical policy transformations, which have enabled a range of important media developments. Even the highly critical Inter American Press Association report (IAPA 2011) observes advances on the legal front in several countries, such as in Brazil, where President Dilma Rousseff enacted a progressive law on public access to information. And some of the most encouraging developments have been in relation to citizen and community media and in scaling back the dominance of corporate media monopolies (interviews with Isabel Ramos, Paula Biglieri). There is a long history of grass-roots media across South America despite limited opportunities possibilities for such media to operate legally. Nevertheless, some of the most progressive examples of community media policy innovations in recent years have emerged in the region. In several countries, non-profit community media have not only been legalized, but have been moved out of niche positions and elevated to a leading force in social communication (Hintz 2011: 147).

Policy change has coincided with increased academic interest in non-mainstream, alternative, community, radical, citizens' or civil society-based media practices, partly enabled by the emergence of new media technologies. Yet, with the growth of the sector, policy questions have become more prominent. According to the AMARC, 'the lack of proper enabling legislation is the single principal barrier to [community media's] social impact'

(AMARC 2007: 5 – cited Hintz: 147). Arne Hintz traces uneven but encouraging advances in community media legislation often driven by civic society mobilization across the continent from Argentina to Bolivia, which have helped to expand citizens' access to communications infrastructure (2011: 152–156). There is no space to review these different developments here, but the case of Uruguay is worth exploring briefly as it is sometimes held up as model for progressive change.

Uruguay

In Uruguay, the coming to power in 2005 of the progressive Frente Amplio (FA), which did not have close ties with traditional media, allowed a broad coalition of media activists, business groups, journalists, labour, educational, civic, human rights and women's groups to successfully lobby for media reform on a platform of media democracy as a human rights issue. This process of coalition building and advocacy culminated in the passing of legislation on community radio in 2007 (Waisbord 2010b). The law assigns one-third of radio frequencies to community, non-profit stations. The coalition also successfully pushed through a press law in 2008, authorizing public access to government information. As Waisbord notes:

> [...] civic mobilization was crucial in the processes that resulted in legal reforms. Civic groups jump-started public dialogue around the issues and drew attention to the need for change among key political, business, and civic actors. They also maintained a central role during the drafting of the bills and the process of consultation and debate in Congress. Both the coalition for the legalization of community radio and the GAIP [Uruguay's right-to-know movement] intelligently sought to expand the social support for their proposals, took advantage of political opportunities, and found allies in the Vazquez administration.
>
> (ibid: 139)

The level of direct involvement by citizens in drafting the media reforms in Uruguay call to mind the 'radical and maximalist forms of participation' discussed by Nico Carpentier (2011: 42), which are opposed to the token 'consultative' processes that so often characterize political decision making. Carpentier draws on Arnstein's ladder of social engagement (1969) and Mouffe and Laclau's 'agonistic model of democracy', which is opposed to 'antagonistic' relations between enemies and is based on an explicit model of 'radical pluralism' to interrogate and develop the concept of participation (Carpentier 2011: 38). This elaboration of the notion of 'participation' in developing democratic media systems represents an important intervention, relevant to Europe, Latin America and other regions interested in implementing media reform.

Despite the continuing power of the executive to hand out broadcast concessions, questions about the independence of the regulator and persistent media concentration (Hintz 2011), Uruguay has risen to 32nd place in the Reporters without Border's press freedom, ranking above France, Spain and the United States. The success of civic groups in changing media structures and the enabling role of the state shows that governments can play a key role in guaranteeing media democracy through appropriate policies.

For Waisbord, the reforms in Uruguay show that in a globalized world, key decisions enabling an independent and democratic media are 'intimately linked to the state, the nature of the political regime, the ideological platforms of governing parties, the relations between the government and the press and so on' (2010b: 150). The model of citizen participation in drafting media laws and equal bandwidth allocation according to state, private and civic groups is a model of reform, which is now being taken up with some success across the continent, yet remains little discussed across Europe.

Europe and media monopolies

The grass-roots influence on Paraguay's media reform efforts can be contrasted with highly effective lobbying of the European Union and member state governments by media corporations, which have played a key role in directing and restricting the scope of media policy (Williams 2004). The European Union is an association of democratic liberal states in which freedom of the press is enshrined in Chapter 2 of the Union's Charter of Fundamental Rights, which refers specifically to 'freedom of expression and information' (cited Hutchison 2009: 57). However, despite a strong tradition of public service broadcasting, Europe's democracies are increasingly dominated by a growing concentration of private media power, which political leaders appear unwilling to resist. Kaitatzi-Whitlock (2008) shows how the EU's self-regulating media market system favours the pathology of concentrated ownership, leading to media baronies and *de facto* unfair competition. For example, in Germany the Axel Springer company has over 20 per cent of the daily market and in Britain the Murdoch dominated Newscorp has over 30 per cent of that market by circulation (Hutchison 2009: 54) with revenues of $2.7 billion in 2011 (Newscorp 2011: 84). The situation is similar in France, Italy and elsewhere in western Europe. In the former eastern Bloc countries, the growth of concentration in the newspaper market is startling with the two largest groups in the Czeck Republic and Hungary increasing their shares of the national dailies from around 30 per cent to over 70 per cent (Gulyas 2006, cited Hutchison 2009: 54). Cross-media involvement is another common feature of ownership patterns throughout Europe, and companies with interests in media often have interests in non-media business.

The course of the EU's communications policy was set by the 1989 Television without Frontiers Directive (TWFD), which exclusively emphasized the economic role of communication and enabled a wave of mergers and takeovers across Europe and the 'transnationalisation of media ownership which made company conduct inscrutable' (Kaitatzi-Whitlock 2008: 31). Despite pressure from the European Parliament, the European Commission has decided, in the face of intense lobbying from media businesses, that no action on the question of ownership need be taken at the EU level (Hutchison 2009). This reluctance to tackle the issue of concentrated media power corrodes the right of citizens to information and participation, curtails plurality of expression and has a detrimental effect on the political process. For Kaitatzi-Whitlock:

> [...] the EU gave away the entire field of communication to private, deregulated, global capital forces. Such a political economy locks citizens and democratic politics out as irrelevant. The self-regulating media market system thrives on the depoliticisation and the pervasive commodification of all political agency.
>
> (2008: 42)

The democratic deficit such a policy produces can perhaps best be illustrated by the extreme phenomenon of the Berlusconi period in Italy, which was 'just the most embarrassing case' (Hutchison 2008: 33). Yet, Britain also provides a warning of ceding control of communication policy to corporate interests. As Des Freedman (2008) has shown, media policy is often presented in the United Kingdom and the United States as a technical, administrative matter free of political influence, where, in fact, it is a profoundly ideological exercise that has been shaped in recent years by so-called free market principles and intense lobbying by powerful corporate interests. Here, we see clear parallels between Latin America and the United Kingdom with inappropriate levels of collaboration between politicians and the media posing a threat to democracy (Lugo-Ocando 2008). As the recent revelations in the Leveson Inquiry in London revealed in spectacular fashion, media empires such as News Corp (currently led by Rupert Murdoch) have the power to corrupt police, politicians and the wider public sphere in ways that must be urgently checked.

An alarming paradox illustrated recently by Tambini (2012) is that while in countries like Russia licences to broadcast tend to be given out to friends of the ruling party in exchange for favourable coverage, in Britain favourable coverage is dispensed by powerful media organizations in exchange for regulatory favours, such as rolling back the few laws protecting the media from monopoly control. This, in his view, amounts to 'capture of the state by the media' (1) the inverse problem to that exercising free speech advocates and critics of the 'left turn' in Latin America.

If, in the United Kingdom, private corporate interests can have such a malign influence on our political institutions, then how can the South American model of media reform help us build a more democratic and representative media system? Tambini identifies the control of telecommunications networks, network neutrality, content and competition regulation as key issues and calls for a 'longer term plan and design for media systems that maintains an appropriate balance between public, private and third sector media [in which] the different models keep one another honest' (ibid: 2). Here, the equal division of spectrum allocation being rolled out in Uruguay, Argentina and Ecuador strikes me as an excellent starting point.

Conclusion

The apparent dissimilarity of European and Latin American media systems masks important parallels around questions of the state's relations to communication systems, the scope and concentration of private media power and the role of citizens in developing genuinely participative, democratic media institutions. I would suggest that the area where Europe has the most to learn from Latin American media reforms is in the bold regional efforts to challenge media monopoly and create a media ecology that equally balances the provision of public, private and community media.

Such efforts have the potential to end the historic collusion between state and market interests that 'continues to undermine the possibilities for media democracy' (Waisbord 2009b: 393). Similar moves in Europe would help support the diversification of media ownership, strengthen the capacity of civic organizations and expand the range of views and information sources available to the public. Legislation to reduce the influence of large corporations in the press and broadcasting; the promotion and financial support for community radio and other 'small media'; freedom of information and transparency in the use of public and private resources; and strong, independent and representative regulatory bodies kept at arms length from the state are measures that could strengthen the vital organs of democracy, in Europe, the Americas and other regions around the world.

Notes

1. The democracy index categorizes regimes as full democracies, flawed democracies, hybrid regimes and authoritarian regimes.
2. Eljuri Group, Isaías Group, Vivanco Group, Egas Group, Alvarado Group, Mantilla Group, Pérez Group and Martínez Group (Radio and Television Frequency Audit Commission cited UNESCO 2011).

3

Towards Community and Non-Profit Media Legislation in South America: Challenging Media Power Through Citizen Participation

Arne Hintz

Introduction

A democratic system, according to late media scholar Edwin Baker, requires the 'democratic distribution of communicative power' (Baker 2006: 6). Media concentration – whether in the hands of government or business – assigns the power of interpreting our environment to a small group of actors and increases the risk that media align with the holders of political and social power. Thus, media reform involves the critical review (and, potentially, reduction) of monopolies and oligopolies in the newspaper, broadcast and telecommunications sector.

At the same time, the goal to democratize the media landscape entails the development of new forms of production, which are more open and participatory, and the ability to create one's own media independent from governmental or commercial pressures. It thus requires support for a third media sector, next to commercial and state/public media, that is owned and controlled by citizens and civil society, and whose mission lies in its independent and participatory nature. The most prominent forms of such alternative modes of communication are community and non-profit media.

Community media is 'a broad category of media structures across different technological platforms (print, radio, television, web-based or mixed-media), operated for and by (and/or accountable to) a community (which can be a community of interest, a geographical community or a cultural community) and is characterized by the effective participation of that community in all processes of the organization' (Coyer and Hintz 2010: 277). Ownership and control are ultimately in the hands of self-organized and independent citizens' groups or associations; participants include individuals who are not professional media makers, thus breaking the boundaries between active producers and passive consumers; and voice is often given to groups, ideas and cultures under-represented in mainstream media, thereby supporting the participation of maginalized communities in society's political, social and cultural processes. As a means for citizens to participate in the public sphere, they are core components of a democratic media system (and may, at the same time, provide the non-commercial and decentralized alternative 'cultural apparatus' described in Chapter 1 of this volume). Community radio has been the most prominent incarnation of these media, but community television, alternative news websites and non-commercial social networking platforms have increasingly been part of the mix.

The past decade has seen increased academic interest in these non-mainstream and civil society-based media practices, which have also been termed alternative, radical and citizens' media (e.g. Rodriguez 2001; Downing 2001/2010; Howley 2005; Rennie 2006; Coyer et. al. 2007; Bailey et al. 2008; Kidd et al. 2009). With the growth of the sector, policy questions have become more prominent. According to the World Association of Community Broadcasters (AMARC), 'the lack of proper enabling legislation is the single principal barrier to [community media's] social impact' (AMARC 2007: 5). Thus, some community media organizations (such as AMARC and the Community Media Forum Europe CMFE) and researchers (e.g. Hintz 2009/2011; Hadl 2010; Milan 2010/2013; Reguero and Scifo 2010) have increasingly been interested in the regulatory rules and norms that shape the media landscape, what they offer for community and non-profit media, and where they may hinder their development.

Some of the most inspiring changes to community media policy in recent years have emerged in South America. Originally a region with a vibrant grass-roots media landscape but few possibilities for such media to operate legally, political change in several countries has led to policy change that legalized non-profit community media, moved them out of niche positions and elevated them to a leading force in social communication. Furthermore, while this has increased the potential for citizens to participate in media making, policy change has often been triggered by civil society campaigns and has thus advanced grass-roots participation also in political processes and policymaking. In some instances, citizen groups and civil society mobilizations have moved beyond advocacy and into the centre of lawmaking, and they have applied strategies of 'policy hacking'.

In this chapter, I will trace this double movement of participation in both media production and policy creation in several countries of the continent. I will first introduce the contemporary dynamics of media policy both at a global and regional level and map several necessary components of policy activism and policy change. Then, I will examine the policy environment of community media in several countries of Latin America, and explore the role of citizens in its making. From this, I will draw conclusions for the media policy situation in the region and for the dynamics of policy change more generally. This investigation, I hope, will advance our understanding of an increasingly important component of media change both in the region and worldwide. The policy innovations and participatory dynamics in parts of Latin America, as well as their challenges, offer relevant insights for both media and democratic reform elsewhere around the globe.

Media policy, civil society and the political economy of communication

Political economy and social forces

A growing research body in the academic discipline of political economy looks at actors and structures in the field of media, information and communication and addresses their roles, their objectives and their capacities in shaping the global media environment (e.g. Comor 1994; McChesney 1998/2008; Chakravartty and Yuezhi 2008). The kind of influence that these actors exert has been conceptualized as 'symbolic power', which derives from producing and transmitting symbolic forms (Thompson 1995); knowledge-related influence due to the ability to decide and influence what knowledge is discovered and how it is communicated (Strange 1994); and 'communication power' that serves to control information streams, defines norms and ideas and thus helps generate the framework within which we make sense of the world (Castells 2009). A primary concern has been with media corporations that transport and distribute specific value systems (e.g. Herman and McChesney 1997) and, more recently, with large Internet companies that provide the infrastructure for most of our online communication (e.g. McChesney 2013), as well as their role in elite networks forming a 'transnational managerial' (Cox 1981) or a 'transnational capitalist class' (Sklair 2000).

However, this disciplinary perspective does not imply an exclusive focus on the interests of dominant actors, nor on material conditions of power. As media actors, activist networks such as Indymedia have achieved considerable influence (Downing 2010), and in policy development, civil society groups have occupied important positions, as we will see below. From Neo-Gramscian understandings of hegemony and counter-hegemony (e.g. Cox 1983) to the analysis of contentious politics and collective action (e.g. Keck and Sikkink 1998; Tilly and Tarrow 2006), several academic strands have highlighted the role of supposedly 'weak' actors in political processes and their capacities to influence these processes.

Global media policy

Media and communication policy denotes the regulatory rules and norms that shape the media landscape, and explores where they originate, how they are created, their values and interests and how they shift. In addition

and Becerra 2005). Across the region, the political environment of media is traditionally characterized by 'cozy relations between large media business and governments' (Waisbord 2010b: 134; also Fox and Waisbord 2002).

Outside of this commercial media core, community radio has been immensely popular across the region. Often, it represents the only media outlet offering local news and programs on local issues, and in local languages. The costs of a radio set are low, collective use is possible, literacy is not essential, the use of radio waves requires only limited investment and it is thus the most accessible media platform (e.g. Girard 2003). The beginnings of community radio are traced to radio initiatives in Bolivia and Colombia earlier in the twentieth century, and since then a vast number of stations emerged across the continent (Rodriguez 2001). However, they were largely excluded from access to frequency licenses due to discriminatory laws and regulatory practices. Most countries of the region lacked precise rules and criteria for granting, revoking and renewing broadcasting permits, supervision of the use or abuse of licences was absent, and the discretionary handing out of licences by the government to specific 'friendly' operators was common. In a context in which the president typically handed out frequencies to political and business allies, community radio could not operate legally (Waisbord 2010b). The alternative allocation procedure of auctioning off licences to the highest bidder was equally inaccessible for non-profit media. Where it was legally allowed to exist, laws were often highly restrictive regarding range and funding. Where radios operated without a licence, they were subject to regular raids and closures (Gomes and Aguerre 2009). The lack of transparent regulatory procedures, particularly of supportive policy frameworks for community broadcasting, has been regarded as a key symptom of an incomplete transition from authoritarian rule and insufficient democratization (Klinger 2011; Mauersberger 2011).

As left-wing governments were elected in several South American countries in the early 2000s (including Venezuela 1999, Brazil 2002, Argentina 2003, Uruguay 2004, Bolivia 2006, Ecuador 2007), following deep economic crises as well as the (related) legitimacy crisis of the neoliberal paradigm, privatization processes were stalled or even reverted. Countries including Venezuela, Bolivia and Ecuador carried out re-nationalization processes in the telecommunications sector, and media policy reform in countries like Argentina and Uruguay established a more favourable environment for non-commercial public service and community media.

Political change was carried by a wave of social movements and protests against the predominant social and economic order. The Zapatista uprising in Mexico 1994 provided a starting point for regional mobilizations as well as global struggles against neoliberalism and the institutions that promoted it. Indigenous uprisings followed in many countries, such as Ecuador, Bolivia, Guatemala and Brazil. The economic breakdown in Argentina in 2001 led to an outbreak of massive protests that took down several successive governments and carried the slogan 'que se vayan todos' – they all must go. A year later in Venezuela, commercial media supported a coup against President Chavez, which was defeated by a popular movement, including community and alternative media. These moments in the recent history of the region, and many others, led to a reactivation of social movements as 'the social and organizational fabric, seriously affected by adjustment policies and new mechanisms for repressing and criminalizing social protest, began to gradually recover' (Leon et al. 2005: 25). Regional linkages and networks between some of these movements were created, such as the international network Via Campesina and its regional grouping, the Latin American Coordination of Rural Organizations (CLOC). Common campaigns emerged, such as the Continental Campaign Against the Free Trade Area of the Americas and the Campaign Against Payment of the Foreign Debt. The intense convergence and coordination of movements was highlighted, not least, by the World Social Forum, which originated in the region.

Communication infrastructure, media structures and media messages have become vital concerns for these networks and campaigns. The right to create media has been a central piece of the communication agenda by social movements in the region, together with access to media and communication infrastructure, both 'old' and 'new', and the democratization of the media. This agenda has been framed by a call for communication rights, which regard communication as a social right rather than a commodity, and as an interactive process, furthering the active participation of the citizenry in social and political deliberations and developments (Girard et al. 2010). Stronger calls for popular participation, non-profit 'third sector' media and the de-concentration of media ownership, have changed the ideological tide away from market logics and towards the 'de-commodification of communication policies' (Gomez Garcia 2013). Overall, the multi-faceted social, political, economic and ideological transformations offered a radically new context for non-profit community media and for citizen participation in both media and policy change.

Community media policy change

Elsewhere: Community media policy around the globe

Operating outside the classic structures of media, such as the traditional 'two-tier' broadcast model of public service and commercial broadcasting, community media has often fallen through the cracks of official recognition. Neither the state/public media system nor the market-based and industry-dominated neoliberal model of organizing media infrastructure provided significant space for small non-profit and citizen-based media (Ó Siochrú and Girard 2002). However, openings for their recognition and support have gradually emerged. Internationally, the MacBride report (the main outcome of the international debate on a New World Information and Communication Order in the 1970s and 80s) recognized the role of local, alternative, participatory and decentralized media (MacBride et al. 1980). At the World Summit on the Information Society (WSIS) of 2003 and 2005, community media concerns were crushed by both authoritarian governments and business agendas, but side-events, thematic WSIS-related conferences and reports strongly emphasized the value of community media (Hintz 2009). Nationally, governments of countries such as Canada and France legalized community radio from the 1970s onwards and, in some cases, provided funding mechanisms (Coyer and Hintz 2010).

Regional policy institutions have picked up the trail over the past decade. In 2001, the African Charter for Broadcasting recognized community media as a 'third media sector' in a three-tier media landscape (UNESCO 2001). Both the European Parliament (in 2008) and the Council of Europe (in 2009) adopted declarations in which they highlighted the role of community media in advancing social cohesion, media pluralism and inter-cultural dialogue, and in which they called for the legal recognition of community media in national media law (European Parliament 2008; Council of Europe 2009). Likewise, the Inter American Commission on Human Rights has acknowledged the centrality of community media for freedom of expression and access to information, calling upon states in the region to 'legally recognize and reserve parts of the spectrum for this type of media, as well as to establish equitable conditions for the access to licences that recognize the difference of non-commercial media' (InterAmerican Commission on Human Rights 2009: 392). Governments in several countries have started to put such calls into practice. The British regulator Ofcom has allocated licences to hundreds of community radios since 2004. The countries with the largest populations in South Asia and Africa, India and Nigeria legalized community radio in 2008 and 2009, and the government of India formulated the ambitious plan to give licences to 4,000 community radio stations over the coming years (AMARC 2010). In the United States, low power FM radio was legalized with restrictions in 2000 and expanded through the Local Community Radio Act in 2010 (Prometheus Radio Project 2010).

Meanwhile, the rise of web 2.0 and social media has offered new opportunities for traditional community media to expand their services through the web and podcasting, and for other media activists to build new participatory and alternative media operations. Commercial social media platforms have been used for activism (Diamond 2010), and non-profit alternatives have been developed (Lovink and Rasch 2013). However, these have not replaced traditional broadcast platforms, and radio activists have argued that our digital futures will not offer access to media unless adequate space for participatory media is provided in the analogue present (Coyer and Tridish 2005).

South America: Towards community media policy

These international developments have not only been reflected in South America. The new laws in the region have often been more far-reaching and innovative than elsewhere and have set new standards for the legal recognition of community media. According to AMARC, the World Association of Community Radio Broadcasters, 'one of the best references of regulatory frameworks to curtail media concentration and promote and guarantee diversity and pluralism' is the new broadcast law in Argentina (AMARC 2010). The law illustrates the dramatic changes between, as well as continuities running through, the 'old' and the 'new' regime. The basis for media policy, until then, was a law that was passed during the military dictatorship and which favoured private commercial media and excluded community media. It had been amended during the neoliberal decade of the 1990s, allowing further privatization, cross-ownership, foreign ownership and a significant increase of the maximum of licences that a company could hold, thereby supporting media concentration (Marino 2009). Following economic breakdown and social unrest, the new Kirchner government began moderate revisions of the regulatory framework in the mid-2000s. In 2009, the new legal environment was created with the adoption of Law 26.522 on Audio-Visual Communication Services. In particular, the law recognizes three sectors of broadcasting – state, commercial and not-for-profit – and guarantees a 33 per cent share of the radio frequency spectrum for each sector. While this provision went far beyond the protection that community media has enjoyed in most other countries around the globe and was welcomed by media activists and communication rights advocates, the law still contained some shortcomings. Community media is legalized but not (yet) equipped with public funding that enables it to operate. The wording of the law refers to 'non-profit' media, which may open loopholes for a variety of media types that are not necessarily participatory and citizen based. Commercial media, not surprisingly, has had more fundamental problems with the new policy. In 2010, the law was temporarily suspended by the Federal Appeal Court of Mendoza, following strong opposition and a publicity campaign by the Clarín media group, the largest Argentine media corporation.

Neighbouring Uruguay passed through similar political and policy transformations. The election of the left-wing coalition Frente Amplio in 2005 represented a fundamental break with political traditions in the country, and the governments of the transition period swiftly adopted two laws legalizing and regulating community media. The laws provide a clear definition of the sector, allocation criteria which are based on the latter's social goals, and highly transparent and participatory allocation and renewal procedures. They also set principles for the administration of the radio-electric spectrum, stating that it 'is a common heritage of humanity (...) and, therefore, the equitable access to frequencies of the entire Uruguayan society is a general principle of its administration' (quoted in Lanza and Lopez-Goldaracena 2009: 4). As in Argentina, one-third of the spectrum is to be allocated to community/non-profit media.

This allocation quota has become a model component of community media legislation and has been implemented in other countries, most recently in Ecuador. The new Organic Communications Law, adopted in June 2013, recognizes and strengthens community media, advances the right to communicate and seeks to limit media concentration. Despite these progressive aspects, other parts of the law have received criticism both by local civil society groups and by international bodies, including the United Nations Special Rapporteur on the Right to Freedom of Opinion and Expression, as they may compromise online anonymity and include problematic clauses for content regulation, and as the new institutional design lacks full independence from governmental interventions (Lavin 2013).

Political change in Bolivia, with President Evo Morales taking office in 2005 and his Movement Toward Socialism (MAS) forming the government from 2006, proved to be an even greater landslide than in Uruguay and other countries. Community media was legalized by decree in 2004, 2005 and 2007. A new constitutional article on 'social media' was introduced, calling for the state to support community media. The government moved beyond mere legalization by creating a national network of indigenous people's radio stations, in response to the particular diversity of social and ethnic origins and languages in the country. This has led to new opportunities for citizens and civil society to create their own media, but also to some confusion as to the role of the state and the definition of community media. Community media is mainly defined as local media and limited in geographic scope; they are not allowed to carry advertising; and no specific percentage of the spectrum has been reserved for them. The new indigenous stations, which are the result of government intervention and dependent on government support, are also called 'community media', which confuses the understanding of that term and concept (Aguirre Alvis et al. 2009).

As the first country with a left-wing government in the chain of recent political changes in Latin America, Venezuela pioneered many of the political and regulatory transformations in the region, including media policy change. A new telecommunications law was adopted in 2000, just over a year after the new Chavez government had taken office. The law regularized spectrum allocation after decades of arbitrary and political license provision, and legalized community radio and television. Since then, the regulator has given out a large number of licences to community media. However, the complex allocation procedure provides numerous bureaucratic hurdles; community media is (as in Bolivia) restricted to a concept of local media, and while financial subsidies are available, they are widely seen as a double-edged sword as they may jeopardize the media's independence (Serjant 2009).

Located geographically next to Venezuela but offering a very different political situation (with a conservative government and market-oriented policies), Colombia, paradoxically, may constitute both a similar pioneer for community media legislation and a further example for problematic political interactions. With around 650 community radio and 40 community television stations, the country has been one of the 'success stories' in the region. However, license conditions are restrictive (Zuluaga and Martínez 2012) and the proactive approach by the right-wing Colombian government regarding community media has been called an 'encapsulation of civil society' (Gomez Garcia 2013), and thus a neutralization of critical voices by means of their co-optation into national strategies.

The largest country on the continent, Brazil, conveys an even more problematic picture and demonstrates that policy change has often been limited and interrupted. Community media was legalized in 1998 and, thus, earlier than in most other countries. However, it faces significant bureaucratic barriers in the application process, severe limitations in terms of transmission power and range, a lack of public funding and restrictions to financing models such as advertising. New license grants have to be processed first by the Department of Communications, and then authorized by the National Congress. While this may allow for parliamentary control and transparency, it leads to long delays and an overly complex process. Even though the Federal Constitution from 1988 highlights the social aspects of communication and rejects monopolies and oligopolies, laws and regulations do not necessarily reflect these goals, and commercial broadcast license holders are usually given wide-ranging freedoms. 'The decision is always to renew, even with notorious violations by stations towards their legal obligations' (Moyses and Gindre 2009: 19). Recent government efforts to facilitate community radio development under the 'National Plan of Community Radio' have led to a growing number of licences being allocated (Gomez Garcia 2013). However, most community radios remain in a precarious position, and as they typically operate with little resources, sponsorship by political groups is common, and political dependency is a likely result. Meanwhile, thousands of community radios are broadcasting in Brazil without a licence, making it one of the most vibrant grass-roots radio landscapes worldwide. However, and in contrast to the lack of supervision of commercial radios, unlicensed community radios are heavily repressed. According to some accounts, up to ten radios are shut down every day, and up to several thousand per year (Moyses and Gindre 2009).

Chile, the country where neoliberal restructuring started and where the links between these policies and the military dictatorship were most pronounced, continues to follow a largely market-based approach. Radio frequency licences are typically allocated by auction to the highest bidder and can be sold further; there is no limit to the number of frequencies that an owner can hold; most concessions are granted for 25 years, and renewal is comparably easy. All these favour large media operations and, particularly, the incumbent stations (La Morada 2009). Until 2010, community radio was only allowed as so-called minimum-coverage radio, and limited to one watt of transmission power, which usually restricted coverage to the immediate surroundings of the station. Concessions were given only for three years, and public funding was not provided. Given, furthermore, the significant bureaucratic and financial hurdles, the 'minimum-coverage' option was not a feasible opportunity for most non-profit community and social groups. A new law was passed in 2010, which expanded license terms to ten years and transmission power to 25 watts (40 watts in rural areas). However, the spectrum reserved for community radio remains very limited (about 4 per cent), technical and administrative hurdles remain high, and restrictions on advertising make it difficult for radios to operate with an economically sustainable basis. Radios exceeding these limits or operating without a licence suffer severe repression (Mauersberger 2011).

Part of the Southern cone thus offers us a problematic case that is not unsimilar to the situation in Central America. In Mexico, for example, a wide variety of mostly small mini-broadcasters service rural and indigenous populations as well as urban groups and student movements. But their legal status is not acknowledged, and they are unable to obtain licences and resources; thus, they operate under clandestine and illegal conditions and are subject to criminalization and closure. As in Chile, emerging proposals for policy reform may alleviate the situation somewhat but face strong opposition by dominant actors in media and policy (Klinger 2011).

This brief tour of several South American countries highlights a number of promising developments and some innovative and far-reaching policy reform but also shows us significant challenges. Apart from the shortcomings of specific laws and regulatory practices, a common characteristic is the persistent weakness of regulatory mechanisms and the discretion of governments in administering the radio-electric spectrum. Although transparency has largely been improved, new allocation processes have been set in place and new regulatory institutions established. As in Argentina and Uruguay, regulators in many countries lack independence from the executive, and governments retain power to hand out broadcast concessions. New laws and institutional arrangements, as in Ecuador where the chairs of the new regulatory bodies are to be appointed by the president, may even create further channels for political influence. A fragmented, complex and sometimes contradictory regulatory landscape hinders the implementation of policy reform in countries as distinct as Brazil and Bolivia and creates a grey area that favours the traditionally close connections between the business sector and political elites (as in Brazil) or requires the executive to retain significant discretion in interpreting and applying the law (as in Bolivia, see Aguirre Alvis et al. 2009). Similarly, Venezuelan media policy, as that of other countries of the region, remains characterized by an 'institutional weakness of the regulatory process' (Urbina Serjant 2009: 8).

The role of civil society activism

Civil society mobilizations have played an important role in creating policy change, and civil society agendas heavily influenced the new policies on community and non-profit media. In Argentina, the civil society initiative 'Coalition for Democratic Broadcasting' was formed in 2004 and brought together unions, universities, human rights groups and community media to advocate for the new audiovisual media law. The coalition developed a set of key demands, and a coalition member and university professor was charged by the government to draft the new law. This first draft was discussed at 28 open hearings, comments by civil society groups were included in the document and a demonstration of 20,000 people brought the final text to Parliament where it was adopted, making it a true 'law of the people' (Loreti 2011).

The wording of the Uruguayan law was based on a draft submitted by civil society groups and drew heavily from a model law developed by AMARC. Its adoption was influenced by significant pressure from a broad civil society coalition of media, labour, educational and human rights organizations, and by AMARC's advocacy work. As in Argentina, community media advocates crossed the lines between inside and outside the policymaking realm: AMARC expert Gustavo Gomez became (temporarily) the National Director of Telecommunication (Light 2011), while the new regulatory advisory body COFECOM in Argentina elected Nestor Busso, a representative of community radios, as its president (Mauersberger 2011).

In Bolivia, AMARC participated in the initial allocation process of new licences to community media, and civil society groups were involved in formulating the respective policies. Extended possibilities of participation, however, only existed during a brief window after President Morales came to power and were later reduced or revoked. In Chile and Mexico, campaigns by national community media organizations and other local and international NGOs managed to weaken the hardline positions by the respective governments and initiate (limited) reform (Klinger 2011). Broader policy norm change was supported by national initiatives such as the 'National Conference of Communication' in Brazil, a multi-stakeholder event in 2009, which was based on earlier efforts such as the 'National Forum for the Democratization of Communication' and which developed a 'historic agenda in the field of communications democratization' (Cabral 2011: 2).

These instances of policy activism offer us significant insights into the dynamics of policy change, the role of civil society activism and the relevance of the strategies for intervention that were discussed earlier. To start with, these cases demonstrate the importance of a policy window. In some countries, economic crisis led to public criticism of established practices, the retreat of traditional political forces and the break-up of policy monopolies. In all countries, political change provided opportunities for policy change. Civil society groups used these policy vacuums to advocate their agendas and propose new solutions. Framing their goals in terms of the democratization of communication and the right to communicate, they referred to widespread concerns across the region. All initiatives were based on strong alliances amongst civil society and public-interest groups, and they developed strong movement–government connections. In some cases, movement members occupied strategic positions inside the institutional apparatus and helped facilitate policy change from there; in other cases, allies in power served as vital connection points for movements.

The existence of a strong transnational advocacy network – AMARC – helped to connect different national efforts and create consistency. While AMARC's presence is stronger in some countries and weaker in others (and political conflicts with other civil society coalitions exist), it was vital for sharing agendas and facilitating institutional relations. The value of transnational exchange and of transnational policy norms that guide national policymaking has been confirmed by the experiences of similar initiatives elsewhere, for example the Community Media Forum Europe (CMFE). The CMFE has served as a channel for community media to raise their concerns on the European level, and as an effective lobby mechanism to foster the recognition and promotion of community media in Europe, and its efforts have led to influential declarations by regional institutions (see above).

Both examples, AMARC and CMFE, are instructive also because they have moved beyond mere advocacy. While the CMFE formulated detailed proposals for policy reform, AMARC developed a model legal framework, the *Principles on Democratic Regulation of Community Broadcasting* (AMARC 2008). In both cases, the proposals were used by relevant institutions as guidance for policy development, and parts of them were implemented. This kind of civil society-based law development extended to the national level, as we have seen in Argentina where movement members wrote parts of the law and a broader range of citizens and civil society groups contributed comments. This is significant as it transcends the advocacy role that has traditionally been assigned to civil society, and thus moves citizens much more to the centre of policy development.

In formulating their proposals, these policy initiatives have drawn from legal precedents in other jurisdictions, institutional declarations and best practices from around the globe. The creators of the Argentine law, for example, selected components from AMARC's framework, other national laws, and norms set by international institutions, such as the UNESCO media development indicators (Loreti 2011). This practice of assembling, revising and 'upgrading' legal instruments can be observed in other regions and regarding other policy fields as well. Perhaps the most far-reaching example has been the Icelandic Modern Media Initiative (IMMI), which developed a full package for reforming the national media and communication laws by cherry-picking laws and regulations from other countries, creating a puzzle of tried-and-tested components and adapting them to the national situation. The IMMI proposal included, for example, components from the Belgian source protection law, the Norwegian Freedom of Information Act, Swedish laws on print regulation and electronic commerce, the EU Privacy Directive, the New York Libel Terrorism Act and the Constitution of Georgia (Hintz 2013). Similar practices are applied elsewhere, from local initiatives, to create municipal and provincial transparency laws in Germany to regional networks that propose legal frameworks for net neutrality in Europe, and to a range of 'policy hackathons' that serve as temporary spaces for activists to develop, for example, new privacy policies.

These forms of 'policy hacking' thus encompass very different experiences in different parts of the world, yet share a common approach: Just as hackers and technical developers change and upgrade code, these initiatives develop new 'legal code'. The relation between technical and legal expertise has been observed in other networks, such as the open source movement, where 'tinkering' with technology and the law draws from similar skills and forms of reasoning (Coleman 2009). However, as our examples demonstrate, the practice of 'policy hacking' may not exclusively relate to the policy field of digital technology but apply also to more traditional and analogue media.

Finally, the international dimension of 'policy hacking' addresses a further concern in policy studies – policy transfer and diffusion. While the transfer of policies from one jurisdiction to another is usually discussed in the context of (inter-)governmental activity, the cases mentioned here demonstrate a citizen and civil society-based practice of policy transfer. The development processes for new community media laws in countries, such as Argentina and Uruguay interacted with each other when Argentine activists integrated parts of the initial Uruguayan reform into their proposal for a new comprehensive law and Uruguayan activists, in turn, used that law as a model for further reforms. Groups and coalitions elsewhere have tried to replicate these model laws in their countries, thus influencing legislative development across the region and up to the Northern edge of Latin America (e.g. for Mexico, see Klinger 2011).

Conclusion

In many countries of South America, the last decade has seen dramatic changes in media policy. Whereas previously communication regulation was characterized by a mix of authoritarian political traditions and neoliberal ideologies, and geared towards political and business elites, new legislation in several jurisdictions has helped to expand citizens' access to communication infrastructure and has provided more transparent regulatory procedures. A key piece of policy change has been the legalization of community and non-profit broadcasting and its integration into the national media mix as a legitimate and important third sector. It has constituted a crucial factor in the democratization of the media landscape, as it enables a variety of social sectors, from indigenous populations to urban youth, to engage in media production, contribute their voices to public debate, and thus participate in public spheres.

Social movements and civil society networks have been crucial in advancing policy change. Taking advantage of policy windows that have emerged due to political change, they have influenced norm change, participated in policy debate and contributed to policy design. In some places, they have moved beyond classic advocacy-oriented roles by developing legal frameworks, writing the law and implementing policies in collaboration with governments and regulatory institutions. Applying practices of 'policy hacking', they have used international precedents for developing policy proposals and have sought to transfer and diffuse policies across the region. By experimenting with citizen-based forms of lawmaking, they demonstrate the enhanced role of civil society actors in the policy process and push the boundaries of citizen participation. Their interventions highlight trends in the construction of legal and political frameworks for the media. They underline that national policymaking has to be understood in the context of an international and multi-actor environment, and that ideological change, social mobilizations and the strategic roles of civil society organizations, as well as individual experts have affected policy change. Further, the new community media laws in many countries of the region provide model legislation, not just for other countries in Latin America but also for other parts of the world, including the 'Global North'. Contrary to classic models of a North-South policy transfer, policy innovation originates, in this case, in the South and may move from there to the North.

Yet, despite many improvements, the situation for community media remains difficult as serious obstacles continue to exist. Legalization has been slow and incomplete in several countries, little or no public funding is available, bureaucratic barriers often make the process of obtaining a legal licence a daunting exercise and various restrictions on community media's operations, such as regarding coverage and content, persist. In particular, the weakness of regulatory agencies and their lack of independence from the state are visible across all the countries discussed here. While promising new laws and regulations have been established, institutional change has not kept pace, and media authorities continue to depend on the executive power. This may be advantageous as long as a government is community media friendly, but when that government leaves office, regulatory practices may be changed or revoked. The structural and institutional environment that frames policymaking therefore requires consolidation to make the current transformations sustainable. South American community media policy is thus highly instructive regarding both the strengths and the shortcomings of its ambitious attempts to democratize the media and enhance citizen participation.

Part II

The Politics and Cultural Practices of Media and Power in South America

4

The Fight for Public Opinion: From the Mediatization of Politics to the Politicization of the Media in Ecuador

Mauro Cerbino, Isabel Ramos, Marcia Maluf and Diana Coryat

Introduction

This chapter analyses new scenarios of confrontation between the government and private media, focusing on the case of Ecuador. We argue that such confrontation has served to erect a platform upon which the government and the private media fight for public opinion.[1] Our intent here is to examine the political significance of this confrontation, particularly with respect to its consequences for governability, and for shaping public opinion.

Similar government–media disputes can be observed in the region, in so-called neopopulist governments, most notably in Argentina, Bolivia and Venezuela (Follari 2010). As Robert McChesney argues in this volume, these disputes, and the media reforms being implemented by these governments, are unprecedented not only in the region but also globally.

Theoretically, the government–media confrontation can be analysed using Ernesto Laclau's (2005) concept of 'populist rupture'. As Laclau (2006: 57) has argued, a political rupture occurs when:

> ...the inescapable condition is that there is a dichotomization of social space, that social actors see themselves as participants in one or the other of the two opposing camps. To construct *el pueblo* (the people) as a collective actor means a call to 'those from below,' to a frontal opposition with the existing social order. This implies that, in one form or the other, the existing institutional channels for the processing of social demands have lost their efficiency and legitimacy, and that a new hegemonic configuration – the new 'historical block' to use a Gramscian expression – supposes a change of regimen and a restructuration of public space.

For Laclau, any form of rupture, which implies the configuration of new hegemonies, necessarily contains an element of populism. Although Laclau's own work does not focus on the role of media, we extend his theory to argue that one can neither conceive of a populist rupture nor any type of governability without taking the media into account. We therefore examine to what extent mediated action is constitutive of a populist rupture, particularly through the mediatization of politics. Moreover, we argue that the Ecuadorian government is deploying a mediatized representation of politics, particularly through its confrontation with private media. Further, this chapter seeks to demonstrate that such confrontation is enabling populism to be deployed in the dispute for public opinion.

In contemporary societies, it is not possible to comprehend any form of political representation or hegemonic configuration without considering the role of the media. For this reason, the battle for public opinion between the government and the media is politically significant. In Rafael Correa's government, public opinion is influenced not only by private media but also by the government in the same mediated terrain. In other words, public opinion is politicized through the mediatization of the government's political communication.

Verón (2001) argues that the transformation from *mediated societies* to post-industrial societies in the process of *mediatization* involves a process of social change in which the media takes on enormous importance. In a *mediated* society, communication technologies are gradually integrated into the social fabric; in *mediatized* societies, all practices and social relations are transversed by mediated communication, and the social fabric is characterized by complex communicational processes across distinct, significant registers. Verón's argument is inscribed in what he calls *audiovisual democracy*, a specific form of functioning of the social body, which is strongly marked by the key role of television in the production of political events. From this perspective, the defining function of television as a cultural phenomenon is precisely the construction of events of a political order. According to this framework, the mediatized experience is constituted in the space of socialization *par excellence*, as the majority of people cannot access much of what goes on in the world without mass media.

For Verón (2001), the mediatization of politics requires specific attention to the 'ties of devotion and dispute'[2] in all the variations that exist between politics and communication. Concretely, this refers to the ties of mutual dependence that are generated between political discourse and journalism, which range from devotion and unconditional collaboration to dispute and permanent confrontation, as in the case described herein. Most recently, the phenomenon of mediatization of politics in Ecuador has an added component, a permanent campaign of confrontation waged by each side. As will be made clear later in the chapter, this situation has been accompanied by the disappearance of boundaries between political discourse and communicational discourse. Verón also argues that in the context of *audiovisual democracy*, one can observe an increasing modification of social practices as a result of the process of imbrication between politics and media.

The use of media by politicians, as spaces in which they debate political ideas in a rational and argumentative fashion, is conceptualized by various authors (Narvaez Montoya 2005; Mouchon 2002). However, the fascination with and dependence on audiovisual economies to capture votes and govern does not sufficiently explain the phenomenon of the government–media confrontation, which has been playing out in Ecuador since 2007. It is also necessary to understand the populist rupture that has occurred in Correa's government and, therefore, to historicize the relationship between previous governments and the private media. As such, the first section of this chapter examines this relationship, and the myriad ways in which the state's policies and institutional framework have fostered the privileged position held by private media, above other kinds of media, journalists and audiences. The second section then analyses how Correa has gone about disrupting that privileged place held by private media through discursive and legislative means, by focusing on scenarios of contentious dispute between these actors.

This chapter also seeks to contribute to a conceptualization of public opinion, by articulating political theory and communication theory. Contrary to liberal conceptualizations of public opinion (Crespi 1997; Lazarsfeld 1957; Neumann 1995), we argue that public opinion has become repoliticized through the populist rupture and ensuing government–media confrontation. Such a framework seeks to provide a deeper understanding of the role that media plays in the neopopulist representations of the Correa government.

The relationship between the media and politics before Correa

Prior to Correa's presidency, the relationship between the Ecuadorian state and private media was one of complicity, with little variation among successive governments (Hallin and Mancini 2008). The implication of said relationship was that private media held a 'naturally' privileged position over other kinds of media, and also over audiences. Such asymmetry of access to mediated space, and to content production destined for mass circulation, reflected the profound inequalities in Ecuadorian society. Moreover, the privileged place held by private media was consolidated legally.

The legislative and communicational politics developed and maintained by governments of different parties have been inscribed, as Tilly (2008) argues, by social inequality, the result being that economic and enunciative privileges have been bestowed upon private media businesses, over the rights of journalists and audiences. Following Tilly, we argue that the historic complicity between private media and these governments generated a framework in which governability was strongly influenced by private media and the elite interests they represented. Furthermore, these private media enterprises prospered under the support of these governments. A brief analysis of the legal norms in Ecuador regarding the printed press and broadcast media cleary indicates that private media has been strongly supported by successive governments, democratic or dictatorial, regardless of their ideological position or political project.

Benefits historically assigned by the Ecuadorian state to private media can be classified according to four criteria: first, those that imply the transfer of funds from the state to private media; second, those that contribute to the profitability of private media through an injection of resources derived from regional and municipal governments, political parties, media employees and common citizens; third, legal measures that have provided the media with privileged, institutional access to decision-making processes that affect the sector; and finally, regulations that facilitated the concentration of media properties, the formation of conglomerates and exercise of oligarchic practices.

In this section, we examine the legally mandated benefits that have facilitated the transfer, direct or indirect, of public resources to private media. Initially, the print media, and later television and radio, were recognized by the state as industrial activities, which meant they were added to the long list of businesses (all of which were economically and politically connected to the traditional elite) that benefitted from the *Ley de Fomento Industrial* (Law of Industrial Development).[3,4] It is important to bear in mind that the abovementioned law, implemented in the mid-twentieth century, was conceived of by the state as a mechanism for industrial development by import substitution. According to our understanding of this law, it would be difficult to apply it to the mass media. In spite of the designation as 'cultural industries,' it remains to be demonstrated empirically, and in a serious national debate, just how mass media has contributed to the development of the country as national industries.

Additionally, since the 1960s, private media companies have received from the state a series of economic stimuli including tax exemptions, the granting of tariffs for the importation of goods and services and the opportunity to participate in national programs of industrial promotion. They also received financing with preferential credit through state financial institutions, such as the *Banco de Fomento* (Development Bank) and *La Corporación Financiera Nacional* (Corporation for National Finance). The advantages accorded to private media companies, beginning with their recognition as 'transformative industries,' also translated into important transfers of public funds to private businesses.

A review of the main benefits that had been accorded by the state's industrial development policies illustrates the magnitude of such transfer of funds, particularly if one takes into account that such policies and practices have been in place for almost 50 years. This transfer of benefits included the following: a full exemption of taxes; the exoneration of tariffs for ten years; the import of equipment and parts that are not produced nationally; a reduction of 20 per cent of the fiscal or municipal taxes on sales during the first three years to new companies; exoneration of taxes on investments, scientific research, staff training and donations; and the ability to quickly depreciate machinery and other equipment.[5] In a similar vein, the military junta that was in power from 1963 to 1966 exonerated, through two decrees, commercial radio and television companies from paying taxes on sales and profits.[6] Additionally, during the government of José Maria Velasco Ibarra, in 1971 media companies were granted a 50 per cent reduction in postage rates.[7]

The second group of incentives facilitated the granting of resources to private media companies through the application of diverse laws and regulations, which allowed such entities as municipalities, provincial boards, political parties, banks and even private individuals to purchase advertising space, especially in newspapers. The requirement to publicly publish in the press announcements, edicts, sentences, resolutions, citations, sanctions and so on was implemented mainly through successive election laws, from regulations of judicial power to a diverse array of administrative regulations. Even if the funds that were mobilized on behalf of these publications were not directly derived from the government's media budget, substantial funds came from local branches of government, commercial and financial enterprises, non-profit associations and family finances. Moreover, the state made these monetary transfers obligatory.

The fact that the 1975 Radio and Television Law expressly prohibited community media from selling advertising space, including those related to judicial and administrative publications, only serves to underscore the historic privilege that commercial media has enjoyed, and that, as we have tried to demonstrate, has been legally sanctioned by the state.

Beyond the economic advantages mentioned above, the Ecuadorean state has legitimated private media owners' participation in political and administrative matters, when decisions would directly or indirectly affect their business activities. For example, the existence of the position of a national lawmaker 'for journalism and cultural institutions' consecrated in the Constitutions of 1929, 1945 and 1967, almost always occupied by owners or executives of private media companies, illustrates the collusion between state institutions and media owners.

As such, it is not surprising that between 1956 and 1960, Jorge Mantilla Ortega, an investor in *El Comercio*, one of the most important media conglomerates in Ecuador, exercised this role, and, a few years later, his brother Carlos became a member of the 1966 Constituent Assembly, thus obtaining political representation for private media. Beyond the aforementioned ties, distinct governments have placed designated journalists and media owners in strategic ministries and attractive diplomatic posts. Given such legal frameworks, it is not unusual that business associations related to radio and television were called on to form part of CONARTEL, the *Consejo Nacional de Radio y Televisión* (National Council of Radio and Television) in 1995.

This position, with voice and vote in the council that regulated their activities, was secured in the 1995 reforms to the *Ley de Radiodifusión* (Law of Radio and Television).[8] Since the founding of CONARTEL until 2008, no formal claims against private media have ever been filed by the state, due to the evident conflict of interest it would have represented.

To conclude this overview of the close relationship that governments have had with private media prior to that of Rafael Correa's mandate, it is important to emphasize that existing laws have not only made it possible but have also fostered the concentration of media, and hence have contributed to the formation of media conglomerates that generate the concentration of audiences, such as the expedited decree that dates from 1935[9] that allows newspaper companies to establish radio and television stations. Moreover, this legal framework has exonerated these radio stations from the payment of all taxes related to equipment purchase, installation expenses and hiring of personnel. In other words, the decree established advantages accorded within the norms of industrial development for 15 years (as discussed above).

The current Broadcast Law, whose regulatory body includes media owners, granted even more privileges that fostered media concentration. In the first place, it did not set limits on the number of frequencies that could be associated with one owner. The legal precept that made this possible was called the *sistema de radiodifusión y televisión* (system of radio and television broadcast) and was defined as 'the combination of the *estación matrix* (headquarters) and its *repetidoras* (that transmit the same programming simultaneously) for an undefined period of time'[10]. Hence, the law provided a path towards the concentration of audiences. Secondly, this law assured that media companies obtained earnings through the private appropriation of public resources, as it permitted the rent, sale and transference of radio and television channels, whose owner, as in most nations, is the state.

The enormous benefits that the state has transferred to private media have helped them to grow more powerful, when not directly delegating power to them. These benefits have foreclosed opportunities for media that are not defined by private ownership, while building the capacity of private media to condition an array of government actions. Moreover, such process of power acquisition, at times, has jeopardized those same governments' legitimacy.[11] The economic and political benefits were bequeathed to these companies by the state without any demand for quality, public relevance or social interest in the informational and entertainment products disseminated by them. Neither did the state insist on their adherence to labour laws and obligations. In other words, the Ecuadorean state did not offer those who work for media corporations the same protection as offered to media owners, nor has such protection been offered to ordinary citizens or communities.

Correa's undoing of media ties: Scenarios of dispute

The confrontation between presidential power and private media has been played out in three scenarios, each with its respective contentious episodes. The first scenario of contention is evident on a rhetorical plane; the second scenario has been carried out through legal actions against the media; and the third scenario enacted through the introduction of normative changes that have interrupted the complicity between the state and the media, as previously described in this essay.

Before describing the three scenarios of dispute, we revisit Laclau's concept of populism and populist rupture. Laclau (2005) associates the emergence of populism with certain characteristics: the construction of a chain of equivalence of unmet social demands, the production of ideological symbols through which a collective identity is articulated and the emergence of a leader who becomes a binding factor. In a populist rupture, the leader seeks to address social demands, exhibits radical opposition to the historic block that that had excluded a large swath of society and politically interpellates collective identities.

In our view, the attention to social demands, a political act, is actually impossible without making use of the media. To achieve that end, some aspects of media logics and tactics that Correa has adopted include the use of simple, binaristic language; informal speech; expressions that circulate in the popular imaginary; references to problems of everyday life; and a moralistic, quasi-paternalistic stance towards the citizenry. And, in order to appeal directly to el *pueblo*, he makes use of his personal charisma and employs discourse that generates emotional impact. These logics, as illustrated below, have prompted Ecuadoreans to affirm that, in contrast to previous governments, 'this government does indeed consult with its citizens'[12].

In the past few years, the mimetism between politics and mediatized communication has surpassed the few established and imaginable limits. The Ecuadorean government has responded by radically reshaping political communication. Since the inception of Rafael Correa's presidency in 2007, two specific strategies have emerged. Firstly, governmental communication has one spokesperson – Rafael Correa.

Secondly, this political communication has been strongly sustained by propagandistic and rhetorical devices that challenge a certain way of conceiving of politics and of administrating public resources. However, while the Correa government harshly criticizes private media, denouncing its political, corporativist actions, it paradoxically employs similar strategies. On the other hand, the media, which has long ceased to hold democratic institutions accountable (it is arguable that it ever did), lost ground with regard to balance and journalistic quality. Private media began to prioritize political action, by engaging in direct confrontations with Correa, including openly propagandistic and corporativist actions.

Mediatized communication has thus been converted into one of the principle points of conflict in Ecuador, in a context of current state-led reforms. This conflict has reached such a point that, to offer an example, in the most important presidential speeches regarding the government's agenda, Correa dedicates an extensive amount of time to characterizing the press as 'mediocre,' 'corrupt' and 'representing the interests of the partidocracia'. In some cases, Correa has taken media companies and journalists to court.[13]

Indeed, we have been witnessing an unprecedented scenario in which mediatized communication plays a key role in shaping social and political representations, and in which the propagandistic media strategies of both the executive and private media respond to similar communicational logics. The result has been that debates concerning issues of national and public interest have been subordinated to a contentious, polarized context in which only two political actors – the president and the private media – are represented and have a voice. The benefits of this game of mirrors are equally distributed: The government has capitalized on the deteriorated perception of the media by its audiences (quite recent in Ecuador), as well as from the erosion of political opposition.[14] At the same time, corporate media sells apocalyptic and futuristic stories about a government it describes as 'authoritarian,' 'despotic' and even 'dictatorial,' openly positioning itself as its opponent. Such polarization has resulted in a heated battle for hegemony over public opinion, rejecting corporate media as the place in which public opinion is formed and expressed. Correa construes the media as political actors that lack legitimacy, in contrast to his own legitimacy, which was won at the polls and through referenda.

> ... [the public] know[s] that what they [private media] say are lies, and published opinion is not the same as public opinion (...) *el pueblo* will support its government.[15]

While Correa enjoyed the relative support of the most important national media during his campaign, since his first months in office, there were a few episodes that, in hindsight, could be read as a turning point in which Correa began to identify private media as the principal enemy. These events were combined with Correa's eagerness to create media legislation, which was absent from the agendas of his predecessors. It certainly appeared as if the tacit pact that historically sustained the media and distinct governments had reached its endpoint.

It is possible to identify the rupture of relations between Correa and private media as taking place on March 9th, 2007. A national newspaper, *La Hora*, published an editorial entitled 'Official Vandalism,' referring to the dispute between the president and the Congress. From that moment on, the disqualifications of the president by private media grew *in crescendo*, and the confrontation escalated. A few months later, in an interview that Correa gave to three journalists of different media companies in the Government Palace, one of the journalists, Emilio Palacio, was expelled for asking a question that Correa considered inappropriate. Later, the same journalist would write an editorial entitled 'No to the Lies', which would lead Correa to file a lawsuit against him. This act evoked tremendous interest in the public opinion, and caused a wave of repercussions in the media.[16]

The cornerstone of contentious dispute has been the president's weekly television show, *Enlace Ciudadano* (Citizen's Link.). This program has become the government's most effective means of confronting private media, and enacting a populist rupture in mediated terrain. It has become a key mechanism of interpellation in which Rafael Correa, as leader, has been able to embody the demands of *el pueblo*. As we have argued here, such interpellation would be impossible without mediatization of politics. The *Enlace*, denominated as 'The President speaks with the people,' involves direct address by Correa to a live audience. The show has been broadcast nationally on Saturdays on a regular basis since 2007 on both state/public television and radio, as well as on privately owned regional and local media. It is an exercise in political communication about all things public, in other words, themes of collective interest. It is mainly directed at two different audiences. On the one hand, it is aimed at strengthening 'the collective identity of the *prodestinario*' (Verón 1987: 17) through the construction of an inclusive 'we' directed at 'the Ecuadorean people'. This enunciative modality seeks to construct a 'reality effect' (Barthes 2002: 186) that strengthens the imaginary about decision making enacted within a communicative context, as if the 'new politics' were being implemented within the reach of all citizens. Secondly, this same discourse addresses a '*contradestinario*' or adversaries (Verón 1987: 17), the national press and journalists who are called such names as 'mediocre,' 'representatives of the interests of the partidocracy,' 'ink assassins,' 'corrupt,' '*pelucones*' (literally, 'the wigs,' a colloquial expression referring to the elite that has been made popular again by Correa) and 'the corrupt press'. These Saturday *enlaces* have evolved as privileged sites in which the president verbally confronts the national press and its journalists. The following statements by the president are exemplary in this regard:

> In general, the common practice had been to create an economic group, and use the media, not to inform, but to defend the interests of that group. The lack of objectivity, the decontextualization, and the warping of information has been pathetic at best. As a President who confronts a certain press, if a dog bites me – the next day the press interviews the dog!
>
> (Presidential Address by Rafael Correa at the University of Columbia, September 23, 2011)

> The corrupt press in our country, in the name of freedom, makes us slaves to what it silences and what it says. Half a dozen families are the owners of the national media; that is the vulnerable situation in which we find ourselves.
>
> ('President urges the media to proof if the government lies in national channels.' (audio), *El Ciudadano*, November 10, 2011)

After three years of programming, the *enlaces* have incorporated a new segment called 'Freedom of expression is now for everyone'. Through a series of news reports that have been edited to resemble television news, the president criticizes private media's coverage of the most polemical topics of national interest, making special note of their politicized nature. The addition of this segment has revealed the importance that national media, as agent with its own political discourse that has enormous power to shape national public opinion, has for the government.

For the officials in charge of managing government communication, the function of the *enlaces* has been to identify the government's political positions, as opposed to merely providing information about the government's deeds and accomplishments, which are also circulated through commercials and public service announcements. According to Vinicio Alvarado, Secretary of Communication:

> Every Saturday, the President exposes himself to public scrutiny, recounting, for good or for bad, what he did, minute by minute, each day of the week.... We firmly believe that, just as shareholders of private companies have a director that is accountable to them, the government has the obligation to tell the citizens what he does, what he plans to do, and what he thinks is for the good of the nation.[17]

In the *enlaces*, there were two main announcements that affected private media. The first was Correa's request that the Secretary of Communication ban government advertising in private media. Such action increased and consolidated the tendency in which, from 2007 to 2012, the executive had slowly decreased government advertising except in the two most important national dailies, Quito's *El Comercio* and Guayaquil's *El Universo*.[18] To strengthen the impact of this announcement, a few weeks later, Correa announced that government ministries were prohibited from giving interviews to private media.

Evidently, these two measures have had both symbolic and economic effects. In the first instance, government advertising had traditionally represented a significant source of income to both newspapers and television. In the second instance, government ministries were among the most utilized news sources, and therefore these decrees directly affected the performance of those media.

Although it is not the first time a government filed a legal case against a journalist or media company, during Correa's administration these cases multiplied. In addition to the previously mentioned defamation case based on an editorial published by *La Hora*, which was subsequently thrown out by the court, there was a judgement brought against Emilio Palacio and the daily paper *El Universo*. A case was also brought against journalists Juan Carlos Calderón and Cristian Zurita, who co-authored a book entitled 'Big Brother,' which contained the results of an investigation into the business of the president's brother. While it is beyond the scope of this chapter to discuss the contents of these publications, the charges brought against the journalists were for slander and defamation. Moreover, in both cases the appellant (Rafael Correa) demanded a huge sum of money as compensation (US$80 million and US$10 million, respectively), as well as imprisonment. Even though the judges sided with the president in both cases, Correa, in a highly symbolic gesture, granted them pardons. However, the pardons were not granted with the intention to resolve the conflict with the media, but rather to reafffirm to Ecuadorean citizens that the press was not what it claimed to be.

The third contentious scenario related to the passage of new regulations that affected the interests of media owners, including the levying of a tax on the paper upon which newspapers are printed, the prohibition of shareholders of financial institutions from owning shares in media businesses (elevated to the level of a Constitutional edict) and the prohibition of shareholders of media companies from simultaneously holding shares in other kinds of businesses. Other actions included the establishment of a new minimum wage for press workers, an increase in the number of labour inspections of media businesses, the elimination of internships (which often included non-salaried positions) and an investigation into the addresses of some media companies in 'fiscal paradises'.

Another scenario of dispute: The debate about *La Ley Orgánica de Comunicación*

In spite of the resistance and campaigns waged by private media, the 2008 Constitution inscribes, for the first time, a framework of communication rights. The communication rights agenda that was debated in the Constituent Assembly was led by various media collectives and communication organizations that came together to present several proposals. Subsequently incorporated into the new Constitution, proposals included the definition of the broadcast spectrum as a public resource administered by the state in an equitable fashion, and the guarantee of universal access to information and communication technologies. The 2008 Constitution also stipulates that the state must guarantee the existence of public, private and community media, and it seeks to prevent the monopolization (direct or indirect) of mediated space. Additionally, it demands that information about facts and events of general interest circulate publicly, and be 'truthful, verifiable, timely, contextualized, plural, and uncensored'. Without a doubt, these precepts have enriched the way in which communication rights are conceptualized in Ecuador.

Following the constitutional mandate, the Correa administration tried to pass *La Ley Orgánica de Comunicación* (LOC) (the Organic Communication Law) to secure the exercise and enforcement of the communication rights agenda inscribed in the Constitution. Discussion of this proposed law in the assembly was possible due to the strengthening of the state in the context of communication and media.

Public debates about the proposed law were transformed into an increasingly intense scenario of confrontation, given the already openly hostile relationship between the government and private media. One of the consequences of this context was that the government could not sufficiently engage citizens in this debate, in so far as private media companies were able to unify their agenda and involve other actors around their corporativist claims.

This 'contentious episode' (Tilly 2008) had particular characteristics, given the political and economic repercussions that the approval of this law could set in motion with regards to the functioning of private media. One characteristic was that the strategies and actions on the part of the actors in dispute were made visible and took place almost exclusively in mediated spaces.

As in other confrontations, they used similar communicational devices, and the polarized debate was played out in a highly mediatized fashion. This contributed to the conversion of the private media companies into privileged voices regarding the proposed law. One of the ways that they manifested their opposition to any attempt to regulate their activities was with the *leit motif* 'the best law is one that doesn't exist'.

Given that the government seemed incapable of creating discursive spaces outside of the media in which to circulate ideas and opinions about ways in which a communication law could benefit citizens, they also ended up prioritizing the production and diffusion of media-oriented material, in effect locating themselves within the same terrain as the private media. The unfortunate result was the impoverishment of the debate, with little citizen participation.

The private media's reaction to the proposed law

The rejection by private media to the government's intent to create a new legal structure for the sector propelled a series of corporativist actions. Rather than produce content that could contribute to a democratic debate, on the basis of which audiences could form their own opinion about the contents of the proposed law, they collectively promoted a protracted, large-scale campaign against state regulation of their activities. The principal characteristic of this campaign was the implementation of common strategies. For example, in 2011, two national dailies jointly decided to run editorials against the proposed law on the front page of their respective Sunday editions (the day of the week with the greatest circulation).[19] In the case of 'news reporting' about the proposed law, private media companies made use of sources significantly close to the interests of media enterprises, including interviews with 'experts' and 'technical' consultants who, except for rare exceptions, argued against the contents of the projected law.

The central argument used in the media's defence has been 'freedom of expression' and the 'free flow of information', through consistent messages circulated in commercials and advertising spaces, which constituted another major component of the campaign which has been carried out through the present in Ecuador. The main problem with this argument is that the claim is based on a limited notion of the concept; in other words, corporate media interprets 'freedom of expression' as its exclusive domain, and equates it with 'freedom of information' (by which it actually means editorial freedom). However, it evades the question of democratic responsibility, which is the defining component of the concept.

Even though journalists work with material that is a public good, their responsibility cannot be equated with that of an 'individual orator' (Fiss 2010). The private media jointly defends 'freedom of expression' as a necessary condition for the practice and strengthening of democracy. But paradoxically, it obscures the difference between opinion expressed by common citizens and those expressed by journalists, and in doing so, it moves farther away from its 'democratic mission' (Fiss 2010: 4). At the same time, it avoids public debates about other rights associated with communication, which the Constitution guarantees for all citizens, and not just journalists or media owners.

Additionally, the conflation between informational content and publicity only serves to highlight the double role played by the private media in contemporary capitalist societies: In the first place, as spaces for the production and circulation of information about contemporary themes of common interest, and secondly, as defenders of certain business and economic interests.

This situation, 'is further legitimated by the social character of communication, under the false pretense that the media facilitate information, communication and social entertainment, when in reality they only serve the process of capital accumulation of media properties and their political domination' (Hernandez and Reina 2010).

On few occasions has it been possible to observe such processes with such clarity, as it has recently been in Ecuador. Following Fiss (2010), we question the defence of corporate interests disguised as 'freedom of expression,' especially when presented as news, information of general interest and expert opinion. Relatedly, we argue that the rise of private media's role as the opposition to the government originates, in the first place, from its intent to defend the privileges that it had acquired under previous governments.

After almost four years of discussion and debate, The Organic Law of Communication was passed on June 14, 2013, following Correa's re-election. At the time of writing, it is still too early evaluate the extent to which the law will secure effective institutional mechanisms that guarantee communication rights for individuals, community media organizations and minority groups.

The creation of state media

Through the creation of state media (denominated 'public media'), the government has been able to build a political communication regime strongly anchored in the figure of Correa, and by appropriating the same model, techniques and aesthetics as private media.[20] It has systematically developed political propaganda, with the objective of creating unilateral and direct contract with Ecuadorean citizens. In what Verón (2001: 127–128) has called an 'official campaign', and what many analysts, following Blumenthal (1982) have since referred to as a 'permanent campaign,' this strategy has been implemented by the ongoing production of information of 'mediatizable' content. In this way, the government makes a daily effort to shape the national media agenda and public opinion. Their arsenal includes an impressive technological infrastructure, huge budgets and an extensive staff.

Political communication has been the principal means of reaching out to and mobilizing Correa voters. The government's three-part strategy consists in its Saturday programming of *enlaces ciudadanos*; the synchronized diffusion of official messages and public service announcements, which all television channels and radio stations are required to broadcast;[21] and the placement of official publicity in parks, concerts, sports events and so on.

In all of these spaces, a strategy of contact with citizen-voters is carried out. These strategies aim to restore the political character of communication, and to preserve the 'conditions of truth of political discourse' (Veron 2001: 129), in other words to render political discourse believable and acceptable. What is interesting is that these mediatized spaces refute the liberal imaginary about the private media, and seek to delegitimate them as political agents that heavily influence the construction of public opinion nationally and internationally.

Correa has contested the privilege that the media has had historically to produce and reproduce social and political representations, while also seeking to recuperate the state's institutionality by implementing sweeping state reforms – including to the media system. This contestation can be observed in his presidential communiques, such as in this *Informe a la Nación en el Parlamento* (Report to the Nation before Congress) on August 10, 2011:

> In the face of their [political opposition] impotence to defeat us at the polls, during these last four and a half years, we have faced both underhanded and open conspiracies by the press, which legitimately occupied the space left by the defeated *partidocracia*. If they were a counter-power with basic decency, I would demand that they make explicit their politics, so that the reader would understand that these media are not informing them, rather they are playing politics.
>
> ('The cowards and assasins are not part of the Citizen Revolution,' *El Universo*, August 11, 2011).

Correa, elevated as the principal, and, in many instances, the first and/or only government official to announce governmental messages, has had the space and incomparable reach to situate private media and recognized journalists on the same plane as the *partidocracia* and the oligarchy. We argue here that he has accomplished this by using simple, impactful speech, and by utilizing the same discursive and aesthetic logics as private media.

Public opinion: A depoliticized or politicized space?

The use of media logic is not necessarily negative, per se. Moreover, such use, especially in the absence of viable political alternatives, could be conceptualized in such a way that transcends public opinion theories that privilege elites as the only sector whose opinions count (Grossi 2004). For example, Grossi suggests that in Crespi's (cite) conceptualization of public opinion, a passive role is ascribed to the general public – understood simply as spectators who react emotionally, and who are incapable of contributing to political decision making (a role reserved for elites). Moreover, they are increasingly disaffected with politics, in part due to the reduced role of political parties as spaces for discussion, as well as the mediatization of the public sphere. In the same vein, Bernard Manin (2006) had previously announced the passage from a democracy of parties to one of audiences, thus acknowledging the power that the media has over political organizations.

A 'mediaphobic' perspective proposed by Exeni (2005) conceives of the media as actors that degrade politics by seeking to take its place and assume its functions, thereby producing a contraction of democracy in which 'the media [subordinates] the political system' (Exeni 2005: 7). Hence, this political configuration would lead to a depoliticized public opinion.

Similarly, Noell-Neuman (1995) argues that public opinion can be conceptualized as a 'spiral of silence' when it has an internal dynamic that is conformist. Or, in Veron's (1998) conceptualization, public opinion becomes depoliticitzed when politics is rendered spectacular by mediated images, thus leading to a loss of the symbolic power of the word and a decline in public debate.

We question, however, whether the convergence between political representation and mediated logics necessarily leads to the subordination of political logics to mediated logics. In fact, we suggest that another possibility exists, one in which a government regains political ground, and distances itself not from mediation, but from the media itself.

Moreover, when that government disputes the media's assumption of power (not just alongside political power, but when it actually considers itself above political power), this could signify that it is recovering its control of governability – including *mediated* governability, in the same terrain as the media. Such mediated governability includes its relationship with public opinion and its intent to weaken the influence of private media. Thus, we argue that public opinion can be rendered a politicized space. Further, the possibility exists that once a government severs its complicit relationship with the media, including in mediated terrain, it could recuperate its capacity to govern, and public opinion could then choose sides.

The Correa government's turn in relation to the media has illustrated a different way in which to understand the role of mediatization, especially with regard to the relationship between government, politics, the media and public opinion. The Correa government has done its best to communicate, through its use of media, the idea that politics is inherently conflictive. To accomplish this, it has exhaustively sought to understand how the media creates an impact, conveys immediacy and guides the moral direction of society. It has employed the same audiovisual codes and languages, but, moreover, it has done so through confrontation. Most of Ecuador's private media suffers from a 'fear of dissent' (Miralles 2011), meaning that its journalistic agendas seek to invisibilize social conflicts and unresolved structural inequalities (Fiss 2008), while negating such inequalities by rendering them 'exotic' or interpreting them through simplistic anecdotes. In response, the Correa government has adopted audiovisual codes as a predominant mode of appeal, to publicly critique the social, economic and political conflicts that exist in the country. Such actions have permitted this government to amplify the political struggle beyond traditional institutions.

We have been witness to the government's reproduction of media logics in order to establish the narrative of conflict. This has meant neither an impoverishment of politics as has been suggested nor the democratization of communication. Rather, it has politicized mediated space and public opinion, through which the government–media conflict has acquired political significance. The government has constructed the media as its principal political enemy, and the media has taken on the role of political opponent. The consequences have meant the metonimization of the friend–enemy logic, in which the media stands in for all political opposition.

The government's confrontation with the media has served, in part, to discredit the private media, thereby disrupting the liberal notion of the media as guarantors of democracy and accountability, and as neutral mediators between the state and society. In fact, the rupture produced by the confrontation, as well as the differentiation between private and public media, has made visible to citizens the political and ideological fissures that traverse the structures and actions of the media. This has allowed citizens to discern between those who share an affinity with the government's political agenda, and those who oppose it, thus revealing the ideological nature of the private media.[22]

Given the historically mimetic character of media and politics in Ecuador, it follows that a process of politicization by the Correa government would lead to a dispute with the media. Such a dispute has resulted in the media being viewed not as pure guarantees of public interest, but as an entity with its own corporate and commercial logics. The repoliticization of public opinion has allowed for governability to be separated, to a certain extent, from the strong conditioning of private media.

The politicization of the media, and its subsequent discrediting, can be clearly seen in Correa's repeated declaration that the media lack legitimacy because 'they haven't been freely elected by the people'. Paradoxically, this statement situates the media as political actors, and at the same time it discredits private media by extending Marshall MacLuhan's argument that 'the media is the message'. Hence, not only the enunciator, but also that which is enunciated, has been discredited.

Conclusion

This chapter has sought to theoretically analyse the political significance of the government–private media confrontation in Ecuador, in light of historic shifts in alliances between the two, as well as configuration of new hegemonies. To that, we extended Ernesto Laclau's concept of 'populist rupture' to understand how such confrontation and dichotomization of social space have not only played out in a mediated terrain but also become mediatized. We have argued that, in contemporary societies in general, and in Ecuador in particular, it is inconceivable to contemplate a populist rupture without mediated action. Moreover, we suggest that public opinion itself has become politicized as a result of these processes.

The Correa government's use of media logics in its confrontation with private media has politicized the relationship between the media and public opinion.

As paradoxical as it might appear, in order to reduce the influence of private media and of media logics (which we have called the mediatization of politics and mediated governability), the Correa government has sought to shape public opinion on the same playing field as the private media. Winning that fight has been the goal of both the private media and the political establishment. In this end game, polarization and conflict have assumed a political value for both parties.

Notes

1. Keeping in mind that, as a large body of literature attests, public opinion is largely formed through the media. See Crespi (1997), Habermas (1981), Lazarsfeld (1957), Lippmann (1946) and Neumann (1995).
2. All translations in this chapter are those of the authors.
3. By Executive Decree No. 1661, published in the Official Register 252, on August 27, 1969, the print media, radio and television were declared 'transformative industries protected by the Law of Industrial Development'. Later, in 1987, the Legislative Agreement No. 105 was passed. With this legislation, radio and television were considered *industrias de la publicidad* (advertising industries, which converted media companies into subjects of credit by the state financial institutions, a status, which the print press had obtained in 1962).
4. All translations from Spanish to English are our own.
5. For more information, the 'brief history' published on the official website of SENPLADES, *La Secretaria Nacional de Planificacion y Desarrollo* (National Secretary of Planning and Development), created in 2007 by the current administration indicates that 'The state planning in Ecuador began with JUNAPLA, *Junta Nacional de Planificación y Coordinación Económica* (National Board of Planning and Economic Development), created through the *Decreto Ley de Emergencia* (Law of Emergency) No. 19, May 28, 1954. In 1979, it was replaced by CONADE, Consejo Nacional de Desarrollo (National Development Council).
6. Supreme Decree No. 533, Official Register 405, April 2, 1965; Supreme Decree No. 1852, published in the Official Register 570, August 24, 1965.
7. Supreme Decree No. 256, published in the Official Register 165, February 17, 1971.
8. *Ley Reformatoria a la Ley de Radiodifusion* (Reform Law to the Radio and Television Law) published in the Official Register 691 on May 9, 1995.
9. Supreme Decree No. 26, published in the Official Register 58, on December 7, 1935.
10. Transitory Disposition No. 5, Reform to the Radio and Television Broadcast Law, R.O. 69, May 9, 1995.
11. For example, the media contributed to the fall of the Bucaram and Gutierrez governments. See Cerbino and Rodríguez 2005.
12. Forthcoming publication by Cerbino, Ramos and Maluf.
13. This has had repercussions internationally, and has prompted criticism by such groups as Reporters Without Borders (RWB) and The Office of the Special Rapporteur for Freedom of Expression of the Inter-American Commission on Human Rights (IACHR). (http://www.oas.org/en/iachr/expression/index.asp).
14. Since the 1990s, political parties and the political process in general had largely lost legitimacy, with three presidents deposed in a decade by peaceful popular revolt. In the elections of 2013, it was clear that this is still the case. In Correa's third consecutive period running for and winning the presidency, he captured 57 per cent of the vote, with the remaining percentage points spread among seven other candidates (the second runner lagged more than 30 percentage points behind Correa).
15. Excerpt taken from Correa's Saturday program, *Enlace Ciudadano* 206, January 29, 2011.
16. The editorial was published by *El Universo* on February 6, 2011.
17. This excerpt is from an interview dated January 28, 2009.

18. According to the authors' monitoring of these papers.
19. To the best of our knowledge, an editorial had never occupied the entire front page of a newspaper in Ecuador before this incident.
20. Correa established the first public media system in Ecuador's history.
21. Other governments have made use of this means of communication, but never to such an extent as Correa.
22. According to a qualitative study carried out in three cities in Ecuador, our research suggests that citizens recognize private media as part of the opposition to the current government, which is shared with traditional political parties and other private enterprises.

5

Audiovisual Services Law No. 26.522: Cultural Practices, Power and Communication

Susana Sel and Pablo Gasloli

On October 10, 2009, the Audiovisual Communication Services Law Number 26.522 was introduced in Argentina in order to limit the economic monopolization of communication. This law originated in the 21 points presented by a social project called *Coalition for a Democratic Broadcasting*, which was created in 2004 by more than 300 social, union and human rights organizations, all concerned by the monopolistic and oligopolistic situation in the commercial media sector. The law was made possible because of its popularity, the support of the majority of the population and the political will of President Cristina Fernández de Kirchner. President Kirchner is a part of a movement of Latin American popular governments, which, in the twenty-first century, are attempting to reverse the neoliberal policies that previously devastated the region.

This new movement seeks to combat monopolistic interests, which, in turn, have resisted change on every available front: political, legislative and judicial. Despite this, the democratization processes proposed by this law and the public policies that support them are advancing. The law, based on the universal human right to communicate and the promotion of plural and multiple voices, also redistributes media space while recognizing new subjects. For the first time, academic and native people's media have become a part of the public service, as community media are recognized as non-profit services. This enables diversity of speech and a plurality of voices and seeks to counter the hegemony of concentrated capital legitimated in the mass media.

This chapter focuses on the changes proposed by the Audiovisual Services Law No. 26.522, the role of the state and the social movements involved in the process resulting from the change in regulations, as well as the political, legal and cultural issues arising from the new legislation. These core topics display a social fabric, which intertwines with political, economical as well as cultural factors, embedded in the regional struggles for the democratization of communications.

The chapter also argues that these struggles represent profound changes, limited by the impunity of concentrated economic power and its media, and that this mediatized communication is inserted into a diverse set of social practices supporting its values. As Williams (1980) argues, this is a culture in which residual, dominant and emergent forms converge.

Audiovisual Communication Services Law No. 26.522

The new law replaces law No. 22.285 from 1980, issued by the last military dictatorship that ravaged the country between 1976 and 1983 under the wing of the National Security Doctrine. The same decree-law was modified during the neoliberal administration of Carlos Saúl Menem (1989–99) and sought to facilitate monopolistic and oligopolistic practices, bringing about an unprecedented level of media concentration. The coincidence of interests between the genocidal military and greedy business interests is observable in the case of 'Papel Prensa', the only company in the country producing paper for newspaper, where 27.5 per cent of its shares belong to the state. In 1977, the military government abducted and tried the Graiver family, owners at the time of 75 per cent of the company's shares. The company was taken over by the government and then handed over to Clarín, La Nación and La Razón. According to Papaleo (2009): 'Clarín bought Papel Prensa while the Graiver family was in custody and tried by a military court. Since then, Clarín has had a clear monopoly in the sale of newspaper paper' (13).

To put an end to these practices, Law No. 26.522 sets precise limits for the creation of monopolies (licensing regime, national production, plurality and diversity) in tune with the most advanced legislation in this area. The starting point is the law's recognition of the right to communication as a human right, essential to development and responsible for keeping alive people's cultures and diversity, a requisite for a full democratic coexistence.

Following the standards upheld by international human rights organizations, the state is understood to play a key role in regulating media activity to guarantee freedom of expression. Moreover, it improves the role of community media in the construction of citizenship, backed by a comprehensive international legislation, such as the many human rights conventions on freedom of expression and information, the *Declaration of Principles on Freedom of Expression* issued by the Inter-American Commission on Human Rights (2000), the OAS Special Rapporteur for Freedom of Expression, the UN and the UN resolutions and UNESCO. The act is based on comparative law that imposes limits to prevent the creation of media monopolies, due to the lack of plurality of information that arises when the sources of information are limited and controlled by few, providing serious obstacles to a functioning democracy, which requires confrontation of ideas, debate and discussion.

The act not only seeks to avoid the inappropriate concentration of media, which gives rise to concentration of political power in the hands of owners or governments, but also promotes freedom of expression in order to:

- Integrate the interests from all social sectors
- Foster diversity through the different kinds of media, sources and contents
- Ensure that the various media – be it commercial, public service or community – provide for diversity, whatever their scope is, that is, local, national, regional and international

On these grounds, Law No. 26.522, Article 1 aims to regulate audiovisual broadcasting services throughout Argentina and develop mechanisms that promote, decentralize and foster competition in order to lower costs, democratize and universalize the exploitation of new information and communication technologies. Article 2, for example, states that the activity undertook by the audiovisual media services is considered of public interest and of fundamental importance to the sociocultural development of the population as it expresses the inalienable human right to express, receive, diffuse and investigate information, ideas and opinions.

As far as service provision is concerned, it recognizes three kinds of providers: (1) state-run, which includes the federal government, the provincial governments, indigenous peoples and Church; (2) for-profit and private; (3) non-profit and private, which includes non-governmental organizations (NGOs), cooperatives, unions, which should be able to operate and have equal access to all available transmission platforms. Also noteworthy is that 33 per cent of the field is set aside for non-profit, private providers and that public media from different jurisdictions has a share in all areas of coverage in the national territory.

Several articles detail the regulations concerning the implementation of the law. Article 14, for example, establishes the Federal Authority of Audiovisual Communication Services as an enforcement authority, a decentralized and self-governed organization within the National Executive Branch, unlike its predecessor, the Federal Broadcasting Committee created by the dictatorship. Two directors are to manage and run this organization, one of them being academic representative from the faculties or courses of Information Studies, Communication Studies or Journalism from national universities. Article 15 creates the Federal Council of Audiovisual Communication to assist and advise in the planning of public broadcasting policy. Article 16 designates that two member representatives must be from national universities. Besides parliamentary control mechanisms, Article 17 stipulates that there is to be an Advisory Council on Audiovisual Communication and Children. Article 19 establishes the Public Defender of Audiovisual Communication Services. Article 124 stipulates the Honorary Advisory Committee on Public Media, consisting of distinguished members from culture, education and communication in the country, two of whom to be appointed by the faculties of Social Communication Studies, or Audiovisual Studies or Journalism of national universities.

A licensing regime is put into practice at a national level (Article 45). With regard to media contents, Article 65 states that 70 per cent should be produced nationally, Article 67 sets a screen quota for domestic films and audiovisual arts and Article 77 guarantees the right to universal access – through the audiovisual media services – to relevant news content and sporting events, be it either football matches or another genre or discipline.

The law also sets out a regulatory framework that recognizes and broadens rights: communication as a human right, as an element for local and national development, which is inclusive, plural and culturally diverse.

These features of the new law, in direct opposition to the concentrated economic interests that find their foothold in the liberal interpretation of the freedom of expression, are resisted by corporate media interests, which are opposed to the enforcement of the law.

The role of the state

This sphere of conflict belongs similarly to the state and the dynamics of social intervention. Article 2 of the Audiovisual Services Law acknowledges audiovisual communication in all of its platforms as a social activity of public service, whereby the state shall protect the right to information, participation, preservation and development of the Rule of Law as well as the values of freedom of expression. In these circumstances, the state positions itself as guarantor of the right to communication, ensuring the exploitation of the audiovisual communication services that could be carried out by three kinds of providers (state-run, for-profit and private and non-profit and private) with equal access to available transmission platforms.

To this end, the state is required to develop mechanisms aimed at promoting, decentralizing and fostering competition for the purpose of lowering costs, democratizing and universalizing the exploitation of new information and communication technologies. In other words, a rule is set with the goal of promoting diversity and universality of access and participation, resulting in equal degree of opportunities for all inhabitants of the nation to enjoy the benefits of this service. Specifically, it sets its sights on satisfying information and social communication, needs arising in the communities where the media is based and where it reaches.

Cristina Fernández de Kirchner's administration (2008–11/2011–14) proposes an economic model based on accumulation and social inclusion, appealing to a new sector of the middle class that fosters the growth of domestic market and reindustrialization. This is the opposite side of the coin to concentrated economic groups, and a diversified oligarchy where the goal is to export, involving only primary resource-related activities and the payment of low salaries. Both the policies from this government and the ones from its predecessor, Néstor Kirchner (2003–07), demonstrate macroeconomic achievements – including growth in gross domestic product (GDP), increase in tax income, fiscal surplus, rise in exports and salaries and decrease in the unemployment rate (over 40 per cent in 2002) – as well as political and social achievements – which includes the repeal of both the Full Stop Law and the Law of Due Obedience, the repeal of the reprieves to genocidal military, modification of the Supreme Court of Justice, incorporation of new retirees to the system, granting of universal allocation per child to the families, approval of equal marriage and more.

Moreover, these policies represent a great advantage to the bourgeoisie participating in this growth model. Limits to income distribution are thereby caused by insufficient independence from the plexus of productive and social relations. Consequently, this appeal to a national bourgeoisie, which enjoyed significant expansion in the early Peron administrations as local capital businesses, makes it possible to recall that many of them turned into oligopolistic firms, which struggled for industrial control at the time with other business factions.

The administration sponsored a capitalist recreation project to try to encourage the restructuring of these local groups at a national level. Even today, many of them are closely associated with transnational capital. The most concentrated economic sectors, which express themselves throughout Latin America via media conglomerates, fight against state policies aimed at economic growth and income distribution – insufficient as they remain. They also fight against foreign policy, which is carried out by the Argentine government. These government actions are regarded as moves towards international cooperation like UNASUR (Union of South American Nations), an organization that, though half-heartedly, supported putting an end to Cuba's political exclusion, making international agreements with countries undergoing profound transformation processes, such as Venezuela, Bolivia and Ecuador. In this fight, the most powerful economic sectors resort to any means necessary to impose neoliberal models.

Thus, because it is impossible to stage military coups to restrain certain advances, a common strategy in Latin America in 1970s, today there are new modalities of 'institutional' coups, such as the one in Venezuela against Hugo Chávez (2002), the autonomous uprising in Bolivia against Evo Morales that took a toll of 30 dead farmers (2008) and the police attack on Rafael Correa in Ecuador (2010). These attempts failed, as have the attacks that take place permanently in Argentina and Brazil. However, this modality prevails with the support of the political, legislative and judicial systems, as was the case in Honduras (2009) and Paraguay (2012).

It goes without saying that during all these coups, without exception, whether they have failed or succeeded, concentrated media groups have acted similarly. In every one of these processes, the big broadcasting corporations have hidden, distorted and misrepresented reality, fuelling the return to old right-wing practices, thus driving, the middle classes to anti-popular positions.

Since the onset of Cristina Fernández de Kirchner's administration, these economic sectors have resisted the implementation of state policies and reform, such as the application of movable deductions to grain exports, an attempt to help the agricultural sector transform the sale of commodities into products with higher added value. The crisis became evident in the elections of 2009, when the government lost its majority. Even in these circumstances, on August 27, 2009, National Congress approved the Law on Audiovisual Communication Services. All walks of society thus marched in support of the presidential election on, what was coincidentally, Broadcasting Day.

The current context marked by a deep capitalist crisis makes it possible to see that most countries in South America, in spite of the difference in their ideological processes, unite in rejection of the economic and political neoliberalism that devastated the region since the 1990s.

Regardless of the fact that these processes could be characterized as neodevelopmentalist, what emerges at this stage, albeit with contradictions, is the confrontation of several segments of the productive capital (so many of them still tied to the financial capital) that share a common ground with the incentives of most of the population, extremely damaged by the painful experiences of the past. The changes have undermined the economic dogma, which dominated previous decades and given the popular classes the opportunity to broaden their tactical goals, giving birth to programs of social and economic transformation that enable the region to usher in a new stage.

The context and cultural practices, that is, the material and symbolic productions responding to the system within which they take place, reveal the tensions present in the social spaces contested. These spaces are pierced by the noticeable influence of the media conglomerates within the framework of popular governments that, even in its diversity, reconsider the role of the state.

Social movements in response to the emergence of the law

The struggle for the democratization of communication has been present in various spheres since 1983, when the painful period of military dictatorship came to an end. This has included professors and researchers from the field of communications of national universities, and the unions of journalists,

FM radio (considered illegal since the law issued by the dictatorship forbade them), the press and others who sought a different kind of communication. For Argentina, 2001 was a year of crisis, but it was also the year in which the World Social Forum (WSF) was created to fight concentrated capital. In the beginning, the WSF was conceived as a meeting point, in order to debate, discuss democratically, exchange experiences, develop proposals and coordinate actions by social movements opposing neoliberalism and domination of the world by capital.

Out of the exercise of the human right to communication and the need for the emergence of plural and multiple voices to democratize it, on August 27, 2004, the *Coalition for a Democratic Broadcasting* (CRD) came into existence. On Broadcasting Day, a social force emerged, which prioritized the building of consensus for a more democratic communication over monopolistic interests. Like the WSF, the CRD meetings are not deliberative since attendees cannot make decisions as a corpus of participants. The organizations that comprise them are those that make declarations and decide on actions that the CRD then publishes. The CRD is a plural and diversified space, non-confessional, non-governmental and non partisan, encouraging pluralism and the diversity of actions of all the organizations and movements that wish to participate. Moreover, it is open to a diversity of genders, ethnicities, cultures, generations and physical abilities.

In this sense, it is possible to conceive of the communication field as an arena of confrontation between struggling social forces, as an expression of an alliance between hegemonic factions and another alliance between the factions of the social movement. The former tries to preserve the status quo and the latter, heterogeneous, fights democratically for equality in the decision-making process with objective actions. In this confrontation, the CRD promotes the implementation of a non-governmental public system and a non-commercial social sector, where citizens can participate actively in audiovisual communication.

Founded in 2004, 21 years after the end of the military dictatorship, the CRD drew up the Civic Initiative for Democratic Broadcasting, comprising 21 points, one for each year of democracy in the country. These points proved to be significant tools in the federal debate and the promotion of contents.

This approach has presented a change to cultural practices, resulting in the appearance of new social actors and the possibility of re-thinking both the public space, which has broadened, and the private space, now demonstrating cracks that threaten the financial will associated with it.

In the face of the silence of concentrated media, which did not perceive this situation, discussions took place in newspapers of social organizations, in public fora, communities, universities and alternative radio stations, in publishing houses, on the radio, as well as on cable and broadcast television. All kinds of events echoed the debate proposed by the organizations.

Officials appointed by President Cristina Fernández de Kirchner at the beginning of her administration, in 2008, in charge of the Federal Broadcasting Committee and the Ministry of Communications and Mass Media, participated in debates voicing citizens' opinions. Within an authentic process of awareness and public debate, the 21 points became the focal point of the debate and provided the basis for the bill presented by the President.

The CRD joined forces with human rights organizations (Mothers of Plaza de Mayo, Grandmothers of Plaza de Mayo, Sons and Daughters for Identity and Justice against Oblivion and Silence, Center for Legal and Social Studies), communication workers of both trade unions and sector unions (General Confederation of Labor and Argentine Workers' Central Union), community radio organizations (Argentine Association of Community Radio Broadcasters, World Association of Community Radio Broadcasters), non-profit, cooperative, religious groups, unions and cultural organizations, as well as small radio and television entrepreneurs (SMEs) and various social organizations. This joint approach to work also respected the operation of the WSF, which provided an arena to think, debate democratically, exchange experiences, develop proposals and coordinate actions by the social movements opposed to the concentration of media conglomerates.

In 2008, after the presentation of the 21 points to the president of Argentina, Cristina Fernández de Kirchner, the CRD sponsored many federal debates on the proposals throughout the country. These debates involved national universities, community centres, media observatories, public ministries, unions, representatives, senators, media officials, municipal deliberative councils from all over the country, broadcasters associations, public radios, student centres, community radios, university departments, civic associations, communication SMEs, judges, commercial press, private universities, confessional radios, social movements, political and social leaders, news agencies, cooperative institutes, communication studies networks, advisors from the legislature, journalists and educators. They were held not only as debates but also as conferences, programs and special transmissions *in situ*. The public declaration of the 21-point project was thus taken up in the legislature and the provincial councils.

With this endorsement, on March 1, 2009, at the onset of the annual legislative session, President Kirchner announced that the law was being sent to Congress. Shortly after, on March 18, she herself presented the bill based on the 21 points drawn up by the CRD in the Argentine Theatre in La Plata. This proposal, which was from the Executive Branch, provided for 24 Participatory Forums of Public Consultation to be held at the national universities of all 24 provinces by the end of July 2009. The goal of these forums was to submit the proposal to popular vote. One thousand two hundred contributions to the bill were received and added to the new draft, which was discussed in the legislature.

From September 8 to 11, 2009, the Legislative Power organized public hearings in the Annex to the House of Representatives, with representatives from different political wings, presiding over the sessions, attended not only by the media sectors directly involved but also by commercial, community and public representatives. On September 16, 2009, the bill was voted on by the House of Representatives, with 20 amendments requested by centre-left representatives. These requests received the support of 147 votes in favour, three against and one abstention. Early in the morning of October 10, 2009, the voting took place in the Senate, with 44 votes in favour and 24 against. The crowd waited outside and celebrated the outcome. That same morning President Cristina Fernández de Kirchner passed the Audiovisual Communication Services Law No. 26.522. Her signature endorsed what is considered to be one of the most historical democratic events in the history of communications in Argentina.

Cultural dilemmas and critical organicism

The social processes associated with the Audiovisual Communication Law have taken on a new dimension, undergoing transformations that, albeit contradictory, demonstrate evidence of what Ianni (1996) terms 'the social issue', comprising racial, regional and cultural as well as economic and political aspects. In other words, the passing of the law presented the country with a social issue that articulated inequalities and antagonisms of structural importance. This is why every production of human sense and values, which include political, economic, scientific, religious, discursive and social practices, is considered culture. These are practices from tightly linked, but different, fields that shape a complex and varied whole of reciprocal influences.

Agreeing with a politically active cultural theory, Williams (1980) and his disciple Eagleton (2001) argue that the meaning of culture includes the set of material (objects) and non-material production (meaning, normative consistency, beliefs and values) by a society. In this sense, the configuration of the social space related to the process that led to the passing of Law No. 26.522 gave voice to the views of more than 300 social organizations. These organizations confronted concentrated economic groups that were imposing cultural practices in the country based on the lucrative and exclusive use of mass media. These practices thus brought about a lack of information expressed in contents of an associated collective imagination, an imagination fuelled by the absence of educational and cultural shows (in the widest sense), which are solely found in the state-run channel and are non-existent on the four private channels.[1]

This imagination is explained by Gramsci (1986) as hegemony, a total social process including culture and ideology. Hegemony, however, goes beyond culture and ideology, as a social process, which is only completed with the specific distribution of its power and its influence. In other words, hegemony is more than culture because of the social processes it involves – in which men and women define and configure their lives, and their ideologies – as system of meanings and values, constituting the expression or projection of a particular class interest. Gramsci, therefore, introduced the necessary acknowledgement of domination and subordination in something that, nonetheless, should be recognized as a total process. Williams (1980) takes up this concept of hegemony to propose that what really turns out to be decisive is not only the conscious system of ideas and beliefs but also the whole social process experienced, which is virtually organized by specific and dominant meanings and values. Ideology, in its everyday definition, constitutes a relatively formal and articulated system of meanings, values and beliefs; it can be taken as a 'universal conception' or as a 'class perspective'.

The complexity of a culture can be found not only in its variable processes and in its social definitions (traditions, institutions and formations) but also in its dynamic interrelations, which are evident at each step of the process, presenting certain variables and historically varied elements. In the historical analysis, it is necessary to examine the complex interrelationships, which exist between movements and trends, both within and beyond a specific and effective domination.

Eagleton (2001), therefore, redefines culture as a network of meanings and shared activities, which foster the 'advancement of consciousness' of society as a whole. A common culture implies the collaborative building of these meanings with full participation of all members of society. For Williams, a common culture exists only when it is shaped collectively, and not when it is the prerogative of a privileged few; it is constantly rebuilt and redefined by the collective practice of its members. This does not take place when the values created by a few are then passively accepted and lived by many, a situation better described by the expression 'culture in common' (Williams 1983: 334). The concept of a common culture is inseparable from radical socialist change, since it requires an ethic of shared responsibility, which is full democratic participation at all levels of social life, including material production and equal access to the process of culture creation.

In this scenario, Jameson (2001) maintains that the characteristics of much of the current cultural production are associated with the dominant cultural logic or hegemonic rule. He defines postmodernism as the force field in which various cultural drives – what Williams has accurately called 'residual' and 'emergent' cultural production – must find their way.

This complex process can be partly described in terms of class. However, another consciousness and social being is always denied and excluded. The alternative perceptions of others within immediate relations, and the new perceptions and practices of the material world, in practice, are qualitatively different from the articulated and developing interests of an emerging social class. The relationship between these two sources of the emergent – the class and the excluded social area – is not in any way contradictory. At some point these sources can present themselves as extremely close, and their mutual relations depend largely on political practice. However, they can also be distinguished, culturally and from a theoretical point of view.

In this sense, it is necessary to focus on understanding emerging culture as something distinctive from the dominant and the residual, in that it is never just a matter of immediate practice, but depends primarily on the discovery of new forms or adaptations. Again, it is important to pay attention to an active and influential emergence of culture, although not yet fully formed, rather than to a manifest emergence, more easily identifiable.

Tensions: Intellectuals and think tanks

It should not be considered odd that a century beginning with the Roosevelt Corollary would finish with a multiplicity of foundations based on 'freedom', 'democracy' and 'rights'. The Santa Fe Documents (1980–2000) from the Republican Party lit up the night of the Empire, and, in its twilight, the intellectuals of neoliberalism managed to find the best way to go from the corporation to the office.

'Think tanks' are today's concrete response to the imperial policy and to the oligarchies' resistance in the continent. Having amassed a fortune with the resources provided by companies and US security agencies, relying on local economic and political support, think tanks bombard the public opinion, pressure and shake Latin American democracies. Such was the case with The Center for the Opening and Development of Latin America (CADAL), American Task Force Argentina (AFTA), the Foundation for Freedom, the Freedom House, Liberty of Expression and Democracy (LED) foundation and several others that have financed, supported and organized movements to destabilize Latin American democracies, mainly in Venezuela, Argentina, Paraguay and Ecuador but also in other countries throughout the region. Supported by the CIA (CADAL), vulture funds (AFTA), communications monopolies and concentrated interests, think tanks flood the universities as well as the mass media with their views.

Quoting González Prada (1985): 'How many deeds not accomplished by the speech of a parliamentarian, the decree of a minister or the revolt of a military officer, were achieved by the simple article of a journalist!' The unprecedented coverage by the hegemonic media of the discussion of the law managed to curb the process of justice democratization. Many groups went up against each other due to this issue. The media match confronted TN (news channel owned by Clarín group) and *678* (a political news show in the state-run channel). In turn, another round was fought between the group called 'Platform 2012' (associated to the political opposition) and the Espacio Carta Abierta (a group of intellectuals who supported the government).

In an article published in *La Nación* on January 5, 2012, 'Where do I go to if not to the Clarín Group?', Jorge Lanata wrote: 'That bullshit of "let's make a radio for the wichi". Who the fuck is going to listen to a wichi radio? Worse still, who will pay for ads on a wichi radio? And where will operators' salaries come from? This is real life. It is a business like any other industry' (translation ours). This statement voices the Clarin Group's opinion, whereby indigenous peoples' possibilities for communication are regarded in terms of profit. According to this model, communication cannot be a viable business.

The paradigm applied by Lanata – a once-'independent' journalist – is none other than those spread by the foundations: The market sets the course. This can be inscribed among the undermining comments of the hegemonic media, which usually reserves to communities and social groups, their representatives, culture and institutions.

While it is true that as a group Platform 2012 never spoke out against the media law, it is also true that its members participated in all kinds of media debates and disputes armed with pro-establishment arguments. As shown in the report 'Undermining Democracy' by the Freedom House (2009), the arguments against the media policy focused on the distrust inspired by the way the public media is articulated by the state (ideologem of the corruptibility of powers applied in Venezuela, China, Iran, etc.). Against this background, the organization Espacio Carta Abierta published letter no. XIII, recognizing the merits of the law. This reinstated the debate in terms of how democratization opens problematic fronts that should be dealt with: 'The country's political tide led to the media law; this led to necessary judicial reform and to the analysis of everyday life in the light of "fairness", and to the nationalization of several public companies, which all must lead to new styles of discussion' (translation ours).

Law No. 26.522 was achieved thanks to the battles fought in the country by a wide variety of social actors over the past few decades. The passing of the law is a significant milestone in a peculiar moment for politics in Argentina: After the *kirchnerismo*'s defeat in the June 2009 elections, few expected the law to be even considered. The social forces confronting the CRD comprised the same concentrated interests that won the elections and contemplated the possibility that the government would apply the law as a gag on media precisely as a result of the political circumstances.

These groups felt threatened by the likelihood of losing privileges as a result of this kind of law, but they also had in mind other measures taken by the government that damaged their interests. For example, the nationalization of pension funds also disrupted these interests. Suffice to say that among the signatures of those who draw the statement *AEA Expresses its Concern for Retirement Project*,[2] which was published in *La Nación* newspaper on August 31, 2008, one can find the names of many media groups. Likewise, as is evident in the same document, one finds the names of powerful agricultural representatives, a wealthy sector that joined the media campaign organized by the opposition after the government decided to increase movable deductions. It is easy to see in all these issues and the constant actions the association of interests that make up the media groups and has already been described in this article.

The Inter American Press Association (IAPA)[3] also joined the campaign opposing the Law. The IAPA is a business group belonging to large media corporations and operating as an international organization, and is financed by intelligence agencies and performing tasks, which destabilize democratic regimes. This strong social actor, associated with business chambers of the concentrated sector, has been joined by several local representatives, like the Association of Argentine Journalism Entities (ADEPA), Argentine Private Broadcasters Association (ARPA), Argentine Broadcasting Association (ATA) or Argentine Cable Television Association (ATVC). The joint rejection showed the network of interests, especially in the case of ADEPA, since Law No. 26.522 does not regulate print media, only audiovisual media.

This offensive was also joined by the transnational think tanks, presented as groups of intellectuals. However, in reality, these were private foundations formed by businesses political leaders, economists, journalists and professionals dedicated to the production and promotion of neoliberal ideas in Latin America. One of these networks, the International Freedom Foundation (IFF), based in Madrid, with a branch in the Argentine city of Rosario, organized the seminar *'Challenges in Latin America. Institutional weaknesses and opportunities for development'*, March 26–28, 2008, in the midst of the agrarian conflict. It was advertised as a pseudo-academic seminar, but, cloaked a call for a continental reorganization of neoliberal forces and an undermining of 'populism' in Latin America, among which they count the ongoing project that started in 2003 with the Kirchner's administrations. The seminar was presided by the writer Mario Vargas Llosa and notorious international personalities,[4] such as Marcel Granier from RCTV (pro-coup Venezuelan multimedia group) and the worst representatives of the local right wing (Mauricio Macri, Ricardo López Murphy and writer Marcos Aguinis). In the IFF's campaign against a new media law in Argentina, two men stood out: Daniel Vila, president of Grupo Uno, a multimedia conglomerate presided too by José Luis Manzano – a former Menem official – and Francisco de Narváez, right-wing congressman.

In December 2009, a new major social actor appeared: the magistrates of the judicial system. Some of them have political ambitions and economic interests; others are remnants of the dictatorship. What they had in common were shared interests with the media conglomerates. These magistrates heeded the requests of the monopolies to curb the enforcement of Law No. 26.522, already voted on and passed by the legislature (Senado Argentino, 2010).[5]

The emergence of Law No. 26.522 has not completely transformed the current horizon of social debate, but it has at least paved the way and shed light on the existing links between the state, concentrated media groups and society. The discomfort caused by the law has led to countless protests, which were then technically adapted and reproduced by the channels owned by media groups. The protests also revealed the tensions produced by the current scenario.

If the state assimilates these social movements, the nation will then be rebuilt with a mixture of dialects within a regime marked by tolerance and dispute. Recent events should not be processed by the concentrated interests that seek to return to the neoliberal model that turned Argentina into a country as fragmented and shattered as a century ago.

This amazing transformation has also affected other regimes in the region. As far as communications are concerned, with the widening of the public sphere, the private sphere, which is traditionally characterized by its mercantile activity, has also reopened to consider non-profit activity such as non-commercial private business. This provides not only vehicle for private production outside the market rules but also vehicle for communication unrestricted by market limitations.

Drafted by leading specialists from public universities, this law has been supported by a political will that overcame the many obstacles posed by concentrated interests. We can therefore assert that the law, in spite of being emergent, has recreated social niches in tune with the transformations of recent history. Perhaps that is why it has been so forcefully attacked by concentrated economic sectors through their interpreters. The same interests, disguised as businesses, intellectuals, representatives, senators or judges, are currently halting one of Argentina's broadest pieces of legislation, the outcome of widespread consultation and debates, which included all sectors of society.

Concentrated power has its methods in the cooperation of media groups with coups – as in the cases of Venezuela (2002) and Honduras (2009) – in the permanent attacks against Cuba, and in the pro-coup campaigns in Bolivia, Paraguay, Ecuador, Nicaragua and Argentina among other Latin American nations. Despite the Free Trade Area of Americas and North American Free Trade Agreement (FTAA-NAFTA), and the defeat at the Summit of the Americas held in Mar del Plata, Argentina, in 2005, the recent VII Summit of the Pacific Alliance in Cali has revitalized the debate on the various approaches proposed as far as Regional Cooperation Agreements are concerned.

President Juan Manuel Santos' speech demonstrated an attempt to break away from previous models and implement what he has called the new 'engine' of regional economy. The group (founded by Mexico, Chile, Peru and Colombia) has added Costa Rica as a full member to this summit; Uruguay, Spain, Canada, Panama and Guatemala, as well as other delegations from the Pacific region, participated as observers. Most members of the Pacific Alliance are incorporated bilaterally via the North American Free Trade Agreement with the United States, allowing the agreement to remain as 'beachhead' throughout the continent; the members have permission to enter the Trans-Pacific Partnership (TPP) as satellites to exercise a geostrategic control of Asia Pacific.

The aim is to meet the goals of the free market to the detriment of social demands and asymmetries between the economies involved, especially the active roles of Latin America and China, whose growing investment in the region has diversified to infrastructure and has financially allowed some countries to escape from the hegemony of the International Monetary Fund. Other think thanks, such as the Freedom Foundation directed by Vargas Llosa, unite in this strategy. All of them aim to put an end to proposals like UNASUR and Bolivarian Allianza for the Peoples of Our America and at returning to the imperial domination of the Free Trade Agreement.

From the point of view of imperialists, popular democracy after the Cold War dominated Latin America from Cape Horn to Rio Grande and has even begun to creep into the United States itself. From this perspective, 'cultural destruction' is considered by Gramsci to be the most disturbing of all destructions, as it is based in the belief that changes in the culture bring about political and economic change. The experiences of the twentieth century demonstrate that it was possible to build a social force capable of imposing another model of society, inclusive and supportive. This is precisely what the capitalist think tanks have attempted to stop.

If the law is still actively and influentially emergent, though not fully articulated, it is necessary to define new political expressions and new cultural practices that can transform its emergence towards the association of communicational practices for a more integral culture.

Notes

1. Channel 7, the state-run channel, produces 9 per cent of cultural and educational contents according to www.afsca.gob.ar
2. The public figure for Clarín Group, Hector Magnetto, is vice president of the Argentina Business Association, which was created in 2001. Julio Cesar Saguier, president of La Nación, is another member of the entity associated with Citibank, Techint and a soy group headed by Gustavo Grobocopatel. See the article on http://www.lanacion.com.ar/nota.asp?nota_id=1065095
3. On the history of the IAPA, read the article by Franklin Ledezma Candanedo, a member of the American Association of Bolivarian Journalists, Chapter of Panama – AAPEBCAP) in: http://www.pcv-venezuela.org/index.php?option=com_content&task=view&id=5905&Itemid=1

4. José M. Aznar from Spain, Roger Noriega from the United States, Vicente Fox and Jorge Castañeda from Mexico, Julio Sanguinetti from Uruguay. For more information please see: http://www.libertad.org.ar y http://criticadigital.com/impresa/index.php?secc=nota&nid=1035
5. Senado de la Nación Argentina. 2010. *Preocupación por las trabas a la implementación de la Ley de Servicios de Comunicación Audiovisual.* http://www.senado.gob.ar/prensa/8352/noticias

6

Media and Empowerment in Venezuela: Towards a Participatory Public-Media Space

Ximena Gonzalez Broquen

Introduction

Since the election of President Hugo Chávez in 1999, the Venezuelan government has promoted a model of participatory democracy in the area of communication, which includes the people, in terms of not only *access* to information but also their *participation* in its construction. From this point of view, this chapter categorizes, analyses and questions the different public media policies implemented by the Venezuelan government since 1999. The chapter first considers the regional media context and compares it to the Venezuelan media context, and then analyses the legal and policy frameworks that were created with the objective of developing a participatory media sphere. The chapter then examines how these policies are implemented in the day-to-day lives of Venezuelans. This is followed by a discussion of how these ideas are extended to other jurisdictions through regional processes. For this purpose, I argue that three empiric transverse axes can be used as a reading key to systematize these different initiatives.

The first axis is that of *the democratization of representation,* which, through the democratization and social reappropriation of the radio-electric spectrum, focuses on the reorganization of the national legal framework, the different measures of social re-appropriation and re-nationalization of public-media space (promotion of the local and independent users committees, etc.). Secondly, the public-media space – the state's support for the development of so-called third sector communication – is the *axis of the democratization of participation.* This boosts the transformation of the representative public-media space into participation by the people. The third is the *axis of integration,* which promotes the constitution of a grand, national media space, which is discussed through an analysis of Telesur as a common space of processing, construction and representation of cultures, identities and continental realities.

The purpose of this analysis is to examine, via these three axes, how media space in Venezuela is being reorganized and re-balanced, in terms of the design, construction and implementation of a number of paradigms, including economic (anti-monopoly, anti-mercantilist), social (community and people's participation in communication), cognitive (education for people's communication) and political (participation, communication coordination and integration) paradigms, progressively remaking of the media into a space of empowerment.

Finally, the chapter argues that the field of communication cannot be reduced exclusively to a matter of human rights: Communication is much more than the right to free speech. In order to contextualize the study, it is necessary to begin by presenting an outline of the regional and national media context, to understand the construction, design, creation and implementation of a participatory public-media space in Venezuela.

From the regional media context to the Venezuelan media context

The context of South American regional media has very distinctive characteristics. Countries that currently promote the most progressive measures in favour of the freedom of communication and media diversity, such as Venezuela, Ecuador, Bolivia and Argentina, are often presented by mainstream media, locally and internationally, as dictatorial and authoritarian, as countries where freedom of expression is constantly trampled.

This paradoxical situation is reflected in the fact that in Latin America, large transnational media corporations have taken advantage of the wave of deregulation and privatization since the 1980s and 1990s, imposing their media dominance on the continent, through the purchase of assets in private media, and the consolidation of agreements with regional media groups. This situation has led to the domination of regional media space by the private communication sector, and therefore the domination of the socio-political *media* representation on the continent.

Four major groups currently rule regional media spaces: The Clarin group (Argentina), Diego Cisneros Organization (O.D.C) (Venezuela), O Globo (Brazil) and Televisa (Mexico). These groups have assets in television, cable TV, DTH TV, video, radio, CDs, newspapers, magazines, news agencies, film production companies, media promotion and distribution companies, telecommunications, Internet service provision and investments in different areas of the economy,[1] which position them in the global commercial market and a provide them with a dominant position in the region.

The interests of these groups, and major commercial media in the region, contrast sharply with the measures promoted by the governments of 'progressive' countries, which are based on communication, social redistribution or recovery of domestic natural resources. This is the reason why the private media sector has created an atmosphere of continuous attack and attempts to discredit these governments.

Two examples of this situation are illustrated by the Inter American Press Association (IAPA), and the Diarios de América newspaper group. The IAPA is based in Miami and includes the owners and shareholders of the major private media groups in Latin America and 1,300 publications in more than 30 countries and over 45 million copies (Denis de Moraes 2011: 117–118). IAPA systematically attacks the governments of Venezuela, Bolivia, Ecuador, Nicaragua and Argentina. Meanwhile, the group Diarios de América holds 11 of the major newspapers in 11 South American countries whose editorial lines systematically attack the governments of Chávez, Morales, Correa and Fernandez de Kirchner (Moraes 2011: 121).

In addition, a detailed analysis of the discourse of these media groups makes it possible to see how the stance in their editorial lines, namely the defence of freedom of expression and human rights, are constantly violated in allegedly dictatorial and authoritarian regimes in the aforementioned countries. It is important to understand that these attacks reflect the fact that these governments have promoted socio-political measures that directly affect the private interests of traditionally dominant classes (nationalization measures of public property and natural resources towards the eradication of poverty on health, education, among others). They also affect the interests of private media groups by establishing laws that promote the diversity of Latin American media space.

The measures implemented in favour of diversity are based on a tripartite view of the media space: It is legally conceived in Venezuela, as explained below, as well as in the cases of Argentina (Law on Audiovisual Communication Services adopted in 2009), Uruguay (The Communication Law of 2010 provides a third of radio broadcasting frequencies for community media, and The Community Radio Broadcasting Law was enacted in 2007), Bolivia (with the funding provided by the Bank of Economic and Social Development of Venezuela (BANDES), Bolivia created the first indigenous radio network, with over 30 FM and AM radio stations) and Ecuador (The Law of Radio and Television of Ecuador, passed in 2002, prohibits the discrimination against community radio stations that currently have the same guarantees of the private sector), a measure that is further consolidated in the Communication Law in Ecuador in 2013. In all these cases, the tripartite view of the media space is divided among the public (state), private (for-profit) and community or associative sector, which is referred to here as the third sector of communication. This comprises the non-profit sector, including NGOs, community associations, organizations and social movements, universities and foundations, among others.

This tripartite division reflects the desire to reach a balance between these three sectors, in order to ensure the diversity and plurality of the media sector. The laws of these countries – against the *de facto* domination of the media space by the private sector – thus tend to promote the development and consolidation of the public and the third sectors, through measures aimed at protecting and promoting local independent and community production (establishment of production quotas for national and independent production, grants, donations and allocation of space for community radio broadcasters, etc.). These laws also tend to rebalance the public management of licences and broadcasting concessions and diversify modular frequency (FM), limiting the concentration of cross-media ownership. Ecuador, Venezuela and Bolivia have the most detailed anti-monopoly laws. The chapter on communication in the 2008 Ecuadorian Constitution makes the state responsible for the anti-monopoly struggle, whereby shareholders, officials or legal representatives of banks, companies and financial groups cannot maintain ownership or equity in the media. In Venezuela, the Law on Social Responsibility on Radio and Television (Ley Resorte), which was passed in 2010, prohibits owners of banks access to the ownership of media corporations and participation in the purchasing of shares, and the Constitution of 2007 in Bolivia prohibits monopolies and oligopolies in media companies.

All these measures serve to confront local, regional and transnational media monopolies. The situation of confrontation of private media against the Venezuelan government, in particular, has reached such polarization levels, resulting in the coup d'état of April 2002, in which the private media was the *actor* directly involved in the preparation, set-up and execution of the coup. In fact, the role of the private media in the coup meant that it was not only allies but also direct *actor* in the development and execution, which led to what is now referred to as the 'media coup' (Britto García 2006: 81–106).

How could this happen in Venezuela? It is important to mention the relationship between commercial media and politics in Venezuela during the so-called fourth republic (prior to the election of President Chavez), in which the owners of large private media companies virtually came to replace political parties. The commercial television in Venezuela has been in the hands of two of the richest families in Venezuela and, in the case of Cisneros, around Latin America and the world. On the one hand, there is the group Bottome and Granier, owners of Radio Caracas Television and Radio Caracas Radio, and, on the other, there is Cisneros family, which owns the TV channel Venevision.

Over this period, the owners of large private media companies virtually came to replace political parties. On October 6, 1993, Deputy Henry Ramos Allup (member of Acción Democrática party) declared (one year before Berlusconi became famous): 'Venezuela is not ruled by the Executive or the Legislature, or Fedecamaras or the CTV (Confederation of Workers of Venezuela), but by social media. It is no secret that the reform of the Constitution was principally defeated in 1992 by the social media, newspaper and radio' (Pasquali 1995: 245, translation mine).

Furthermore, there was a very tight relation between communication corporations and politicians. As Earl Herrera states:

> (...) Owners and CEO of communication consortia reached the Congress, legislatures and municipal councils (...). From the economic and media power, they directly began to have political power quotas (...). As senators and representatives they were part of the board that passed, reformed or repealed the laws of the Republic. Consequently, they would never approve anything that even brushed the interests of the media from the point of view of their messages or far less the tax field.
>
> (Herrera 2007: 28)

When Hugo Chavez won the elections in his first term, private media owners lost their power over the government, as well as their associated economic benefits, given that the state decided not to retain their advertising. The state left them off the lists for the new legislative power. Moreover, the government, together with other sectors of society, entered into an important debate on the need to establish a legal framework that regulates the telecommunications sector. This process started with discussions and drafts of an act in late 2000, with a version of 138 articles, widely discussed in working groups that brought together different sectors involved in communication problems: private, public and community (intellectuals, social organizations, institutions related to health, culture), which ultimately led to the version presented in 2003 and approved in 2004, the version being 35 articles divided into six chapters.

The private media, which, for years, promoted anti-political discourses in order to replace parties (Britto Garcia 2006: 308–315), considers regulations as a threat to their economic interests. Thus, they have come to control of the opposition, making them 'platforms to express instigation and calls for many social mobilization initiatives against Chávez administration, (...) and illegally replace the political role of opposition parties' (García de Madariaga and Domínguez 2006: 320, translation mine).

Thus, private media has become *de facto* opposition political actors:

> Days before the two-month oil sabotage, the general secretary of Acción Democrática, one of the two traditional parties of Venezuela, opposed to Chávez government, said to El Universal that the politicians of the *Coordinadora Democrática*, the group of opposition parties, which opposed the Chávez government, were preparing a political strategy and then media owners came in the evening and changed it.
>
> (Herrera 2007: 29, translation mine)

Media corporations thus took on the role of political actors and behaved as 'the stars of a coup d'état that they disguised as a spontaneous social uprising, a general oil strike disguised as general strike and days of unjustified terror' (García de Madariaga and Domínguez 2006: 327).

To this day, private media continues to perform the role of political actor, as evidenced by the candidacy and opposition campaign for the upcoming elections, in order to destabilize the country, using psychological manoeuvres that seek to create an atmosphere of terror and chaos in Venezuela. For example, the opposition candidate for the presidential elections of October 7, 2012, Henrique Capriles Radonski, was a founding member of the party 'Primero Justicia', which took a leading role in the 2002 coup. Interestingly, this party was formed as a result of a TV show called *Justicia para todos* (Justice for everyone), led by Julio Borgues. Capriles Radonski is also part of a family linked to the business and productive sector of the country; they own industries (Cadena Capriles), entertainment (Cinex) and real estate and service companies.

In response to this situation, the Venezuelan government has encouraged the development of measures aimed at the recovery of the media in favour of objective information, rather than leave media space in the hands of a putschist private sector that does not represent the plurality of Venezuelan society. The following section analyses the basis of these measures from the discussion outlined, concerning the three axes of democratization of media representation, the democratization of participation and the grand national media integration.

The three axes of media democratization in Venezuela

Democratization of media representation: Towards the recovery of media space

The first series of measures promoted by the Venezuelan government focus on what has been identified as the axis of the *democratization of representation*. A new legal framework was the basic tool to establish a real national media space, conceived and organized as a public good. The main legal measures can be classified into three groups: the transformation of the general legal framework, the re-organization of content and user's responsibility.

Prior to the enactment of this new legal framework on communication, the legislation for the regulation of broadcast media in Venezuela was very low, and inspired by regulations from 1940 to 1941, which were renewed in 1984. The new legal framework protects the media space as a space of public interest. It is important to note that the Constitution of the Bolivarian Republic of Venezuela is the legal framework for all laws, and it was the first legal measure promoted by Chavez through a broad participatory process.

It mentions the freedom of expression in Articles 57, 58, 60, 61, 78, 101, 108, 110 and 113, as well as the free and pluralistic nature of communication, the right to freedom of information without censorship and the right to reply, the right of children and adolescents to receive adequate information for purposes of their overall development, the protection of every citizen's honour and private life, the right to freedom of conscience, the freedom of issuing, receiving and disseminating cultural information, the obligation of public and private media to promote citizen's education, the dissemination of information and knowledge of cultural values concerning local identity, the public nature of information services and the prohibition of monopolies.

Some laws were enacted within the first legal framework: the Organic Law on Telecommunications (published in the Official Gazette No. 36.970 on February 12, 2000), the Regulations of Radio Broadcasting and Community Network Television of Non-profit Public Service (published in the Official Gazette No. 37.359 on January 8, 2002), the Law on Social Responsibility on Radio and Television (published in the Official Gazette No. 38.333, on December 12, 2005), commonly called RESORTE law) and, in 2011, the Law on Social Responsibility of Radio, Television and Electronic Media[2] (published in the Official Gazette No. 39.610, on February 7, 2011).

Within this broad and renewed legal framework, some measures have been promoted in favour of the national recovery of ownership and the use of the public radio-electric space, through regulations based on social responsibility of media. This includes the issuing of licences, the classification of programs, schedules according to the language in the areas of health, sex and violence, time limits of advertising, promotions and propaganda, open-signal broadcasting with 12 percent of channels for free, tax measures and sanctions, national and independent production, promotion of democratization and citizen's organization and participation.

The first step has strengthened, with the re-appropriation and 'physical' recovery of the domestic radio-electric spectrum, the creation of new local public TV stations such as ANTV, TVES, VIVE TV, AVILA TV, Telesur[3] and the legal recovery of such space (*non-renewal of RCTV's*[4] *licence and signal, the recovery of the signal to create the public channel TVES, and the recovery of the radio spectrum*[5]), as well as the creation of a local newspaper (Correo del Orinoco) and two regional newspapers (Ciudad Caracas and Ciudad Valencia[6]), the creation of *Radio ALBA 96.3 FM, Radio del Sur, Radio Asamblea Nacional, Radio Ciudad Valencia,*[7] and the Venezuelan News Agency,[8] all of them integrated into the new National System of Public Media.

Another extremely important legal aspect in favour of this democratization of media ownership is the implementation of anti-monopoly measures, as well as the creation of a Social Responsibility Fund (Chapter 6 'The Social Responsibility Fund', Article 24 of the RESORTE Law) managed by the National Telecommunications Commission. In order to strengthen Independent Local Production and to support Independent Local Producers in developing their products, since 2005, the Ministry of People's Power for Communication and Information and the Social Responsibility Board – through the Social Responsibility Fund – has funded over 500 projects submitted by Independent Local Producers (MINCI 2012).

It is important to understand that the purpose of these measures was not to eliminate private media, but to fight the monopolization of the public radio-electric spectrum and to rebalance public and private media share. Previously

> the distribution of broadcast capacity and the effective power between the private and public sector gives an idea of the concentration of ownership in the private sector. In fact, it controls 74% of the broadcast compared to 26% of the state, and 85% of broadcast power compared to only 15% of the public sector with a global advertising market amounting to 160 million dollars, and 70% is focused on TV (Hernández 2005: 36). Nowadays, it is still favourable to private sector. In fact, there are seven private open-signal channels (Televén, Globovision, Venevision, La Tele, Vale TV, Channel I and TV Family) compared to five owned by the state (VTV – ANTV-TELESUR-VIVE TV-TVES), 26 out of the 28 pay-TV channels are private, five belong to the opposition (El Universal, Tal Cual, El Nacional, El Nuevo País and Diario 2001), one is neutral (Últimas Noticias), only one has a favourable editorial towards the Bolivarian process nine Diario VEA) and one public newspaper belongs to the state (Correo del Orinoco).

The second wave of measures involved *the regulation of content*. In this area, a legal framework was developed to promote the creation, recovery and broadcasting of local, regional and community media content. The second step towards the democratization of media representation was composed of measures to encourage national production, including the creation and approval of the concept 'National Independent Producer'[9], as well as the regulation and limit definition[10] of mandatory broadcast of national production content[11] through the media, which also covers advertising,[12] music[13] and language protection.[14]

Finally, through the establishment of user committees (according to data provided by MINCI, 1,200 user committees have registered since the approval of the Law on Social Responsibility in Radio and Television until December 2009), society was responsible for the analysis and evaluation of Venezuelan radio and television programming. They have the right to demand from public–private media service providers information about their programs, the right to make requests, complaints or claims that must be answered within 15 working days, the right to access the records of the messages broadcast to participate in the formulation, implementation and evaluation of public policies, the right to participate in public consultations for the implementation of this law, the right to submit projects on education for critical perception of messages or researches related to communication and messages broadcasting, the right to access free spaces on radio and pay-TV broadcasting and the right to promote opportunities for dialogue and exchange among radio and TV providers, the state and users. This has allowed the progressive creation of a truly social control of media space.

The physical recovery of the radio-electric space, the promotion of local media content creation & broadcasting and society's responsibility in the use and respect of media space are three pillars that allow us to see how Venezuela created the necessary legal framework to have a media space designed as local public space.

However, the impulse given by these legal frameworks and measures are not enough to give life to such space, not only as local public space but also as a common space for public concerns.

From the analysis of the second axis, it is possible to view the axis of participation as a true democratic public space that can be conceived not only as a space of representation but also as a space for participation and interaction.

Democratization of media participation: The third sector of communication

This next level of analysis explores how media is being gradually organized in Venezuela as an *integral space for participation*, as space where media matters are conceived in terms of social organization. The idea of creating a third communication sector, that is to say, a sector that is neither private nor public, is not new. However, few countries have been given the necessary legal, political and socio-political conditions for this purpose, given that the existence of such a sector is contrary to the interests of large media companies, and often, of the states.

In Venezuela, there has been a legal framework through the implementation of the 'Regulation of Sound Radio Broadcasting and Community Network Television of Non-profit Public Service',[15] which defines, protects, promotes and supports the existence of a true independent media sector. Furthermore, a draft of the law on Communication for People's Power is being debated in Congress. The purpose of this new law, which is currently being discussed, is to 'encourage, develop and consolidate people's communication as a fundamental human right, as well as to regulate the organization, operation and joint initiatives of organized communities, movements and social organizations for the participatory, protagonist and emancipating communication' (http://www.asambleanacional.gov.ve/index.php?option=com_leyesficha&Itemid=239&lang=es).

The 'Regulation of Sound Radio Broadcasting and Community Network Television of Non-profit Public Service' raises a number of rules and principles regulating the requirements, characteristics, limitations and obligations of such media as community media. The definitional aspects of this regulation demonstrate that it regulates community media as community foundations, defining their main purpose as media communication services for communities, establishing incompatibilities of functions, regulates advertising and allocations of their patrimonies so as to protect their independence, establishing their necessary influence in local matters and their democratic, participatory and pluralistic approach to administration. It also establishes a number of obligations concerning programming[16] and content, whereby these need to be focused on community. At least 70 percent of its daily transmission time is devoted to the transmission of community production. In addition, it states that every community media channel has to participate in community media training.[17]

Although it is the fundamental basis for the impulse, definition and regulation of the third sector, regulation as a whole it is not enough to be entirely feasible. This is why the Ministry of People's Power for Communication and Information (MINCI, Spanish acronym), in coordination with institutions that provide and regulate media licences, have launched a series of programs that support the process of creation, feasibility and monitoring of such media.

These initiatives include programs that support the legal framework of such media, including programs to review and evaluate support requests and promotion of projects submitted, processing support requests and promotion of projects before other institutions. They also include technological endowment programs granted to communities, whose media projects have enabled the resources to buy the necessary equipment through the technological endowment program for alternative and community media, as well as programs for community ownership of technological media tools (training, socio-technical and education programs for popular communication). They also provided financial support programs through the granting of public advertising and sponsorship to such community media.

According to data provided by MINCI in March 2012, the National Telecommunications Commission (CONATEL, Spanish acronym) has enabled 280 community media (244 community radio and 36 community TV stations). From 2004 to the present date, MINCI has technologically endowed 205 community radio stations, 72 community TV stations and 69 film production groups and has invested about $50 billion since 2004 in endowment and funding granted to community radio and TV broadcasters of the country.

Community media promotes the development of content and formats made, produced and broadcast for and on behalf of the local communities. This allows the progressive constitution of a new group of signs, a new social and cultural model for communities. It's about doing radio, television, journalism *with* the people and not only about people.

It is therefore very important that this local community media is *organized* as a true third sector; they have to communicate with each other. Channels such as the nationwide VIVE TV are exclusively a community media, and it is an organization platform for these media. VIVE TV is the channel that supports hundreds of groups and social organizations in our country and in America, guaranteeing that more than 15,000 communities have direct participation in the different programs of VIVE TV (See information in: http://www.vive.gob.ve/quienes.php).

The National Association of Free and Alternative Community Media (ANMCLA, Spanish acronym) gathers about 150 community media[18] and is another alternative for this organization. This association is not defined as *a* collective, but as a *collective network*. It conceives the organization of the media, taking into account *the transverse nature of media as an integral space*, through a number of initiatives, such as the creation of popular communication schools, the alternative news agency with its popular correspondents, the popular printing network, radio and TV centres of production, among others.

What is evident is the reformulation of the media and public communication as collective processes of social transformation. Social transformation from the media, which implies an authentic and lasting re-appropriation of social media tools, a re-appropriation of ICTs as tools for development, not only of community media content but also for communities themselves. Infocenter networks (free Internet access centres) in Venezuela represent a good example. Infocenter Foundation has constructed in Venezuela 840 Infocenters (of which 30 are mobile),[19] which are organized as true community centres for the organization and development of communities, through a clearly participatory and inclusive model. Infocenters are the headquarters of activities for community training and development. These centres develop a number of activities that go beyond the mere use of Internet for personal or mercantilist purposes.

Through a series of community experiences of use and appropriation of ICTs, Infocenters have served community development in many aspects: a new community communication, a technological training as an instrument of technological democratization (with specific attention for people with disabilities),[20] community organization, health prevention, preservation and environmental recovery, recovery and organization of local culture, collective reconstruction of community history, development of activities aimed at making good use of free time of children, development and creation of self-sustaining social community network and so on.[21]

The Integration and creation of a grand national integral media space

Regional media represents a powerful field against which the construction of public and integral media spaces is very difficult, for the reasons mentioned above. It is therefore imperative to consider how it might be possible to construct an international media space, which challenges the neoliberal logic of international media corporations. In order to build an integration that is not limited to its economic component, it is necessary to construct trans-regional public media spaces designed as *common* spaces, as integral public spaces. These spaces need to be organized for people's empowerment, taking into account the identification, representation and construction of a series of values based on the defence of the rights of peoples and communities, and not just individuals.

By reconstructing media as a space for people's integration, Venezuela is promoting the internationalization of media as a public space for representation, and the construction and organization of the collective in and beyond the country to create a regional public space. The integration of the peoples across America is *also* taking place through the construction of a grand national media space, aimed at constructing the relationship among South Americans, as a comprehensive and political space.

Through the creation of international media integrators, such as Telesur, a South American multi-state company created in 2005 with the support of six countries (Argentina, Bolivia, Cuba, Ecuador, Nicaragua and Venezuela) and 11 permanent correspondents (Bogota, Brasilia, Buenos Aires, Caracas, Mexico City, Havana, La Paz, Lima, Managua, Quito and Washington), and La Radio del Sur, which began broadcasting on February 10, 2010, as a communication tool at the service of regional integration among the countries of South America, Central America, the Caribbean, Mexico, Africa, Asia and even the people of the United States, Canada and Europe,[22] a regional public space is being constructed to allow the representation, processing, construction and recognition of the socio-political realities of our America. This media tries to picture a sovereign media space of the South American reality. It would be a space that fosters the re-appropriation of its reality. This responds to the need to regionalize the democratization of media representation.

The following discussion considers Telesur, which is the update of a project such as the one described before. In fact, as it appears on the website of the channel (http://www.telesurtv.net/noticias/canal/index.php), Telesur is a 'socially-oriented Latin American media aimed at leading and promoting the union processes of the South Americans'. Telesur defines itself as a 'voice and space for the construction of a new communication order' that 'encourages the production, promotion and broadcast of contents of the region, thereby promoting the recognition of Latin American imaginary', from the construction of a media space 'composed of a diverse and plural programming as diverse and plural as the Latin American population'.

Thus, Telesur is a media source aimed at the construction, broadcasting and recognition of a representation of the regional socio-cultural and socio-political diversity, constructed by the citizens of the region. As a result, there is an integration designed as an identification of the differences that make possible the construction of the collective understanding. As the slogan of one of its programs states, it is all about *'knowing each other, recognizing each other in order to be integrated'*.

This integration is thus organized through a common public-media space for the peoples of the continent. That is to say, it is a common space for the representation and interaction of its diversities, systematized in the media in favour of the collective construction. In fact, Telesur literally allows these people to recognize each other through its policy of representiativity in programming.[23]

Telesur's main axis is to provide information in the wider sense. If Telesur can be seen as a regional communication strategy alternative to CNN, it is far from being reduced to that. In fact, Telesur is recognized by its programming grid as a public space for the representation of identities, cultures, histories and realities that make up the South American continent. Through its programs, it attempts to promote cultural diversity with the view to consolidating historical memory and collective identity of South Americans, in favour of development and organization. The democratization of content production promoted ensures the construction of the representation and democratization, through the development of a sovereign Latin American public- media space.

However, it is also important to understand the role of Telesur as communication strategy aimed at the development of media power, oriented towards development and safeguarding of the democratic stability in the region. Telesur's role in the coverage of the coup perpetrated in Honduras in 2009 is an example. Telesur played a major role, since the first hours of the coup.

The coverage brought to the attention of the international community what was happening, and forced international agencies to take a stand. The Organization of American States (OAS), the EU and the UN were obliged to condemn and label the coup as a result of the information provided live by Telesur from Honduras. This example demonstrates that the creation of a regional public-media space provides opportunities for empowerment with regards to the representation of people's reality, not merely symbolically, but with a very specific level of a political reality.

The actions of a channel like Telesur[24] can thus be understood as twofold: It has an international geopolitical role and an interregional symbolic function. First, through the representation of the current regional presence, it also constitutes a space for the defence of democracy at the regional level. Secondly, it establishes Telesur as a space for the construction of South American communities organized to construct a repertoire of their own signs, based on the local context. It is evident that these two levels only exist because of the structural relationship between them.

Conclusion

The creation of a participatory media space based on the media empowerment of society is central to developing and deepening a more participatory democracy, as the case of Venezuela. Taking into account the international and regional situation, the measures taken in Venezuela provide pioneering examples in this field.

The reorganization of the global media space is not an easy task. However, it is essential to securing the progressive processes that are occurring in many southern countries. Participatory democracy must create another communicational model, organized as a participatory and inclusive process. It is not enough to write minutes and denounce the neoliberal ideological hegemony that the large media empires have put into practice. If these communicational paradigms are not radically broken, there is the risk of reproducing the same situation under democratic realism.

Venezuela is facing this challenge, on an inevitable trial-and-error basis, via an arduous process of re-creation. The global media offensive against the initiatives enacted from and in Venezuela is very powerful. It is necessary to raise consciousness concerning media spaces at a global level, whereby neoliberal paradigms privatize and monopolize politics, gradually reducing them to an auxiliary function of the global economy.

To this end, it is necessary to remove the blinders that make us face the media exclusively from an ideology of human rights: The field of communication is more complex than the right to free speech. The essence of democracy can be seen through the media. The organization of the public space has the potential to be a real space for collective participation in the construction of the common good.

To allow this space to be controlled by exogenous powers strips people of sovereign power. 'Voluntary servitude', to paraphrase De la Boetie (1986), has set the pace for too long in the development of neoliberal democracies. It's time to face all the challenges of the organization of an authentic political power based in the people. To this end, it is necessary to fight one of the most important battles of this century: the media battle. The challenge lies in the creation of a genuine media space for people's empowerment.

Notes

1. The Cisneros Organization (www.cisneros.com) provides information of all companies and their holdings.
2. It is important to point out that the reform of this law does not involve the Internet as the opposition has stated. This law regulates digital media, websites, newspapers, radio and television.

3. Dates of creation: Fundación Televisora de La Asamblea Nacional ANTV: 2005: Televisora venezolana Social TVES: 2007, VIVE TV: 2003, ÁVILA TV: 2006, Telesur: 2005.
4. The non-renewal of RCTV's licence in 2007, when it expired, as well as its disqualification as international media in 2009 are part of the Venezuelan state's legal prerogatives. See Libro Blanco de RCTV 2007.
5. CONATEL called upon radio and TV stations for a data update process that lasted 15 days and ended on June 23, 2009. However, 86 AM radio stations did not attend neither did the 154 FM stations. In total, 240 radio and TV stations did not attend this call, and their licences were revoked. These frequencies are in the process of re-allocation, which is usually processed in favour of community radios.
6. It was created in 2009 for the first two newspapers and in 2012 for the last one.
7. Created respectively in 2008, 2010 and 2012.
8. Created in 2005 under the name Bolivarian News Agency, and in 2010, it became the Venezuelan News Agency.
9. According to recent statements by the Venezuelan Minister of Communication (February 2012), Andres Izarra, 21,000 independent producers have registered in the country to date. See the statement in http://www.diariodelpueblo.com.ve/nacionales.php?vermas=1336 statement
10. Article 13 of the RESORTE Law. *'The local audiovisual or audio production, program, advertising or propaganda, broadcast by radio and television service providers will be those containing in its creation, direction, production and post-production the items listed in below 1) Venezuelan capital, 2) Venezuelan locations, 3) Venezuelan scripts 4) Venezuelan authors or writers, 5) Venezuelan directors or artists, 6) Venezuelan personnel, 7) Venezuelan Technicians, 8) Venezuelan culture values'.*
11. Article 14 of the RESORTE Law *'Radio and television services providers must daily broadcast, during the hours of general viewership, a minimum of seven hours of programs of national production, of which a minimum of four hours must be independent national production. Also, they must daily broadcast, during the hours of supervised viewership, a minimum of three hours of locally produced programs, of which a minimum of one hour and a half will be independent national production'.*
12. Article 14 of the RESORTE Law: At least 85 per cent of advertising will be transmitted to domestic production.
13. Article 14 of the RESORTE Law. *'During the hours of general and supervised viewership, the radio or TV services that disseminate musical works shall guarantee the dissemination of Venezuelan musical works in at least fifty percent of its daily music programming. At least fifty percent of the Venezuelan musical diffusion shall focus on the dissemination of traditional Venezuelan musical works, which may contain, among others a) music from different geographical areas of the country, b) the use of Spanish or indigenous official languages, c) the presence of Venezuelan culture values. d) Venezuelan authorship or composition. e) The presence of Venezuelan singers. 'During the hours of general and supervised viewership, the radio or TV services that disseminate foreign musical works shall allocate at least ten percent of its daily music programming to the dissemination of musical works of Latin America and the Caribbean authors, writers, composers, songwriters or singers'.*
14. Article 4 of the RESORTE Law: *'The messages that are disseminated through radio and television services shall be in Spanish'.*
15. Regulations of Sound Radio Broadcasting and Community Network Television of Non-profit Public Service (Official Gazette No. 37,359 on January 8, 2002).

16. Article 26 of the Regulation of Sound Radio Broadcasting and Community Network Television of Non-profit Public Service states, for example, '(3) Ensure that the transmission of messages to the service of the public who seek the solution of the problems of the community. (4) Having spaces to ensure the direct participation of community members, and to ensure the right of individuals to free and pluralistic media'.
17. Article 27, titled 'Training Programs' of the Regulation of Sound Radio Broadcasting and Community Network Television of Non-profit Public Service 'community members shall annually submit to the National Telecommunications Commission training and education programs in audio or audiovisual production that they will teach to the community, in order to train and certify community producers'.
18. See the list in the website of AMNCLA. http://www.medioscomunitarios.org/pag/index.php?id=17
19. See http://www.infocentro.gob.ve/
20. The program has trained over a million people so far, and, in January 2011, it was awarded the UNESCO King Hamad Bin Isa Al-Khalifa Prize.
21. See the systematization of these experiences in http://sistematizacion.infocentro.gob.ve/
22. For further information see http://laradiodelsur.com/
23. See http://www.telesurtv.net/programas
24. La Radio del Sur, inaugurated in February 2010, is designed and organized in the same order of ideas, with the particularity of being formed as a radio network. Regarding Alba TV, we see the importance of alternative media networks in the creation of South American media spaces for social transformation.

7
The Internet for the Public Interest: Overcoming the Digital Divide in Brazil

Carolina Matos

Introduction

Latin America is quickly becoming one of the world's fastest growing Internet markets, with access to computers rapidly expanding in countries like Brazil. The Internet and new communication technologies have been hailed by various scholars and cyber enthusiasts as key elements that can bring development to countries of the Global South, and contribute to the reduction of inequalities between nations (Cardoso 2010; Silverstone 2000). The 2005 *Pesquisa Nacional por Amostra de Domicilios* of the Brazilian Institute of Geography and Statistics BIGE underscored the existence of 32.1 million Internet users in Brazil. This represents 21 per cent of the population of ages ten years and over. In the 2008 study, this number went up to 55.9 million, or 34.8 per cent, and is rapidly growing.

If there is one thing the Internet does offer, then it is the possibility, or the hope, of a *more democratic and participatory society*. Arguably, the exclusion of citizens from the World Wide Web has economic, social and political implications, and poses serious implications on an individual's rights to participate in a democracy and to engage in political life. To be digitally excluded is not only a violation of citizens' information and communication rights, but it makes the emerging economies of South America and Brazil loose out in jobs and investments. In this chapter, I argue how democratic politics in Brazil are facing a paradox: New technologies are opening up avenues for participatory democracy at all levels, from providing citizens with a growing platform for advocacy, political mobilization and organization, as was evident during the 2013 June mass protests held throughout the country, to the ability to scrutinize the activities of politicians and of Congress.

For a country that traditionally closes its elite activities to the rest of the population, the web is beginning to play an important role for the public sector in its relationship with citizens, making governmental actions more transparent and thus creating the means to undermine political corruption. The Internet is emerging strongly also as a tool for politicians to engage with citizens, promoting particular causes and working on issues usually marginalized from the mainstream media, like gender politics. The persistence of digital exclusion nonetheless poses serious limits to the capacity of the web to deepen democratic politics in Brazil. To start with, political mobilization, which takes places on the web, is still largely restricted to politically aware and educated citizens as well as decision-making elites, although from the 2006 elections onwards the web has become increasingly popularized in the country.

This chapter explores key theories concerning the problems and impacts of the digital divide (i.e. Norris 2001; Nederveen Pieterse's 2010). The debates presented here are divided into four parts: The first investigates the benefits of networked politics and its limits; the second looks at the relationship between economic growth and the persistence of high numbers of digitally excluded in Brazil, as well as the government and civil society initiatives to tackle this, while the last part of the chapter provides a summary of the positive aspects of the uses of the web in Brazil for the public interest. It provides a brief discussion of the ways in which female politicians, such as Marina Silva of the Green Party and Dilma Rousseff from the Worker's Party (PT), used the Internet for political campaigning during the presidential elections of 2010. It also examines briefly the 2013 June protests and the ways in which various different sectors of Brazilian society used new technologies to mobilize and organize the demonstrations or report on them live, denouncing police brutality.

One crucial argument raised in this chapter is how the Internet has emerged and, in the June 2013 protests, managed to consolidate itself, as an *alternative and political blogosphere* and a reaction to the partisanship and officialdom character of the mainstream media, with requests for media democratization and further reforms. Thus, the Internet in Brazil has a positive role in invigorating public debate, and is contributing to the undermining of media concentration, boosting political pluralism and stimulating political participation. This emerging vibrant, contradictory *blogosphere* is paving the way for the construction of diverse representations of disadvantaged groups. I begin this discussion by providing a short summary of the theoretical debate on the positive aspects of networked politics, as well as their limits, in the democratization process.

The benefits of networked politics: The limits and challenges for democratic politics

How can we understand the relationship between the Internet and the public interest? It seems clear that the relationship between the Internet and democracy must be understood in relation to other social, economic and political factors. Various members of society, on one hand, use the web for the public interest through an individual engagement with politics as well as to scrutinize the activities of governments, whereas governments, on the other hand, in their relations with citizens, make use of new technologies. Politicians for instance are finding in the web an avenue to advocate their party policies and mobilize citizens, whereas disadvantaged and marginalized political groups and social movements view it as an opportunity to work on misrepresentations and mainstream stereotypes or to organize protests to pressure governments to fulfil their promises.

Firstly, it is important to recognize that democratic politics play a minor role in *cybperspace* in comparison to commercial transactions. The Internet is heavily dominated by commercial corporations over independent individual blogs, NGOs and other party websites. Drawing from a wide range of political theories, Norris (2001: 107) asserts that the types of political organizations found online are closely linked to the process of democratization of a given country. This means that there is a clear connection between income and economic power, new technologies and wider political participation.

Digital politics can be understood here in the broader sense, in other words, as the carrying out of political debate between voters, or as non-partisan discussions or forms of civic engagement by sectors of the community gathering online to deliberate on ways of improving their own lives. High expectations have been placed by cyber enthusiasts on the capacity of information and communication technologies of benefitting minor parties and other political voices marginalized from the mainstream, creating an alternative sphere of debate, which can work as a counterweight to dominant *status quo* discourses (Ward, Gibson and Nixon 2003), or offer more in depth discussions on governmental policies.

Debates concerning the rise of the Information Society nonetheless have been deeply contested, usually cast in either an optimistic or a pessimistic light: The former group sees the web as having the potential of reducing traditional inequalities between developed and developing societies, whereas the latter believes that it is destined to reinforce current disparities. More utopian or highly optimistic theories on the Internet (Clark and Aufderheide 2009) argue however how the web has profoundly shaped contemporary life, from the selling of books to the ways in which politics is being practiced worldwide.

In the summary of the report *Public Media 2.0: Dynamic, Engaged Publics*, Clarke and Aufderheide[1] (2009) underlined how digital public media 2.0 will become more of a key component of democratic public life. They see this new media as being directed to the public and produced by it. This has been the case of the grass-roots mobilization around the 2008 Obama electoral campaign, seen as proof of how the medium has opened up new avenues for civic engagement, and especially amongst the younger segments of the electorate. Such arguments seem to hit at the very core of the technological determinism theories, and the utopia surrounding the supposedly 'magical' powers of the Internet and of social networking sites to change real life problems, such as reducing poverty and combating race and gender oppressions.

The fact of the matter is that the power structures of the old media, and their tendencies towards concentration, have not disappeared and have actually been reinforced in a context of increasing expansion of new technologies, mergers between companies and other inequalities produced by globalization. Thus, the Internet can be seen as being more a space to advertise products to consumers and trade than one that improves the democratic quality of public life (Margolis, Resnick and Levy 2003: 65).

A comparison can be made between the expansion of digital democracy in Brazil in the 2010 elections and the uses of the web in the Obama 2008 presidential campaign. According to data gathered by the *Pew Internet and American Life Project* survey, some 74 per cent of Internet users, or 55 per cent of the adult population, went online in 2008 to get news and information about the election. More than half of the population used the Internet to get involved in the political process. Two-thirds of voters between the ages of 18 and 24 engaged in political activity on these sites in 2008. Similar to the actions of many Americans in 2008, but taking into consideration the lower levels of Internet use in Latin America, many Brazilians in 2010 went online to share their views on the dispute with other bloggers, as we shall see, with many politicians also attempting to copy the 2008 'Obama effect' by actively going on the Internet to attract voters.

Thus, it is more accurate to say that the web is emerging everywhere around the world, either in Egypt, Brazil or the United Kingdom, as a valid space for opposition groups, or parties who feel marginalized from the mainstream, from either the Conservative or Progressive side of the political spectrum. The Internet can have either negative or positive functions, such as reinforcing prejudices, in the same way as it can be empowering for many disadvantaged groups, neglected at the margins. We saw this happen in Brazil during the 2013 June protests, when different youth groups who do not usually receive space in the mainstream media voiced their demands through social media.

The Internet can thus provide room for opposition groups to attack each other, or to strive to debate particular socio-economic and political issues that can have an impact on policy decisions. From whatever perspective we take, it seems to be the case that these 'multiple discourses', which are being articulated on the web, can assist in the creation of a more *vibrant* public sphere of debate in the *Habermasian* sense, and this is especially important for transitional or emerging democracies like Brazil.

In Brazil, as is the case with more advanced democracies, the mainstream media has embraced new technologies, with a growing convergence between media platforms occurring since the 1990s. The majority of blogs accessed on the Internet are those of journalists from the mainstream newspapers, such as Ricardo Noblat's blog from *O Globo*. Nonetheless, the web in Brazil is also offering many spaces for new websites and other civic organizations to make use of it to propagate their political causes, from the emergence in the 1990s of media websites like *Observatorio da Imprensa* (www.observatoriodaimprensa.com.br) and *Comunique-se* (portal .comunique-se.com.br) to alternative media sites like *Midia Ninja*, which gained notoriety with the live reporting of the police repressions against demonstrators in Rio and Sao Paulo in the June 2013 protests.

The Internet is thus offering more opportunities for citizens to access details on party policies and the biography of politicians, contributing to scrutinize the activities of Congress and providing more transparency in party funding, radio and TV concessions and approval of laws. The democratic capacity of the Internet includes not only its interactive potential, as well as its ability to stimulate more engagement, but also its role in invigorating the public sphere, helping to unite civil society in various debates, including wider investments in public services and education, as the protests in Brazil made clear. Thus, for emerging and new democracies like Brazil, the Internet can have a very positive role, one which is closely tied with the advancement of democratization. The limits to *cyberdemocracy* are nonetheless persistent, and the efforts to tackle the digital divide need to be expanded if there is a genuine aim of granting communication and information rights to less privileged groups in the country.

The Internet for the public interest and the digital divide in Brazil

Various theorists have explored the numerous benefits to democracy of the web, ranging from its capacity to increase interconnectedness between countries, peoples and communities to permitting the rapid transmission of global events, assisting in the creation of global citizens and the formation of global civil society united in favour of particular political causes (Ward, Gibson and Nixon 2003; Norris 2001; Nederveen Pieterse 2010; Cardoso 2010). Some of the key concerns raised in the digital divide controversy between information-rich and information-poor countries have mainly consisted in how to include larger sectors of the world population in the knowledge economy, providing the means for further democratization of access and connectivity to all citizens in developing and advanced democracies alike.

Scholarship worldwide has shown that the hype with new technologies has not resulted in a diminishing of economic and social inequalities between and within countries. However, it can contribute to democratization and political engagement, and most importantly, it can strengthen the voice of the developing world. The digital divide literature is vast and cannot be fully covered here. My main purpose in this chapter is to highlight some of the core dilemmas concerning the digital divide debate by looking at the work of key authors (Norris 2001; Castells 2010; Nederveen Pieterse 2010; Thussu 2006) who have articulated a relationship between digital inclusion, education and economic development.

Norris (2001: 103) is sceptical about the role of the Internet in strengthening democracy. In her book (2001: 37) on understanding the digital divide debate, she makes use of a sophisticated framework, which combines both institutional as well as individual data. She underlines three levels of analysis: (1) the *macro-level technological environment*, which determines the distribution of the Internet access within each country; (2) *the meso-level context of political institutions*, including parties and government departments and (3) *the micro-level individual resources*, which affects patterns of online engagement. Norris's key findings suggest that *economic development* is an important avenue for understanding Internet connectivity and consumption. In this chapter, I precisely equate the lack of digital inclusion of certain sectors of the population, a factor that both has an impact on further economic development and is emerging as a barrier for wider political participation, with the ways in which the web nevertheless is contributing to form a vibrant and influential counter-public sphere in Brazil.

A pattern that emerges here is that most rich nations that already have many radio and television stations are the ones with more access to networked computers. As Norris (2001) states, *UNESCO* emphasis is that most of the world's population lacks basic access to a telephone, nevermind a computer, resulting in societies that are marginalized at the periphery of communications. Nederveen Pieterse (2010) and Norris (2001: 59) thus envision the digital divide debate as being less about providing more computers in schools and libraries in developing countries and more about creating the means for wider education in IT (information technology) skills and literacy levels. Education is thus seen as a significant force in social development, capable of assisting in the creation of the skills that will facilitate a wider use of computers in these societies.

Nonetheless, prospects regarding the Internet's capacity of contributing to the development of poorer countries and reducing economic inequalities seem grim. The report of the *Global Economic Prospects and Developing Countries 2001*, published in December 2001 by the World Bank, predicted that the distance between the rich and poor countries in terms of Internet access would continue into the next (current) decade. As Norris (2001: 5) notes, the Organisation for Economic Co-operation and Development (OECD) has underlined how the benefits of the Internet have not yet trickled down to Southern, Central and Eastern Europe, not to mention the poorest areas in sub-Saharan Africa, Latin America and Southeast Asia. The developed world has nearly 50 telephone lines for each group of 100 people, while in low-income countries this proportion is of 1.4 telephones for each group of 100. Also, 90 per cent of the users reside in the industrialized countries, with nearly 60 per cent of the users concentrated in North America, in Canada and the United States (in Norris 2001).

The fact that the development of software technology is still heavily concentrated in the United States attests to what Nederveen Pieterse (2010) sees as a tendency of ICT4D (information and communication technologies-for-development) to reaffirm the dependency of developing societies on these same technologies. The situation of dependency has not changed much. In the end of 2012, France and Brazil negotiated a deal for the production of supercomputers in the country, a technology transference project, aimed to contributing to areas of geo-military advancement and oil production, creating a technological centre in Brazil. Problems of infrastructure, funding and centralization of projects, however, are some of the challenges that Brazil faces, impeding it to advance its digital inclusion programmes. This is a common problem faced by other countries of the South, as scholars (i.e. Thussu 2006: 238–240) have underlined.

According to the statistics provided by the International Telecommunications Union (ITC), the number of Internet hosts in Latin America grew at a rate of 136 per cent, ahead of North America (74) and Europe (30). The numbers vary according to the source, methodology and the quantity of participants. According to a more recent research conducted by *ComScore* (May 2010), the number of Internet users in Brazil increased to 73 million users, including children from the age of 6. The numbers continue to grow: Statistic provided by the institute of research *Ibope Nielsen Online* stressed that in the second semester of 2012, there were 83.4 million users.[2] One of the reasons for the increase was the increase of income of people who, from 2007, had their first contact with a computer through the *lan houses*[3] and afterwards bought their own. The numbers are not that far apart from the 35.5 per cent who use the Internet in Chile, although it is much lower than China (49.2 per cent), according to the *2006 World Internet Project* (in Cardoso 2010).

The reduction of the divide between the digitally included and excluded carries important political, social and economic dimensions. It has the potential to boost prospects for economic development and literacy, serving as a tool for the expansion of educational levels and IT skills. In Brazil, there are approximately 17 million literally illiterate people and another 30 million called functional illiterates. A computer has little capacity to serve as an engine of economic growth and educational inclusion of the person using it if there is no proper electricity, or the person does not know how to use the technology properly.

Governmental efforts to increase Internet connectivity have become more pronounced in the region in the last years. The first mandate of Lula

(2002–06) included wider digital inclusion and access to new technologies as a national public policy capable of guaranteeing citizenship rights. It launched ambitious programmes such as the project Citizen Connected – *Computador para Todos*, part of the 'Programa Brasileiro de Inclusao Digital' (*Brazilian Programme of Digital Inclusion*),[4] equating the use of technology with local development and the deepening of democracy.

At a moment when Brazil's economy is pointed out as being the sixth largest one in the world, the government of Dilma Rousseff is facing the difficult challenge of boosting digital inclusion, having promised to take broadband Internet access to 75 per cent of the country by 2014 through the programme initiated during Lula's administration, the 'Plano Nacional de Banda Larga' (*National Broadband Plan*). Other non-governmental experiences of digital inclusion conducted by NGOs include the work carried out by *Viva Rio*, an organization that is being responsible for implementing spaces of access to the web in shanty towns and poorer neighbourhoods throughout the state of Rio, as well as offering IT training.

There are sharp regional inequalities in access, with the cost of broadband being very high. Institutional problems include the lack of proper infrastructure throughout the country, making it difficult to install a wider structure of broadband access. Governmental actions on digital inclusion include the participation of the Ministry of Education, through the Secretary of Distant Learning, the ministries of Communications and Science and Technology. The GESAC project (*Governo Eletronico Servico de Atendimento ao Cidadao*) is a key example of a programme that aims to include citizens from remote Brazilian areas, serving more than 10,000 localities. All areas are attended with a connection kit, which permits access to the Internet of high speed through satellite. The participants include schools and *tele*-centres, such as the famous *lan houses,* part of the governmental digital inclusion programme, *Computador para Todos* (Computers for All), and which created credit lines for low-income families to purchase computers.

Governments have not been capable of providing access to *all* citizens to Internet access. Businesses have had to play a role here as well. Data provided by the consultancy firm *McKinsey and Company* has underlined that an increase in 10 per cent in broadband connections can lead to a growth of 0.1 per cent to 1.4 per cent in the GDP of the country. The same study argues that if the access to the web in Latin America reached the same level as Europe, 1.7 million jobs could be created in the region.[5] Moreover, Lugo-Ocando (2008: 5) argues that there is not enough evidence to suggest that the massive investment in information and communication technology and telecommunications during the past ten years throughout the continent has made much difference to the lives of millions of Latin Americans in terms of narrowing the social and economic gap between the rich and poor on the continent.

In terms of the uses made by the public sector and government of new technologies to communicate better with citizens and stimulate their participation (i.e. *E-government*), responding to civil society's demands to wider transparency in the administration of public funds, it seems evident that the Internet has a role in the undermining of political corruption throughout the public sector as well a positive impact in making the activities of the Ministry of Communications regarding radio and TV concessions more transparent and democratic.

Castells (2003: 128, quoted in Gomes de Pinho 2008) affirms how research has underlined that the democratic potential and possibilities of the Internet have remained unfulfilled throughout the world, with the exception of the Scandinavian democracies. That said, Castells (2003: 276, quoted in Gomes de Pinho 2008) also affirms that most of the social and political movements in the world, of all political leanings, use the web as a tool for action and organization. Considering Brazil's still authoritarian and hierarchical nature, with a highly concentrated mainstream media that remains partisan and struggles with professionalism, it seems evident that the Internet is emerging as a powerful political and informational tool, occupying an important role in political mobilization and organization and assisting in the creation of a more democratic, but at the moment (counter) public, sphere, raising issues to be examined next.

From political campaigning, gender politics to citizen's protests: The uses of the web for the public interest

Writing about the potential of *cyber-democracy*, Levy (in Moraes 2003: 367) has underlined how social media and virtual communities open up a new public sphere where liberty of expression flourishes. The Internet has managed to open up a communication space that is 'inclusive, transparent and universal', and which is different from the 'modern' public sphere space associated with newspapers and the traditional media, culminating in an expansion of the mediated public sphere where communication takes place from everyone to all. Arguably, the power of the Brazilian blogosphere as a counter-public sphere and as a vehicle that is contributing to boost media pluralism, political diversity while also undermining the concentration of the media and its position as the ultimate definer of the public agenda, has grown considerably in the last years in the country, as we shall see.

Brazil's political arena still provides room for the articulation of conflict and for the competition of ideas, for the battle for the agenda of public opinion, the predominance of a particular form of thinking over a topic in opposition to another and for the use of media actors to endorse particular political views. If the key themes of the 2006 elections were political corruption and the reduction of inequality, the 2010 presidential Brazilian race was marked by the shadow of the legacy of the two Lula governments (2002–06;

2006–10) and by the entry in the dispute of two strong women candidates, Marina Silva and Dilma Rouseff.

Research demonstrates that party websites do not make much difference in terms of changing voting patterns. Focus group studies in the United Kingdom, Sweden and the Netherlands have revealed mixed reactions (Nixon and Johansson, 1999a and Crabtree, 2001 in Ward, Gibson and Nixon 2003: 25). Many surveys also indicate a reluctance of parties to engage in open dialogue with voters. As Gibson and Ward (1999: 364) correctly point out, '...providing online channels for participation...is not the same as empowering members'. The authors do recognize that the Internet can make more of an impact in emerging democracies, including destabilizing one-party regimes and serving as a counterweight to one-sided media discourses. I believe this is primarily the role that the web is having in Brazil as well as throughout Latin America, and as evident in a variety of ways during the 2010 presidential elections and the 2013 June protests.

Although the Internet has been featuring in the everyday life of middle-class sectors of Brazilian society and in much of Latin America since mainly the mid-1990s onwards, its adoption by politicians is a much more recent task. According to Jose Calazans, analyst of the research institute of the Ibope Nielsen Online, the Internet in Brazil is in its third phase of evolution. The first phase, from 2000 to 2003, has been characterized by a restricted access by people of high income; in the second phase, from 2004 to 2006, there was a growth in access, but it was restricted to the A and B classes; and in the third phase, from 2007 to 2012, there was a growth also of social networking and websites largely due to the improvement in the economic situation of Brazil. This helps explain why since the 2006 presidential elections the Internet has began to occupy centre stage in political campaigning, as well as in the life of politics in the country.

Since the 1990s, various websites have began to proliferate Brazilian Internet space, from specialized media channels like *Observatorio da Imprensa* to other political websites, with government administrations and politicians also creating their own websites to provide information to citizens or to engage them. Certain Brazilian civic websites, like *TVoto*; *Repolitica*; *Eleitor 2010*, *Transparencia Brasil* and *Vote na Web*, have began to occupy a niche and prominent space in the Brazilian political blogosphere, contributing to stimulate public debate and civic engagement and to assist citizens with knowledge of the political process. The aim of the website *Vote na Web* (www.votenaweb.com.br), for instance, is for citizens to closely follow the work of Brazilian MPs, including checking the proposals that are sent to Congress and monitoring how many voted on particular issues.

A major component of the 2010 presidential elections in Brazil was the massive presence of the Internet in political campaigning as a means of promoting candidates and providing varied information about their political personas to voters. Prior to the start of the 2010 elections, there was a lot of debate on the nature of the impact of new technologies on the outcome of the race, with scholars like Lima (2007) defining the web's role in political campaigning in Brazil as having contributed to promote active niche circles of debate. In the 2006 race, the female candidate of the then far left party (Socialist and Liberty Party), Heloisa Helena, emerged as a leading front runner in the race that culminated in Lula's re-election.

Since the impeachment of former president Fernando Collor in 1989 and the publication by the press of corruption practices by members of the Lula government in 2005, there has been a rise in political cynicism and growth in corruption scandals in Brazil. Such a volatile political environment has created a fertile ground for the emergence of strong women leaders, many of whom are perceived by the public as more trustworthy, with both the 2006 and 2010 presidential elections marked by the presence of strong women leaders, from Heloisa Helena to Marina Silva and Dilma Rousseff.

The fact of the matter is that many Brazilian women are still seen by conservative Brazilian elites – as well as by traditional western standards, patronized as 'Third World women', mixing a toxic combination of racism, sexism and classism – as a unified group of young, attractive and 'intellectually inferior' creatures who deserve to be exploited for capitalism's profit. Similar to the current obstacles discussed above concerning the problems of expanding digital inclusion, the persistence of gender and race inequality in Brazil also pose a serious impediment for further advancement of political democratization.

However, there have also been, in this realm, important conquests in the last decade. Women in Latin America currently govern over 40 per cent of the population: Dilma Rousseff in Brazil, Cristina Kirchner in Argentina and Laura Chincilla in Costa Rica. In the last ten years, women have conquered important levels of political participation and rights throughout the continent. Countries like Brazil have seen a rise in participation of women in the workforce, with more women occupying senior positions in businesses and government, including in the newsroom. As Buvinic and Roza (2004: 1) point out, Panama elected a woman president in 2003, Mireya Moscoso (1999–2004), and soon afterwards Chile and Argentina followed by electing the former president Michelle Bachelet (2006–10) and Cristina Kirchner (2007), wife of the previous president Nestor Kirchner (2003–07), respectively.

A 2000 Gallup poll conducted for the Inter-American Development Bank with a random sample of 2,022 voters in six major Latin American cities (Bogota, Colombia; Buenos Aires, Argentina; Mexico City; Rio de Janeiro and Sao Paulo, Brazil; San Salvador) revealed that the average voter had positive opinions concerning women's place in politics (in Buvinic and Roza 2004: 8). The authors (2004: 12) added that in a 2001 poll conducted in Brazil, the majority surveyed believed that women in senior positions were more honest than men. Nonetheless, despite the presence of high profile female candidates in the 2010 elections, according to the Supreme Electoral Court of Justice (TSE), a total of 79 per cent of men (15,780) ran for various political positions (governor, senator and MP) against only 20 per cent of women candidates, or 4,058.[6]

According to the 2012 ranking of the World Economic Forum (WEF), Brazil has gone up in 20 positions regarding gender equality, falling from the 82nd position to the 62nd on a list of 135 countries. The four criteria included economic participation and opportunity, access to education, health and survival and political participation, all issues widely explored during the 2013 June protests in Brazil, which were seen as an expression of dissatisfaction with the limits of the modernization reforms carried out by the Fernando Henrique Cardoso', Lula and Dilma's governments. Brazil received most of its points in the areas of education and health, but scored badly in economic participation (73rd position between the countries) and political participation (72nd). The study states that the advancement is largely due to improvements in primary education and in the percentage of women in ministerial roles, which has gone from 7 per cent to 27 per cent.[7]

Nonetheless, political participation is on the rise throughout the continent. Statistics from the World Bank revealed that in 2010, the percentage of women with political responsibilities in Latin America was of 24 per cent, the highest percentage in the world, bigger than in Europe, where it was of 15 per cent. Latin American women also occupy only 33 per cent of the best paid professions, with discrimination in the marketplace persisting.[8] Thus, despite such advancements throughout Latin America, most still face economic hardship, social, cultural and political barriers to not only full political participation but also equality in mainstream society.

Poster (in Moraes 2003: 330) has argued that the web promotes and reinforces already-existing political formations, with the *Zapatistas* from Mexico, for instance, expanding their political ambitions through the web. One defining feature of the 2010 presidential campaign that saw Dilma Rousseff win in the second round with 55.7 million of votes (56.05 per cent), against 43.7 million given to her rival, Jose Serra of the PSDB (43.95 per cent), was the revival of the clashes between sectors of the mainstream media with Dilma's candidature on the Internet.[9] The web here was widely used by political parties for attack campaigning and the exchange of accusations between the two main rivals of the dispute, the PT (Worker's Party) with Dilma and Jose Serra's PSDB (Social-Democratic Party).

One month before the 2010 October elections, Marina Silva (www.minhamarina.org.br) was pointed out to be the most popular candidate on social network sites due to her influence on the youth vote, according to experts. She held the biggest number of participants in her online profiles in social network sites such as *Orkut* (46,584) and *Facebook* (41,977), while Serra dominated in *Twitter*, with 455,186 followers, appearing ahead of Marina (244,057), Dilma (235,519) and Plinio Sampaio of the Partido Socialismo e

Liberdade (PSOL) (41,064).[10] Dilma widely explored the women's vote during her campaign, with her website (www.dilma13.com.br) containing links to various other women's blogs, including *Hip Hop Mulher, Galera da Dilma, PCdoB Mulheres* and *Viva Mulher*.

One of the most talked about events of the presidential campaign was the ironic and humorous reaction of *bloggers* towards the newspaper *Folha de Sao Paulo*. Bloggers ironically criticized what they thought was a biased campaign coverage that attempted to assign blame on Dilma for errors committed by particular individuals or ministers of the former Lula government. In response to a story published by *Folha* on how light consumers paid R$ one billion *reais* for an error committed by Dilma,[11] a group of agitated bloggers created a popular tag on *Twitter* called *DilmaFactsbyFolha*. The *bloggers* went on the web to question the objectivity and partiality of the newspaper by coming up with fictional headlines that attempted to emphasize the partisanship character of the accusations, and by attributing random blame to the candidate for various disconnected and irrational facts, producing fictional headlines with ironic sentences like the following: '*Folha* has proof that Dilma was responsible for the collapse of the Roman Empire'.

Part of the same youth groups in Brazil in cities like Rio, who massively supported Dilma's election in 2010, made use of new technologies and of social media websites like *Twitter* and *Facebook* to organize protests against the government and other Brazilian authorities during the 2013 June demonstrations, which were held throughout the country. Substituting the old 'face to face' assemblies associated with traditional forms of mobilization and party organizations, different sectors of Brazilian society were disillusioned with the government's promises for wider social reform and economic growth. From anarchist groups like the *Black Bocs*, accused of acts of vandalism during the demonstrations, to leftist, conservative and other youth movements, these groups took to the streets in the main capitals of the country, from Rio to Sao Paulo, in what was perceived as a burst of outrage against political corruption and public spending on stadiums for the 2014 World Cup, while public transport, health and education continued to be underfunded. Social media was widely used beforehand also for the organization of the March Against Corruption protests of 2011 and 2012, in the aftermath of the 2005 *mensalao* corruption scandals that saw senior Lula advisors in a tight spot.

Social media and the Internet emerged during these protests as vehicles of *grassroots mobilization* and of *digital citizenship*, having helped to assist disperse groups of people from different social backgrounds and economic income to unite via *Facebook, Twitter* and other websites around common causes of frustration with the pace of change in the country. These groups urged a deepening of the social reforms being carried out by the Dilma government, expressing disillusionment also with the corruption practices of local administrations and with the limits of the democratization project of the last centre to centre left-wing governments in the country, from Cardoso to Dilma.

Moreover, the partisan character of the mainstream media and the notion that organizations like *TV Globo* have had a role in maintaining the *status quo,* impeding further democratization of the country's political and social institutions, were criticised during the 2013 June protests. These were translated in the attacks of many demonstrators against the vehicles of these media companies. Pressured by civil society players, mainstream newspapers like *Folha de Sao Paulo* and *Estado* and *TV Globo* changed their editorial line from attacking the protesters to supporting the demonstrations. The alternative media website, *Midia Ninja,* emerged as a key vehicle of the counter-public sphere during the most tense moments of the June protests, acting on the scene and amongst the demonstrations, covering the protests live and denouncing police repression and brutality.

Theories on the potential of the web for *cyberdemocracy* claim, as we have seen, that the web has limits regarding its capacity to reduce offline inequalities, but that it can act as a persuasive tool for political campaigning, contributing to lay the seeds for the articulation of counter-discourses about particular disadvantaged groups that in short, especially in the mid and long run, can assist in the *empowerment* and in the changing of attitudes towards these same groups. Arguably, we know that the Internet can offer opportunities for smaller parties and candidates to get to know voters better, providing ordinary citizens with a voice and a chance to criticize political and media institutions, as evident during the 2010 elections. It can also be perceived as being an extra tool in mobilization and in the empowerment of voiceless citizens from diverse political ideologies, including apolitical and *de-politicised* groups, as the 2013 June protests revealed. It remains to be further researched how the Internet can function as more of a vehicle for wider participatory democracy in Brazil, and one that is truly committed to the public good.

Conclusion

Clearly, any discussion regarding the strengthening of the web as a public sphere of debate in Brazil, as a vehicle for the public interest and a tool in wider democratization, cannot be separated from other social and economic reforms and from the level of political maturity of the country. In spite of the limits of access and connectivity, the Internet during the 2010 elections functioned as an important tool to counterweight the discourses articulated by the mainstream press, and this was evident again during the June protests in Brazil. *Blogging,* the creation of websites by various groups of Brazilian society, and the articulation of debates on social media sites like *Twitter* and *Facebook*, with the latter being seen by many as a new online political arena, have contradictorily emerged as a significant force that can contribute to the undermining of media concentration, boosting political pluralism and providing diverse representations of stigmatized and subordinated groups that have little space in the mainstream media.

As I have sought to underline in this chapter, the various uses of the web in Brazil attest to how it is emerging as an alternative space to play out politics away from both the mainstream media and Congress, assisting in the scrutiny of politician's activities and pressuring in favour of the approval of particular welfare reforms. At its best, the Internet can provide an avenue to fortify media pluralism and undermine media concentration; it can help disseminate a host of political ideas and articulate discourses that are rarely seen in the mainstream media; it can be used as a tool for wider civic engagement and political mobilization during election campaigns; it can serve as a vehicle to scrutinize governmental power, making administrations more accountable and transparent, as well as assisting in the support of certain causes, including the undermining of authoritarianism and political corruption.

Notes

1. Conducted for the Centre for Social Media of the School of Communication of the American University (February 2009), and part of the Future of Public Media Project, funded by the Ford Foundation.
2. See 'Internet no Brasil chega a cerca de 71 milhoes de pessoas', (*Internet in Brazil reaches 71 million people*, Portal Vermelho/UOL, October 02, 2012).
3. Lan houses are areas of local network access, of computers displayed together, which have become very popular in Asia and are now proliferating in poor communities throughout the country. There are approximately 130 lan houses in Rocinha, a large shanty town in Rio and one of the biggest in Latin America. Research published by the Brazilian Internet Steering Committee (CGI.br) underlined that 48.08 per cent of the people from the classes D and E have accessed the Internet from commercial places like *lan-houses*. ('Lan houses: a new wave of digital inclusion in Brazil,' by Ronald Lemos and Paula Martini, September 2009, Publius Project.)
4. See document 'Acoes governamentais em inclusao digital – analise de utilizacao do FUST' (*Governmental actions in digital inclusion – analysis of use of the FUST*, report of the Ministry of Communications, 2005). http://portal2.tcu.gov.br/portal/pls/portal/docs/2055288.PDF).
5. See 'Exclusao digital pode prejudicar economia brasileira, dizem especialistas' ('Digital exclusion can damage Brazilian economy, say experts', *BBC Brasil*, March 16, 2010).
6. 'Eleicoes 2010 – As outras candidatas' (*The other candidates*, Ligia Martins da Almeida in *Observatorio da Imprensa*, September 21, 2010).
7. See 'Brasil sobe 20 posicoes em ranking de igualdade do genero' (Brazil goes up 20 positions in the ranking of gender equality), *Portal Brasil* (October 24, 2012).
8. 'Mulher latino-americana: muito por fazer, muito por ganhar' (*Latin American women: a lot to do, a lot to gain*, Revista Dialogos do Sul, March 08, 2013).

9. Brazil gave women the right to vote in 1934, although most of Central and South America, as Desposato and Norrander (2008) assert, gave women suffrage laws only after the World War II.
10. 'E se a eleicao fosse nas redes sociais?' (*And what if the elections were on the social networks?, Comunique-se*, September 29, 2010).
11. 'Consumidor de luz pagou R$ 1 bi por falha de Dilma' (*Light consumer paid R$ 1 bi for Dilma's error, FSP*, September 05, 2010).

8

The Endless Battle: Populism and Mainstream Media

Roberto Follari

The battle between corporate media and South American governments offers a new opportunity to study populism (Follari 2010). This chapter argues that media corporations have come to play the role of political opposition in several Latin American countries, particularly in South America. The actions of political parties, which oppose governments that possess a liberal left ideology or populist views, are particularly problematic for political systems, as their close relationships with oppositional media corporations heighten the conflict without offering adequate tools to resolve it. The chapter acknowledges, however, that this does not take place in a specifically organized way, as media corporations have become political actors without an official place within the system of representation.

This chapter draws on the theory of populism of Ernesto Laclau (2008a), which views populism as a politics in which antagonism is inherent and seeks to represent the social and the people or 'plebs' versus the elite. I also draw on Pierre Bourdieu's (1997) understanding of 'field' as a relational and conflictive setting whereby 'agents' and their social positions are located. Bourdieu's work is important as it presents a sociology of micro and macro concerns, both theoretical and the empirical, in search of causality in relation to the social, in economic, cultural and symbolic terms. In addition, the concept of 'field' permits us to grasp the specificity of a determined professional space,[1] without reducing it to mere economic factors or social structures, which form part of this space. At the same time, the concept of field helps us to take into account how they condition this professional space.

The cases discussed here make it clear that the ideological tensions between hegemonic private media and popular governments are very strong. However, they are not the only conflicts in these political realities, which need to be examined by taking into consideration the various dynamics contributing to the persistence of this struggle between state and corporate power. The notion of 'power' in this case is that of 'structural power', in society, as used by Laclau, and not the Foucauldian notion of micropower.

This chapter will first discuss populism's conceptual foundation, given that both journalists and intellectuals who argue against populism tend to believe that such foundations are non-existent. Even for those supportive of the political processes of Evo Morales and Rafael Correa, today these might be considered idiosyncratic situations, irregular expectations if we consider them from a theoretical perspective. This is very clear from the position of Marxism, at least in its conceptual framework and, of course, also from the perspective of political liberalism. In other words, both Marxists and 'republicans'[2] reject populism, viewing it as lacking theory, and as a type of practice without the backing of conceptual references.

Conceptualizing populism

To begin with, this chapter aims to examine and revive conceptual frameworks concerning populism, which, in contrast to existing theoretical writing in this area, remain insufficiently developed. This lack of conceptual development occurs because neopopulism is a political reality created by the state, and derived from the exercise of political power. Neopopulism, as discussed here, is characterized by strong leadership, active participation in social movements and rejection of neoliberal economics and governance (Follari 2010: 27).

Certainly, neopopulism can be considered a concrete modality of populism; for this reason, the terms used to characterize populism also apply to neopopulism. However, populism can be distinguished from neopopulism. The former can be characterized as anti-imperialist and nationalist, but not necessarily related to leftist ideologies; these include the governments of Peron in Argentina, Vargas in Brazil, Cardenas in Mexico and Velasco Ibarra in Ecuador. Neopopulism, as it is used here, refers especially to the South American context, assuming a left-leaning ideology, critical of capitalism as a system. Neopopulism, as presented in this chapter, refers most especially to the twenty-first century governments of Correa, Chavez, Kirchner and Morales.

This chapter argues that neopopulism is not the result of a theory arrived at by 'lying in wait'[3] for those hoping to ascend to power, but is the opposite: It is about *practical* arrangements involved in the exercise of political power – which is not all power – that involves looking for secondary conceptual justification.

Power is not only political, and it does not come only from state; there is power that no one chooses or controls, unless political powers intervene. These include the power wielded by embassies of the most powerful nations, multinational enterprises, churches and media owners (Follari 2010: 40–41). It takes a certain level of concentration of democratic political power to break up powers that have no inherent electoral representation. This is part of what distances populism in general from many academic theoreticians.

First, there is status (and an anti-academic *pathos*, evident in the 'sandals yes, books no' of early Peronism). Second, populism is created by the state, not an organization, which may come to power gradually. The theory by Laclau, which we take into account concerning 'power' in this instance, is restricted to the apparatus concerning the administrative management of the state.

For these reasons, the personal leadership of populist leaders works so well, allowing for the precise concentration of power without the previous formation of political organization. This not only suggests that theory comes after practice, rather than before it, but also suggests that theory rejects the spiritualism for which the outline in the plane of *mental representation* must take place before any realization happens. So, without being objectified, theory concerning 'real populism' (Durán Magliardi 2013) supposes populism to be empiricist and erratic.

The aversion of much of academia to populism does not exempt us from the need to look for solid theoretical justifications of populism, which are useful both in academia and in politics. This supports the revolutionary John William Cooke's[4] statement concerning Peronism during its resistance period, having being violently displaced from government as a 'terrible fact of the bourgeois nation' (Cooke 2011: 2).

In this conceptual analysis of populism, it is important to consider more closely the founding work of Ernesto Laclau (2005), which contains several fertile suggestions that can be adapted to multiple contexts both historically and in terms of concrete examples, which are often insufficiently highlighted. For example, there exists an idea that political actors are redefined by populism, to the point of their identity being established solely in connection with populism (Groppo 2009). This is evident in several countries with existing neopopulist regimes. Here, we consider 'neopopulist' the governments of Chavez, Kirchner, Morales and Correa, distinguishing these 'left' populist governments from the conservative populism of a former Ecuadorian president, Buccaram, for example.

In the case of Venezuela, the Venezuelan opposition acts as a whole, forming a contradictory conglomerate and varied diasporic opposition, disguising its multiplicity in the decision to be 'one opposition' against the Bolivarian movement. In Argentina, for a long time, there was only one opposition, including the left (Solanas, Lozano, etc.), the moderate right and the far right of Macri, to social democracy and the radical centrist party. They were nothing other than opponents, without defining their own specific identity or programmes (except on a formal level); they abdicated any identity that was not 'anti-government'. This point could be argued further, if our intention were to focus solely on populism.

Another point, more common in literature on the subject, is Laclau's reference to the plebeian aspect of populism. This represents the 'dangerous classes' of former times, the masses that are viewed as threatening the peace of stabilized systems, something inconceivable to elite social classes. It is important to emphasize this point when considering the level of irrationality, which is evident in the attack against governments and which we are discussing here.

What is at stake here is the rejection of what Laclau (2005) terms 'the plebs'. This explains why even the best arguments do not convince the dominant social sectors, which have benefited from populism, despite openly detesting it. These social groups do not take into consideration economic achievements or personal improvements, but view the situation as intolerable in the public arena by those who think they should be hidden, denied and possibly liquidated or removed. The 'rest' are the social residue, which are the disinherited, wretched people of the earth. They are viewed as manure to the clean and perfumed space of the hegemonic classes (and often the middle classes too), which imagine themselves as forming part of an ideal, decent society.

The 'poor maintenance of form' thus appears as a permanent leitmotiv that hegemonic actors use against neopopulist governments, calling on them to follow vacuous form and republican procedures that simulate the defence of democracy. In reality this concept simply serves to defend dominant institutions as they face a 'zoo barrage', should a government choose to protect neglected social sectors.[5]

However, there are several differences between my view and Ernesto Laclau's perspective on this issue. For example, I do not concur with Laclau that psychoanalytic categories can be applied without the social mediation of a specific object. Laclau argues that the reference to 'fullness' is an impossible psychological situation, implying that the notion of 'totality' refers to an impossible social (Laclau 2008a: 20–21). Here, two different categories are superimposed because, epistemologically, it can be assumed that the notion of whole has nothing to do with the idea of fullness. Wholeness does not mean all the facts and all the things, but a horizon of intelligibility for the analysis of a situation or social institution (Lukacs 1969).[6]

Our object of study, however, is not the concept of populism (or the leftist neopopulism in Latin America, referred to above). Rather this chapter seeks to analyse the *relationship* of South American political regimes with corporate media, which is tense and troubled, as observed in earlier writings (Follari 2011: 23–38).

Media in politics: Enough but not too much

The weight of the media in politics ranges from the notion that media plays the role of informational instruments with little weight as political actors, to the extreme opposite: The media far exceeds its communicational role and is therefore very powerful in that specific role.

In a previous work (Follari 2011), my analysis was limited to the power of the media and its ability to convince and manage public opinion. We did not determine which specific political weight that 'moment' might have for the constitution of points of view. Nor did the work specify how policy functions are at times supplanted by the media apparatus, which, as we reiterate, has not been elected by the citizens to exercise political role, usurping spaces that are not incumbent to them.

There are two issues with the first point: (1) Media does not manipulate all people to think from their point of view (Morley 1996). This work is further developed in a study by Follari (2011) and establishes that the media is able to convince only where the audience has no relevant prior information, or where there is no prior conviction opposed to the message content. In such cases, which are many, the broadcaster may be sure that the messages have high penetration and that they have acceptance of their contents. However, if there is no relevant information contrary to the message, or there are no existing convictions inconsistent with the message, the media will have no impact except to raise a question or cause a drop in the level of conviction, whereby its content is usually rejected.

In sum, repetition and a permanent combination of messages in a single ideological direction may lead to long-term change of opinion, while a single message could not have had this impact. However, this situation occurs only with some audiences: those who in their daily lives find some 'cognitive dissonance' – as social psychology terms it – concerning his or her convictions and social functioning. For instance, if many friends and/or family think otherwise, then this person will not have a 'counterweight' from other members of any group to think like him or her. In synthesis, media does not 'affect' those who have different beliefs, and they affect even less audiences who hold antagonistic views or belong to certain groups and share opinions with others who support them. However, media may convince the rest of the population, which in some cases may be a very significant percentage.

(2) The media has changed significantly. Radio and TV in the days before the satellite were merely used to consult or watch during one's free time. Today, the media is ubiquitous. We are connected to media everywhere, at all times. Media has a global reach; we can see Saudi and Japanese television simultaneously. They are available online, on mobile phones, in a restaurant or in a government office. It is naïve to claim that there is 'a moment of speech' and other different practices, thus assuming that the media is only involved in the first, in the interpretive aspect. We know now that perception is inseparable from language[7] (Kuhn 1980), which is not absent in silence, but is involved in the overall structure of meaning. Thus, all that takes place is 'always interpreted', because meaning is constitutive of all practical tasks, particularly in the case of public opinion and citizen standing, as is the case of political practices. The media's over-determination of social meanings has increased substantially, following Baudrillard's (1988)

metaphor, in a world where the meanings float alone.[8] Therefore, there is a strong involvement of the media in politics even though it was initially limited to fulfiling the role of message transmitters and information providers.

With regard to the point concerning the involvement of media in politics, we can analyse the known mechanisms of distorting information: the use of ideology, which becomes more perverse if it has not been made explicit; attacks on governments, saying that they are ideological, without taking into consideration how the media and its own points of view are also partial;[9] and the use of assessments presented as facts (e.g. common reference to Moreno, member of the government of Cristina Fernandez de Kirchner, as a 'controversial' or 'aggressive' person or worse).[10] Titles are denied in the text, or insufficiently reaffirmed therein are other mechanisms, as are secondary facts presented as primary ones and vice versa, according to the interests of the newspaper, radio or TV station. Facts are directly ignored, when they are not suitable for the presentation of a middle position; weight is given to adjectives over journalistic decision; enigmatic references are made to 'observers' who always say exactly what the media wants to present; and direct lies or simple injuries are presented, as has been demonstrated in the trials conducted in Ecuador,[11] but which is easily observed in many other cases.

A detailed study concerning these semiotic, syntactic and semantic mechanisms remains to be carried out with regard to the interactions of media in relation to populism. This is not part of our research, but this brief list highlights the wide range of mechanisms used in building daily news, news that – as it is well known today – are never based on a single finding and that always (and could not be otherwise, but just hide it) come to be a particular form of organization and constitution of meanings around the facts stated in each case.

The mass media beyond the mediated world

The following discussion explores the political influence of media corporations in South America. The argument proposed here is that while on the one hand media oversteps its role of becoming political actors, it is in fact limited due to the fact that it is not elected. In Ecuador, for example, the oppositional journalist, Carlos Vera, left journalism to take up a political opposition role, working with firms that could enable a referendum to revoke the mandate of the president. He had little success on this mission, and today he has insignificant weight both as a journalist and as a politician opponent.

In Argentina, the corporate media has performed activities suggested by major media owners that generally take place more covertly in other latitudes. For example, an executive of the newspaper *La Nación* visited President Nestor Kirchner while he was in office and presented him with several ultimatums that they required of his government, in order to transit smoothly his constitutional period. This has been reported in detail[12] and carries extremely serious institutional repercussions.

Furthermore, until recently, presidents in Argentina had been conditioned to not openly discuss the trials for crimes and attacks on human rights during the dictatorship years. They were urged to follow the economic policies synonymous with neoliberalism, in order to maintain international policies akin to those of the United States, among other things with deep pro-imperial and pro-capitalist ideological roots.

President Kirchner, however, rejected doing this, because of the blackmail that it entailed. In a newspaper dedicated to the government, a headline predicted that the government would not last the year, thereby threatening a coup in Argentina (Escribano, 2003). Considering the widely read source, which is Argentina's *La Nación* newspaper, this news was something that could not be taken lightly.

Also, at a time when the main contenders began to emerge for the presidential elections, which finally took place on October 2012, the chief executive officer (CEO) of Clarin Group, Hector Magnetto, gave a dinner party at his home, bringing together the main political opponents. Although their conversations were not made public, while examining the political and ideological line followed by the paper it is possible to see how the political opposition and Clarin came together, in a single united front that was set on defeating Kirchner, whereby the media group took the lead, especially after the passing of the Audiovisual Services Law in 2009.

These examples demonstrate a high degree of political interference by the media, in the case of Argentina (and which is also present in other countries with neopopulist governments, the details of which are beyond the scope of this chapter). However, we must admit that these institutional distortions and abuses by the corporate media often occur and have several limitations. It is widely accepted that admonitions, 'suggestions', blackmail and threats have been more effective than most conventional political tactics. However, it is also true that such extreme behaviour by media corporations has generally not been required with regard to the political classes. If we consider their ideological positions, politicians have generally not been a problem for the media.

These are common codes used against governments that distance themselves from the pro-establishment, as in the case of neopopulism. However, there are also cases whereby media corporations confront institutional limits: Politics can be done through the media, but not all other forms of non-media interventions are possible for these surreptitious political actors.

It is thus possible to enumerate mainstream corporate media's achievements and limitations as follows: (1) It acts like political opposition, thereby replacing political opposition. It is the real opposition, which slips into opposition parties and social organizations that are less prominent than the media in this role. It is evident that political opponents generally are a reduced minority in the legislature, and they are absent or only have presence in regional executives powers. Media, however, does not have these limitations; it operates throughout the country and reaches every level. (2) Media does not just replace political parties and organizations, but, politically, media corporations are often involved in the leadership of these organizations. This is clear in Argentina, as we have mentioned, but we can also relate the situation to the cases of Venezuela or Ecuador, where political opposition has taken up the discourses of the media in an oppositional and closed way, without assuming specific party positions. For example, opposition, which takes place through the unilateral demonization of government, may be viewed as functional by politicians – even as an autonomous decision – but truly it is an agenda imposed by the media, which limits the quality of proposals from the opposition. (3) Today the media is more than a 'fourth power' as it used to be considered in the past, as argued above. Now, the media is closer to becoming a 'first power'.

Media is able to pillage any public figure in a few minutes by mentioning imposed points, as well as to alienate citizens against someone by presenting them as guilty crime suspects, despite lack of proof.[13] Mainstream media is potential builders of common sense, often far beyond the awareness of citizens, and – consequently – enjoy little control over the role of social construction of meanings and ratings.

We have already addressed some of the media's limitations with regard to its ability to persuade. These include encouraging the audience to share and accept the judgements implied or expressed by the message. There are other constraints, however, which do not increase the media's capacity for generating conviction, but problematize its ability to operate as political actor.

Media corporations may be able to challenge the authorities and blackmail, threaten or influence them. When the authorities possess the same ideological leanings, it is also possible to request favours. However, media corporations can never fully occupy political roles. They do not occupy the seats of legislators or ministers. Those who do so may have relationships with the media, but they are not media representatives, and therefore they should not be held accountable to the media corporations, in the first instance, for legitimizing their role. In other words, media corporations are neither government nor parliament. They may have influence, and they may even have their own agents,[14] but they cannot operate directly. They are limited by their own specific institutional practice, and from that point of view the political limitations of their role are obvious, and should not be overlooked.

Media corporations do not have their own political parties. Of course, they have political parties of their preference (this is the case the right-wing in Argentina with Macri as their leader), but they do not govern parties.

They may mediate between parties to exert their will; however, directly participating in politics would delegitimize them. Thus, media actors' political actions are limited to taking place from outside of the political apparatus. When they become directly implicated in the political arena, they put themselves in an extremely vulnerable position from the point of view of the public, which legitimates them only if they can be seen to be neutral, objective, predominantly linked to an informative function and so on.

Confusion of fields

Bourdieu's notion of 'field' (1997) is widely known as a structured and hierarchical space shared by those who perform a particular social or professional, artistic or scientific activity, whereby a struggle for legitimacy occurs among various groups. Bourdieu points out how the media and journalists subvert regimes of legitimacy, consecrated and owned by intellectual fields (ibid: 125). Unaware of the epistemic requirements of scientific knowledge in the field, some ask brutish and rash questions resulting in illogical arguments, which inadequately resolve conceptual problems.

Being counterparts in the confusion of fields, omnipotent media actors attempt to prescribe policy without directly working on it. This can be seen played out in the political field but presented from their own mediated spaces, without respecting or understanding necessary political specificity of the situations being reported. This includes, for example, the need by political parties to look for electoral legitimacy, in addition to promoting opposition to those who have different interests or political views.

It is in this incurable *non-specificity* of media intervention in politics where we can see corporate media's insurmountable failure. On the one hand, media corporations cannot set up an opposition party, nor do they demonstrate that they understand the internal logic by which political parties form their identity and create possibilities. On the other hand, they assume that the political field plays by the same rules as the media field. What is worse is that the media views the function of politics as imagined by media producers, ignoring the inherent logic of the political field itself.

In the case of Argentina, where the political opposition is censored by the media for not uniting as an oppositional force, it is possible to view this as an oversimplification of the complexity of democratic representation. Outside of politics, there is simply the 'order' for politicians to unite against the uneasily accepted fact that a government can defend popular classes. This is thereby intended, obviating the very different clienteles, the multiple internal groups, the dissimilar histories and diverse identities. There is no way to reduce the multiple groups to one unit, as the charlatans of plurality used to pretend, accusing governments of single-mindedness and lack of openness to difference, intended to occlude any difference in the field of oppositions. Transgressing democratic principles, and reducing the complexity and variability of social policy to a single shade, there is a lack of minimal definition and consistency.

However, if we consider that some journalists and media executives believe they can give orders to politicians – which is indeed evident in Argentina – one finds numerous references to 'what should happen' in the political arena. This transgression of fields and their misunderstanding of the complexity of the political field could be reversed if they could grasp why they should not join one medium, or amalgamate multiple media companies into only one, obviating their different histories, styles, public and economic interests. It would be reductionist to take such a multicoloured hue of histories, which are competing with each other, and reduce it to one, especially if we consider the disparate points of view.

Media owners do not intend to form a single company, when it could be argued, as many media commentators argue to politicians, that in this case there could be one powerful method, which is better than several divided and scattered together. Just as the latter argument is absurd, likewise it is unrealistic to expect political opponents to unite. The current Venezuelan opposition, where some people with left-leaning ideas are comfortable under the hegemony of a right-wing candidate, is an example of this unity/disunity, whereby only directionality revolves around opposing the current government. Whatever might follow, the slightest chance of being unified by a party line, chaos and internal contradictions is generally expected of them if they become ruling parties.

Many of these same parties and individuals have brought on disastrous economic and social repercussions for populist governments. This was demonstrated in the defeat of the opposition in the presidential election in Argentina in 2011, when Cristina Fernandez won 54 per cent of votes (10 per cent more than in 2007). The media apparatus demonstrated its limitations with respect to politics: If a candidate is solid, positive results can be generated independent of the views generated by the media. This depends on the policies proposed by the candidates, and not on the media. These policies, by themselves, failed to make Macri a candidate of the right or Carrio an inordinate candidate with an uncertain ideological position that is attractive to the public.[15] TV spots are not enough for people to believe in a candidate, and less so if the candidate has been identified as 'anti-government', without defining the candidate in positive terms or purposeful profile.

Finally, it is very evident how the mechanism of constantly attacking neopopulist governments has resulted in the paradox of placing them centre stage, thereby positioning them as the only ones who can effectively govern. While corporate television and radio producers inevitably invite pro-government politicians to their programmes, the subject invariably becomes focused on attacking a supposedly omnipotent and evil government. This focus, however, manifests the strategic superiority of these governments with regard to agenda setting, and in the referencing of their political speeches. Therefore, the constitutional weakness of corporate media as opponents becomes evident, as they simply invert mirrors in relation to what these governments propose.

Certainly, it is possible to consistently argue that there is also a pro-government position, as neopopulist governments have also founded their own media, as the case of Ecuador so clearly demonstrates. Private media has also promoted certain programming that was once characteristic of state media, which is strongly evident in Argentina. However, this type of *transgression of field* by governments, defending themselves against attacks from private media, has only had a very modest impact. Private media corporations continue their hegemony in the era of neopopulism. This is because state media is considered 'political' and 'governmental', whereas private media is considered journalistic and supposedly neutral and objective.

While this has led corporate media to win the media battle, it has also made it impossible for private media to act directly in the political field, condemning them to defeat when it comes to operating on the political front, as argued above. However, this does not change the fact that the weight of the production of public opinion via private media is not succeeding in its own right to modify the political battles taking place, despite its albeit significant role within the political context.

The final stretch

Corporate news media does not seem to possess an alternative script. Despite their many defeats in Venezuela, almost a decade of loss of public trust in Argentina and having lost almost all credibility in Ecuador, they repeat the same mantra. Other than badmouthing neopopulist governments, media conglomerates have been unable to present us with viable alternatives outside of neoliberal forms of governance.

It is also true that state and community media have grown in the three countries concerned, as mentioned above, and is no longer as strategically inferior in media terms (in Ecuador, there was not a single public TV channel or radio station when Correa took office in 2007). However, public media has evidently often become government voices, serving almost exclusively to disseminate official views.

This move towards the promotion of officialist views is not desirable, because state media should be representative of universal social interest (this is the case in cultural channels like 'Encuentro', in Argentina, founded by the present government, but not in that of Channel 7, a so-called public television channel) as generally is the role played by Chilean or Spanish state television. However, the legitimacy of being 'governmental' for these channels is now increased due to the role of furious opposition that private TV assumes. It is evident that there is more legitimacy for those voted in by the majority of the population – or highest minority of it – when it comes to the right to express their views, than the unelected owners of media, who have become owners only due to their privileged economic situation. For this reason, I argue that while the private/political opponent model is maintained, it consistently reinforces the public/government as one of the few answers that those who have been elected by the people can give. Media corporations do not see themselves reflected in their specific interests of any government action, thus becoming permanent and systematic opponents of the same.

In turn, the role of corporate media as an oppositional force should clearly warn us of their lack of specificity when it comes to operating directly in the political arena. They are like bad drivers, leading politicians to defeat, ignoring the different logics of the political field in relation to itself. They do not grasp the unique field in which politics is defined and exercised.

If we contemplate the possibility of corporate media returning to playing the role of mediators and consider the necessity of limiting their role as total opposition, it seems that there is a need to re-think their approach, because they have not been successful in bringing down governments on a permanent basis, despite attempts to displace them. The erosion of the legitimacy of neopopulist governments has been marginally successful, but this erosion lacks an alternative capacity for building and only serves to put populist governments centre stage. Greater imagination, beyond the use of insult and aggression as a permanent reference point, is needed in addressing what have become corporate media's irreconcilable political enemies.

Notes

1. In this case, we examine the mediatic and journalistic fields, which are linked without being superimposed.
2. Republican, as it is used here, is not to be confused with the US Republican political party; it is a much broader concept.
3. This patient stalking, linking all life to an expectation of some future almost never attained, is what Nietzsche (2003) argued in a paragraph referring to *Thus Spake Zarathustra* calling leftists 'tarantulas', sons of resentment who can never enjoy the present.
4. John William Cooke was a Peronist militant with leftist ideas. He held a seat in the legislature at the time of the first Peronism (1945–55). Later, Peron, who was exiled out of Argentina, gave him the title of 'personal representative' in Argentina in times of so-called Peronist resistance. Cooke also trained in Cuba and was involved in the struggle against the regime, which banned Peronism. This is known from his correspondence with Peron, published after his death (Peron and Cooke 2007).
5. The term 'zoo barrage' is used by the oligarchy of Buenos Aires before the arrival of the native population from the interior, living in the suburbs who demonstrated for Peron, from the initiation of the Ministry of Labour and Social Welfare in 1943, during the transitional military government led by Farrell.

6. On the main of category of totality, see Lukacs G. (1969).
7. In this line of writing, which goes from 'the theory of linguistic relativity' to Wittgenstein, this idea was consolidated by Kuhn in his work on the philosophy of science (1980, see Chapter 10).
8. On the contemporary saturation of signs, this is a well-known metaphor proposed by Baudrillard (1988).
9. It is worth emphasizing that the most incisive and penetrating ideology is that which is not declared as such, for example, that which is concealed in a 'total reality effect'. This includes those who do not recognize their own ideology, and therefore believe that they are a-ideological speaking. Those, however, accused of being 'ideological' for making explicit their ideology have more freedom in relation to their views. He or she is thus aware of its existence and, at least in part, is conscious of its effects.
10. This is the case of Cristina Fernández's cabinet member, previously employed by Nestor Kirchner, M. Guillermo Moreno, accused of forcing prices down for employers, while raising prices for the public, demonstrating unacceptable personal behaviour while behaving outside the country with pure dissimulation. Governments have consistently kept Moreno as a cabinet member as he knows his way around the toughest negotiations required by government officials.
11. In this famous libel trial, President Rafael Correa won his suit against the newspaper *El Universo*, which published a column by the journalist Emilio Palacio. The Ecuadorian opposition held that – even following the judgement passed in February 2012 – the suit was a governmental attack on freedom of expression, as the information supplied was that the president had ordered the shooting of unarmed civilians in response to September 30, 2010, which is both implausible and capricious. Online columns by Palacio, where he refers to the democratically elected president by the people as 'the Dictator' and to his government as a 'dictatorship', highlight the type of accusations faced by Correa. Admittedly, no dictator allows for the public writing that there is a dictatorship. In dictatorships, the person would be more likely to be put in prison or killed without a trial.
12. This situation was narrated directly by Nestor Kirchner on the television program '6–7–8' broadcast on Channel 7, which is state owned. At that time, he was no longer president of the nation. It also refers to the situation as described in *El Flaco: diálogos irreverentes con Nestor Kirchner*, by Feinmann (2011: 93). This book serves as a political record, although it includes work of the author rather than writing by Kirchner.
13. This is the case of the attack made against a judge of the Supreme Court of Argentina, Zaffaroni, known for his left position and garantists theories. In 2011, a media campaign was launched against him concerning a property he rented to third parties via a real estate business that had prostitution links. Zaffaroni had not the remotest connection with the tenants. However, in the opposition campaign (they looked for associating this judge with the government, while he was a member of the Supreme Court proposed by Néstor Kirchner), the television ran headlines referring to 'the Zaffaroni brothel'.
14. A former deputy of the Province of Mendoza in Argentina narrated that upon reaching the legislature he had to face an 'interblock' managed by Grupo Vila-Manzano (original spread Mendoza and various parts of the country, with a strong presence in media ownership, as well as in other business areas). Manzano, a partner of the group, is a politician who was accused of multiple counts of

corruption in the Menem period, and then went into business. Several members of various political parties were referred to this group, declared the former deputy.

15. Mauricio Macri, leader of the Republican Proposal (PRO), a corporate right-wing party that won the election in the city of Buenos Aires. However, his party has had great difficulty maintaining representation in the rest of the country. Elisa Carrio is a picturesque figure of Argentine politics. She was considered progressive in times of Menem, but became a reactionary, characterized by catastrophic sensationalist predictions, which were not at all plausible.

Part III

Regionalism and the International Political Economy of Communication

9

Media and Multilateralism in South America: How the International Matters to Domestic Media Reform

Katherine M. A. Reilly

Currently, we are seeing major examples of media reform in several South American countries. But accounts of these ongoing processes focus primarily on political processes at the national level, particularly media's place in the renegotiation of the social contract between state, capital and society. While these works provide important analysis of national political processes, they are limited by their tendency to overlook wider regional and international contexts, including regional integration processes such as the Union of South American Nations (UNASUR), the Bolivarian Alliance for the Americas (ALBA) or the Central American Free Trade Agreement (CAFTA). This is problematic because ultimately media reforms should enable more equitable development processes within global capitalist circuits, and not merely greater recognition or representation at the national level. Since patterns of capitalist insertion are often negotiated and implemented at the regional level rather than the domestic level, voice within the domestic sphere may be insufficient to ensure the goal of redistribution. This oversight is particularly relevant, given Latin America's changing orientation vis-a-vis the global economy in an era of global power shift. Given the global financial crisis, China's rise and the decline of multilateralism within global trading relationships, South American states have stepped up their international diplomatic game, while at the same time opening themselves to increased dependency on natural resource extraction, producing new patterns of exploitation and resistance within processes of uneven globalization.

In this chapter, in an effort to move the media reform discussion more in the direction of international political economy concerns, I first discuss patterns of capitalist insertion and processes of media reform. I suggest three different models at work in Latin America: cordial complex interdependence and market-based media reforms (e.g. Brazil), counter-hegemonic network management (e.g. Venezuela) and, finally, informational capitalism–dependent development (e.g. the PPP corridor). I show that the fact of these different models highlights the significance of the relationship between management of capitalist insertion and patterns of media reform. I then go on to discuss, in very general terms, three implications of this international political economy reading of South American media reform: (1) Plurality of voices ultimately rests on successful distribution of resources, which in turn requires a wider analysis of post-neoliberal developmental policies within global trade and production networks. (2) As a result, media reforms need to be strategically aligned with development processes at the national, regional and international levels. This includes careful consideration of policies to develop and regulate media distribution channels, commercial aspects of digital production and circulation and industrial policy related to innovation and digital technologies. (3) These considerations have significant implications for the work of social movements in terms of medium, strategy, message and target. In particular, it is important not to let the current interest in enabling local media (e.g. community radio) displace or overshadow the work required to produce convergence around regional and transnational concerns.

Contemporary approaches to peripheral capitalist insertion

Latin American international political economy has a long tradition of theorizing the international from the perspective of 'peripheral' insertion into capitalism.[1] The roots of this tradition can be found in the *dependista* scholarship of the 1970s (see Beigel 2006 for a comprehensive review of this literature). In this line of thinking, 'One of the primary manifestations of dependency reveals itself at the level of the state, whose consolidation is constrained by the changing nature of capitalism' (Tickner 2003: 329). In other words, domestic economic and political compromises are constrained to a large degree by external economic and political forces. With this in mind, the international *matters* to our understanding of media reform because reforms and their effects will result from social processes that are conditioned by capitalist insertion. This provides the theoretical backdrop for Schiller's (1969) discussion of media imperialism, and in particular the observation that domestic media markets are shaped by international markets in ways that constrain the ability of states to establish autonomous media policy with implications for culture, education, production, politics and so on.

However, older dependency frameworks are limited by their methodological focus on international structures to the exclusion of other processes, particularly at the domestic level (Merke 2011). Structural discourses leave little room for the generation of alternatives – by states or anyone else – especially within peripheral contexts, including through the pursuit of regional integration strategies. Furthermore, dependency theory treats capitalism as if it were something 'out there' to which the social processes 'in here' are subjected. While this approach may have made sense at a time when peripheral states were being actively incorporated into capitalism through highly uneven processes, today the situation is quite different, given the global consolidation of capitalism. As a result, contemporary authors are more likely to speak of 'variegated capitalism' (Peck and Theodore 2007) or combined and uneven development, as a way to capture differing experiences with incorporation into what is now a fully global capitalist system, as well as the active role of states and other actors in ongoing processes of capitalist formation. For economic geographers, this can be understood in terms of the different geo-social processes that work to reproduce capitalism in different ways (Hudson 2004). This approach puts more emphasis on the social production of capitalism, and by extension, varieties of media systems corresponding to varieties of capitalism (Hallin and Mancini 2004) within a globalized system (Waisbord 2013). Thus, Robinson argues, 'more determinant (of causal priority) in conceptualizing regions within the larger unity of the emerging global economy and society than uneven accumulation, while still important, is the distinct configurations of social forces and institutions that arise from these configurations' (2011: 355).

Indeed, in Latin America, social responses to neoliberal globalization have given rise to a variety of new institutional arrangements that have resulted not only in a renegotiation of democratic social compromises (Cameron 2009) but also in new patterns of capitalist insertion. After the debt crisis, decades of International Financial Institutions (IFI)-mandated structural adjustment gave rise to mounting social pressure throughout the region, from the Zapatistas in Mexico to the Piqueteros in Argentina. Meanwhile, throughout the 1990s, newly emergent left-wing political parties created regional spaces for reflection and exchange such as the Global Progress Foundation and *Foro de São Paulo* as they worked to achieve electoral success (Regalado 2007). Both social movements and political parties found inspiration in municipal democratic experimentation under the PT in Porto Alegre, Brazil and the Wide Front (FA) in Montevideo, Uruguay, as well as in various failures in the neoliberal model and flashpoints of points of struggle, such as that occurred in Ecuador and Venezuela in 1997, in Argentina in 1999 and in Peru in 2000. After 2001, social forces began to come together regularly at the World Social Forum, which first took place in Porto Alegre, Brazil. Under pressure from these and many other social forces, the neoliberal compromise began to shift in the region, and we began to see major upheavals in the status quo, including the election of left-leaning political leaders at the federal level. This post-neoliberal moment has come with increased state interventions in the economy, reforms to democratic institutions, and several new processes of regional integration, including ALBA and UNASUR.

However, while these new institutional arrangements came in response to a common set of forces, they have differed in their manifestations across the region. Given that the renegotiation of the social contract at the domestic level in Latin America relies on successful insertion into the global capitalist economy, state management of flows of power and resources – cultural, ideological, informational, physical – both their own and that of others, becomes an important determinant of capitalist formation. It is with this in mind that Merke (2011) suggests shifting the focus away from structural constraints and towards the locus of power-driven decision-making processes at the border between the state system and domestic comparative politics. This can be understood as a 'reintroduction of the state' into international theorizing (Tickner 2008), but with some caveats. First, the post-neoliberal moment opened up new possibilities for autonomous state management of capitalist insertion. For example, Leiva (2008) observes that Latin America's emerging economic model seeks ways to balance fiscal responsibility with social democratic reforms that can contribute to greater equality. But he concludes that achieving this goal will require innovations in the model of social incorporation that address power relations at both the domestic *and* international levels. Second, therefore, recognizing that national ability to manage international flows is constrained, states pursue regional integration projects as a strategy for improving capitalist insertion. Since states offer differing analysis of the best way to pursue management of international flows, we have seen different processes of regional integration emerge in South America since the millennium. And finally, insofar as global power shift changes the context for global governance, it opens windows of political opportunity that savvy leaders can use to advance the interests of peripheral nations. For example, where Veneuzuela has defaulted on international loans, it has simply borrowed from China against future deliveries of petroleum.

Three models of capitalist insertion and media reform

In sum, while Latin American states have become more active in their management of capitalist insertion, and pursue projects that will allow them to better manage these processes, they are still subject to the challenges of peripheral insertion into global capitalist flows. With this in mind, we can identify three broad models of capitalist insertion in the region today, which correspond, I will argue, to differing visions of media reform.

The first is a model of cordial complex interdependence, which draws inspiration from Keohane and Nye (1977), as well as the realist-institutionalist thinking of the English School of international relations theory (Buzan 2004). In this view, states can best enhance their position by influencing norms of collaboration within international institutions. In other words, managing capitalist insertion rests on managing relationships – what Russell and Tokatlian call 'relational autonomy' (2003). Brazil has emerged as the iconic case of this approach in South America, especially as a result of its part in reshaping integration processes. In particular, Brazil played a leadership roll in challenging the Doha Round of the World Trade

Organization (WTO) and the Free Trade Area of the Americas (FTAA) process, has been active in restructuring the International Monetary Fund (IMF) and is the driving force behind South America's UNASUR regional integration process. According to Celso Lafer, where once Brazil sought to build autonomy by distancing itself from the world, today the autonomy that underlies domestic democracy and development 'can only be built through active participation in the creation of norms and guidelines of conduct for the management of global order' (2001: 117; cited in Vidigal 2010). Norms that shape processes of accumulation emerge through what Cervo has dubbed 'Cordial Power' (2008), defined as 'informal dialogue, fluid personal relationships with great international authorities and diplomatic discourse that was sympathetic to social, environmental and peace causes' (Vidigal 2010: 34).

Brazil may rely on cordial power to smooth integration processes and influence global norms, but its weight within international political circles rests on the size and maturity of its economy, and the conversations it enters into are similarly oriented towards questions of capitalist management. Here, we begin to find evidence of how international integration can shape domestic media reforms. The UNASUR process (which encompasses all of South America except French Guiana) advances in part because other South American states want access to Brazil's markets, and benefit from Brazil's leadership on certain international issues. In turn, the weight of UNASUR's backing gives Brazil additional heft on the international stage. This means that maintaining the strength of the economy is key to Brazil's strategy for capitalist insertion, and therefore, Brazil's approach to economic management has been pro-business even as it has worked to distribute greater social benefits to citizens. This is why both the Lula and Rousseff administrations have supported policy reforms that reduce the cost of basic services such as electricity and telecommunications: Cost reductions simultaneously increase business competitiveness, reduce costs to consumers and increase the size of markets for services, since services become more accessible to a wider swath of the marketplace.

This, in turn, is the logic behind a Brazilian-driven UNASUR project, advanced within the South American Infrastructure and Planning Council (COSIPLAN), to build a fibre-optic ring around South America (Zibechi 2012a). The new infrastructure will relieve South American dependency on private commercial broadband links, which are both very expensive (contributing up to 50 per cent of the end-user cost to connectivity in the region) and also pass through data centres in the United States (which poses a security threat). The benefits are apparent for all participating states, but the ring is being financed by Brazil's Brazilian Development Bank (BNDES) development bank, and the regional scope of the initiative will help ensure its financial viability. (Also, the ring will have international linkages to Africa, Europe and America, all running off of Brazil's coast, which gives Brazil a certain measure of geopolitical control over the infrastructure.)

In Brazil's view, states need to work through regional bodies such as UNASUR to build this type of fundamental infrastructure, using state-financial backing and oversight as required. But once the backbone is built, and national broadband infrastructure is extended out to sub-regional centers, end-user pricing should be ensured through competition among local service providers. Ultimately, this means that the market will be the guiding principle for the regulation of broadband infrastructure in the region. It also means, interestingly, that the market will be a guiding principle for the regulation of the *media* sphere, at least in Brazil. Early on in its tenure, the Lula administration touched on the media reform discussions that have been happening in the country since the 1988 Constitution, but discovered that resistance from powerful media players, such as Globo, posed a political challenge (Matos 2008). So, rather than subsidies or regulations, increased competition has emerged as a key strategy for managing incumbent media powers. Fibre optic will allow for the introduction of broadband services, including digital mobile, into the Brazilian media sphere. This, in turn, will allow transnationals such as Spain's Telefónica to compete with Brazil's traditional TV and print-based media powers, through, for example, emerging Spanish-language apps like the TuEnti mobile social networking platform, recently purchased by Telefónica. Pro-business reforms like these offer left-leaning governments a quiet way to address the entrenched political influence of media oligarchies while also securing strategic regional interdependencies. This market-oriented approach to media reform allows Brazil to maintain its 'cordial power' image on the international scene while also addressing domestic power asymmetries.

But Brazil is clearly uniquely positioned to advance a strategy of cordial complex interdependence at the regional and international levels, given the size of its economy. This has led some authors to suggest that Brazil is engaged in a process of regional imperialism within South America (Zibechi 2012b); Latin American states may benefit from Brazil's leadership, but they are also subject to Brazil's processes of political-economic expansion, as well as the assumptions and discourses that surround those processes. This opens the door to a second perspective on capitalist insertion, which argues that the hierarchical distribution of power between states, plus inequalities within international institutions, leave peripheral nations, at best only relatively autonomous, and at worst, absolutely dependent (Jaguaribe 1979; Puig 1980; Tickner 2003).

It is with this in mind that the autonomist tradition recommends fostering domestic economic strengths and new political competencies that will allow for the eventual defiance of dependent relationships. But whereas in the past autonomists recommended autarkic self-sufficiency, the goal of today's autonomists is counter-hegemonic network management. Here, the idea is to influence channels of interdependence in ways that reduce subjection to powerful actors or powerful norms. Castells' idea of network power is useful here. We can think of counter-hegemonic network management as leveraging 'the power resulting from the standards required to coordinate social interaction' (2011: 773) to both take advantage of and shape international interconnections in ways that create alternatives. It is for this reason that we see the most autonomist countries in South America, such as Venezuela, pursuing international partnerships in spaces like UNASUR, even as they work to create the foundations for socialist development models through spaces like Bolivarian Alliance for the Peoples of Our America (ALBA). Unlike UNASUR, ALBA prioritizes trade integration as a strategy of alternative development rather than as a means to pursue profit-driven trade integration.

This very different approach to capitalist insertion has a strong influence over the types of media reforms we see emerging in autonomist South American states. Venezuela, for example, is a supporter of the fibre-optic ring being advanced by Brazil through UNASUR because of the cost reductions and security benefits it will bring. But according to the Venezuelan Minister of Communication, the broadband project is merely a first step in creating regional informational autonomy. Once the ring is complete, Venezuela envisions state-run or sponsored data hubs as well as a regional Internet search engine that will reorganize flows of information throughout South America (Prensa Latina 2012). Venezuela is more concerned with ensuring the ability to set autonomous policy around the production and movement of ideas than creating a market for access to services. In this sense, we can see clear analogies between the UNASUR broadband project and Venezuela's two satellites, Bolivar, which is uses to broadcast the state television channel Telesur 'free to air' throughout the hemisphere, and Miranda, which is used for planning, security and scientific observation. What is important in these projects is not the regulation of a market for secure satellite transmissions, but rather creating a platform that will enhance national or regional abilities to coordinate social interactions in ways that will contribute to social development in the long run.

As a result, in autonomist countries, there is much greater sympathy for state-funded or not-for-profit access to broadband backbones as a way to provide local communications services. Local broadband services could, for example, prioritize last-mile service provision over cost reductions in order to facilitate locally produced, culturally relevant and non-commercial media content. Indeed, the more autonomist countries of the region have expressed concern over private-sector involvement in UNASUR's regional broadband service provision project (Business News America 2012). If competition fails as a means to drive price reductions at the local level, then there is a risk that a small number of powerful big-data players could emerge and put pressure on key states like Brazil or Chile to reduce net neutrality. Since the proposed fibre-optic ring circles the region, changes in one country could have domino effects on pricing throughout the region. This is the struggle that autonomist media policy must deal with in the face of Brazilian leadership on regional infrastructure.

Brazil and Venezuela's differing economic models have attracted the majority share of intellectual attention in recent discussions about Latin America. But there is yet a third perspective on international insertion to consider, which draws inspiration from the peripheral realism perspective put forward by Carlos Escudé (1995). Both the interdependence and autonomy frameworks can sometimes overestimate the scope for independent action available to peripheral nations. Countries like Venezuela, Ecuador or Bolivia can leverage exports of primary resources to finance alternative development schemes, while the economic weight of countries like Mexico and Brazil gives them a place within diplomatic circles. But the same is not true of all Latin American countries, which find that they are by necessity 'rule takers' rather than 'rule makers'. This being the case, autonomist actions may, in some cases, undermine the functioning of domestic democratic institutions, offering a justification for powerful states to further reduce the sovereignty of peripheral nations, potentially with negative economic implications. Recent events in Honduras uphold this vision. In Peripheral Realism's more pragmatic approach, foreign policy should avoid actions that might move powerful neighbours to action, particularly insofar as these actions undermine the achievement of pragmatic economic policies.

As such, it is perhaps not surprising that over the past ten years, some countries in Latin America have offered, in comparison with their neighbours, significantly less evidence of media reform. Given the 2006 Dominican Republic-*Central America* Free Trade Agreement (CAFTA) agreement, for example, Central American states find themselves suspended in transnational production networks that oblige deep structural relations with capitalist circuits. In the Plan Puebla Panama (PPP) corridor countries, national economies are tied to 'efficiency-seeking investments in the industrial sector' related to low labour costs and geographical proximity to consumer markets (King et al. 2012: 159). These relationships rest not only on political agreements that structure the price of imports and exports but also on long-term investments in infrastructure that facilitate the movement of physical goods, as well as complex networked systems of production that tie domestic labour to corporate decision making in other countries. In these countries, where national development continues to rely on insertion into global commodity chains driven by transnational capitalists (Castells 1998), post-neoliberal or post-democratic reforms are not on the table in any serious way. There just is not a context for the implementation of comprehensive media reforms. So, while disappointing, it is not at all surprising to find strong oligarchic patterns of media ownership and state management in countries that are subject to this form of capitalist insertion.

In sum, the fact of these different models highlights the significance of the relationship between capitalist insertion and media reform. Contemporary media reforms are not just an upshot of the renegotiation of the social contract at the domestic level, but also take place within particular patterns of capitalist insertion under the guidance of interventionist states. Given that many Latin American states are working from peripheral locations, they use the levers of foreign relations to negotiate the context for their domestic development, including the context for communication's role in development. The combination of economic strategy and media reform policies will have important implications for the domestic political, economic and social sphere. Given this, in what follows I discuss three broad and general implications of this international political economy reading of Latin American media reform.

Plurality and equality

The first implication of looking at media reforms in international relief is simply this: The real impacts of media reforms on people's specific daily experiences will be constrained by state-led patterns of capitalist insertion. It is extensively argued that the media reforms taking place in Latin America have the potential to increase media diversity, improve democratic accountability, and create spaces through which to imagine alternative (non-neoliberal) development trajectories. These are all great objectives. However, students of democracy have long recognized that it is one thing to access to the right to vote; it is quite another to have access to the freedom and opportunity that comes with economic autonomy. Similarly, it is one thing to have access to the means to communicate. It is quite another thing to have the sort of economic autonomy that allows you to produce independent media, or use that media to achieve economic autonomy. With this in mind, the success of media reform needs to be measured not only in terms of improved representation (voice) and recognition (identity) but also in terms of the quality and extent of redistribution (equality). Here, we run up against some interesting truths.

Clearly 'rule taker' status within global commodity chains has a strong influence on the emphasis of media reforms within some countries. Take, for example, the case of El Salvador, where the left came to power in 2009 under the leadership of Mauricio Funes. Here, current processes of media reform are focused on re-regulating *public* media (specifically Canal ten and Radio National) to ensure, on the one hand, that they will not be used for partisan purposes, and on the other hand, that they will be used to 'promote ideological, political and cultural plurality, social inclusion, human rights, a culture of peace, national identity, historical memory, citizen participation and the construction of citizenship, which commercial media does not provide because it does not generate profits' (Diario Co Latino 2013). In addition, the new law contemplates expanding the reach of El Salvador's public media through international television and radio stations (el Nuevo Herald

2013). This project is clearly oriented towards consolidation of the state, plus the maintenance of Salvador's connections with its large ex-patriot community abroad, which is a major source of remittances, investment, and political and economic opportunities for the tiny economy.

Meanwhile, other media continues to be regulated by El Savlador's neoliberal Telecommunications Law established in 1997 by Salvador's right-wing political party, The Nationalist Republican Alliance (ARENA). This auction-based system of spectrum allocation effectively guarantees that many community media outlets operate illegally in the country, something that El Salvador's Association of Participatory Radios and Programs (ARPAS) is currently trying to rectify through a proposed 'Law for Community Radio-Diffusion' (ALER 2013). The point of the example is this: The priority for media reform in El Salvador is not decentralization but rather re-organization of centralized channels. Even *if* ARPAS is successful in their bid to 'democratize' El Salvador's media, this will be a kind of democratization within limits. We would not be able to fully understand the democratization of media in El Salvador without also making reference to a larger media context that focuses largely on consolidating and securing Salvador's position as a peripheral economy within global commodity chains. Community media will operate in a context very different from the community media of, say, Venezuela.

Where governments take a market-based approach to media regulation, as in the case of Brazil, the focus on cost reductions for telecommunications services risks expanding the market for *consumption* of media commodities at the cost of fostering local and/or autonomous media *production*. This is particularly so given that one of the primary drivers of broadband infrastructure in Brazil is the desire to tap its massive market for digital mobile technologies (Barros et al. 2012). This puts the openness of the Internet at risk by prioritizing 'bundled' online services (Mansell 2013a). In this sense, despite the fact that broadband will enable more people to 'get online', the vast majority of users are likely to access the Internet as prosumers and sources of personal data, rather than as autonomous producers of pluralistic media.

There are also questions about how broadband access will be extended to remote or less-profitable communities in Brazil once the new South American fibre-optic ring is built, and domestic fibre-optic cables are extended out to the regions (InfoDev/Jensen 2011). It is not clear whether non-commercial groups such as municipal governments or community organizations will be granted rights to service provision, and the state will surely face heavy pressure from big-data players who see non-commercial or subsidized service provision contracts as a form of unfair competition. So all together, while the price reductions and business opportunities fostered by telecommunications modernization in Brazil can enable greater market competition, they may do so at the cost of developing local and/or autonomous media.

Finally, the governments that have made the greatest headway in spectrum reform in South America (Venezuela, Argentina, Bolivia, Ecuador) rely heavily on a narrow range of primary resource exports to finance domestic social reforms. These countries have also made slow progress with digital upgrading in manufacturing sectors. In this sense, while spectrum reformers in South America are winning the battle, they may be losing the war. China's gains in the area of high-technology production are eroding Latin America's gains in the same area (Gallagher and Porzecanski 2010). Latin American high-tech exports have remained low waged and low skilled, whereas China's exports have steadily diversified into higher-wage, high-skill and high-value-added consumer products, and 95 per cent of all high-tech exports from Latin America are under threat from Chinese competition (ibid: page 8). Meanwhile, Latin American economies have been strongly influenced by China's demand for raw material exports. Latin American exports to China grew by 370 per cent from the year 2000, and of this 74 per cent were primary commodities (ibid: page 37). This is troubling, because in a globalized capitalist economy, the health of the economy, and ergo, the ability to redistribute economic resources in ways that sustain media autonomy, is intimately tied to patterns of capitalist insertion. Carlo Vercellone explains it this way:

> A development policy based in low value added industrial sectors is a short term policy that cannot be sustained in the long term. What this teaches us is that cognitive capitalism is investment of human beings in human beings.... In this sense, cognitive capitalism signals that need to develop collective institutions and services that both satisfy essential needs and allow for investment in those human capacities that will be an essential condition for development in the long run.
>
> (Miguez 2012)[2]

Instead of this, the combination of media reform, deindustrialization and over-reliance on primary commodity exports puts autonomist states at risk of clientelistic battles over media messaging. When a narrow band of natural resources form the primary centre of capitalist accumulation in a domestic economy, control of the state becomes a primary avenue for control over the means of accumulation. Even with diversified media ownership, polarized messaging can become a tool to fight for control over the state apparatus. In this sense, an undiversified economy is a risk factor for media autonomy and diversity.

In all three cases, simple media reforms, such as spectrum reallocations or market interventions, are not enough: Plurality of voices rests on communicative autonomy, which, in turn, requires strong redistributive policies that provide not just access to infrastructure and media spectrum but also autonomy and capacity to leverage resources in diverse ways. Strong redistributive policies require, in turn, strong economic management. With this in mind, we need to look not only at national processes but also at patterns of regional integration that condition domestic redistribution.

For example, depending on how it is regulated at the domestic level, the construction of a regional fibre-optic ring has the potential to pass cost savings on to consumers, or may be leveraged by states to facilitate community access points that are free or low cost. But at the same time, the development of the fibre-optic ring is part of the economic development plan being pushed forward by UNASUR that prioritizes accumulation through resource extraction. One of UNASUR's most active portfolios, COSIPLAN, has been developing a wide range of regional infrastructure projects. Some of these projects position Brazil as a regional imperialist power by using Brazilian investment resources to finance infrastructure projects, opening up opportunities for Brazilian companies to do the work, and providing resources needed to fuel the further development of the Brazilian economy (Zibechi 2012b). Meanwhile, these projects reinforce over-reliance on exports of natural resources as a foundation for economic productivity in other countries.

These larger patterns of regional economic integration put into question the assumption that media reforms will necessarily result in improved representation and recognition within national spheres of decision making. Regional patterns of economic integration, pursued by states as a way to manage capitalist insertion, establish conditions for redistribution that condition the impacts of media reform processes.

Industrial policy and media reform

Given that the impacts of media reform are related to the social production of capitalism, a second implication of an international political economy reading is that domestic media reforms need to be studied in relation to larger processes of economic management. The relationship between media reform and representation (voice) or media reform and recognition (identity) is obvious. But what is the relationship between media reform and redistribution? How do regional patterns articulate with national processes?

There are different ways of modeling this connection. For example, a cultural industries approach looks at media as a productive sector, which contributes to the economy both directly and indirectly, and can also benefit from state interventions. A knowledge economy approach, on the other hand, considers the nature of the relationship between circulation (patterns of nodes, ties and flows) and production, as well as how infrastructure, technology, processes, policy or ideas mediate that relationship. Clearly, the latter conditions the former, since the nature of circulation will affect the production of culture. But in the real world of policy, these different areas are often addressed separately, especially since cultural policy tends to focus on content, while infrastructure and spectrum policy focus on structure.

Within UNASUR, cultural industries were, until recently, addressed by the Working Group on Culture within the South American Council on Education, Culture, Science, Technology and Innovation (COSECCTI). So far this group has focused on compiling information about the state of culture industries in South America, noting in a 2012 report that 'at the level of various countries, there are more and more examples of transversal efforts that try to guarantee both economic development and cultural development, where the goal is to use the promotion of cultural industries to support integral sustainable development' (COSECCTI-UNASUR 2012; *translation mine*). The group has since been hived off into its own South American Council on Culture (CSC). The newly formed South American Council on Science, Technology and Innovation (COSUCTI) plans to focus its energies on the formation of South American researcher networks, a fund for researcher exchanges and regional trade fairs (Colciencias 2013). In both cases, regional integration is seen as an opportunity to expand the potential for economic returns on creative or innovative work by strengthening regional markets.

These policies articulate in challenging ways with spectrum reform policies taking place at the domestic level across the region. Drawing on Latin America's long history of land reform struggles, spectrum is often framed as part of the national patrimony, which should be leveraged as a way to redistribute economic benefits. Thus, media reform discourses parallel modernist and developmentalist projects that position productive inputs as nationalized resources. Even if we accept this approach, it remains unclear how best to leverage these resources. Should spectrum be treated like land, which should be redistributed to create a foundation for autonomous cultural production? Or should it be treated like an oil well, the benefits of which should be socialized under state control? Out of these debates emerge policies that appropriate spectrum for 'national' use (as in the case of Telesur, for example), as well as policies that redistribute spectrum to communities (as in the case of spectrum reform (Light 2011). There, then, remains the question of how redistribution of spectrum articulates with regional efforts to promote linkages between cultural development and economic development. At what point can community radio form the bases of new cultural industries, for example? If a community radio station produces a documentary, can it make a return on its investment through distribution to other broadcasters in the region?

Meanwhile, these considerations are largely dealt with in isolation from information age industrial policy (i.e. knowledge economy concerns). The key debate unfolding *here* is between those who believe that the benefits of the information age are best ensured through commercial competition between technology and service suppliers, and those who believe that cooperation and collaboration should be prioritized as a foundation for information-age production. At present, the 'bias is toward the dominant model favouring market-led development and focusing on information exchange, information scarcity secured through copyright, and rapid technology innovation and mastery' (Mansell 2013b). It is for this reason, for example, that we continue to see spectrum treated like a resource, the ownership of which can be imparted by the state. This is in 'contrast with alternative models which favour a widening of the information commons to foster information sharing, information abundance, and generative innovation from the bottom up' (ibid). So, for example, we don't see spectrum being regulated as an 'open resource' that, given emerging cognitive radio technologies, could be used more efficiently by sharing white spaces between various different users and uses (radio, wifi, cell, etc.). The latter offers a way of thinking about media reform and economic management that is more ecological in its approach to resource management, and also treats the economic and social value of cultural production very differently.

In the case of Brazil, for example, where debates are currently ongoing about how to manage the 'digital dividend' of unused spectrum resources that has been opened up by the switch to digital TV, incumbent television providers are in a battle with incoming digital mobile providers for control over this space. This has the effect of squeezing out consideration of alternative models or uses of the resource that might create foundations for differing forms of production. This is further complicated by Brazil's leadership role in the region. As leader with regards to telecommunications policy, the decisions made by Brazil often influence policy choices made elsewhere in the region. For example, in the case of Brazil's adoption of a new standard for digital television, not only did discussions on technical issues evolve in ways that 'displaced discussion of the political-communal-public to the technical-normative-private' but also the adoption of technical norms was converted into a geopolitical strategy for 'economic and cultural integration of the region' (Baccaro, Maglieri and Manchini 2012: 228). Specifically, Brazil chose to adopt the Japanese standard as a base for the development of a digital television standard (ISDB) over the American ATSC or European DVB standards. It then modified this standard by upgrading it to MPEG-4 technology, and developed a new middleware software solution called Ginga. In so doing, Brazil reiterated its dominant policy approach by guaranteeing access to services while turning a blind eye to the fact that these services are dominated by a highly concentrated media sector (ibid: 228). The resulting Brazilian standard (called ISDB-Tb) has since been extended to most countries in South America, providing a market for compliant TV sets and set-top boxes, transmitters and other peripherals produced in Brazil. As a result, the Brazilian tendency to favour market-led development is de facto exported throughout the region.

What all of this suggests, once again, is that the impacts of domestic media reforms on redistribution will be constrained by patterns of economic management that are being established through either regional integration or regional policy contagion. It is not enough to ask for reforms to legalize community radio. It is also necessary to think through how access to community radio can be leveraged as a productive resource, *given* particular patterns of capitalist insertion. In particular, there is a common assumption that media reform will strengthen identity and voice, and this will serve as a tool to make states accountable to citizen needs. But policies established at the regional level within bodies such as UNASUR, or policy contagion that happens as a result of the leadership of dominant players, will condition the possible impacts of media decentralization at the domestic level. When states engage in processes of capitalist insertion, or participate in regionalization processes as a management strategy, this can constrain the potential of media reforms to achieve truly autonomous media, and undermine the potential of media to serve as a mechanism of representation or rccognition.

Articulating grass-roots work with regional policy advocacy

Finally, as was made clear by the previous discussion, many of the decisions that implement new approaches to media regulation and economic development are being made through transnational processes. These processes are often beyond the reach of local voices, or happen through processes of contagion that are not adequately captured by the metaphor of the state system. This gives rise to a third upshot of a global political economy analysis of capitalist insertion and media reform, which is that it is important to reconsider the relationship between media reform and processes of advocacy or resistance. In particular, these processes need to orient their work more towards the ways in which regional and/or international processes affect media's contributions to redistribution.

In the 1990s, given Latin America's dual context of national democratization and global neoliberal multilateralism, Internet was the communications medium of choice for an emerging group of 'global civil society' actors (Leon et al. 2001; Johnston and Almeida 2006). But by the millennium, globalization was being actively rejected, as was the idea of global civil society, and its use of Internet to form professional policy advocacy networks (see, for example, Edelman 2005). Latin Americans had become disillusioned with their 'democracies with no options' and came to realize that change would require widespread grass-roots mobilization both to discredit the status quo and to bring new leaders into power. As post-democracy began to emerge in the region, radio experienced a renaissance. Calls for spectrum reform became part of efforts to create spaces of grass-roots deliberation, and to forge stronger connections between the grass roots and the state apparatus. In addition, in order to gain electoral victories and prevent coups against left-wing leaders, there needed to be a sustained process of grass-roots mobilization. It wasn't that the Internet was being tossed aside, but groups like AMARC and ALER saw greater purpose in using it as a platform to reinvigorate community media, particularly community radio, by facilitating news distribution between community radio stations (Leon et al. 2005). As a result, the transnational became a space of information sharing and solidarity in ways that were oriented principally around local identity and class formation for new waves of national democratization.

Today, with post-democracy well advanced in the region, the situation is quite different. In particular, the region's neoextractivist developmental economies finance social spending by exporting natural resources with the support of regional infrastructure programs such as COSIPLAN. But these processes are not driven forward at the national level within the context of reinvigorated domestic democratic institutionality. Rather, they are being driven forward at the regional and international levels, through trade deals and integration processes that are often beyond the reach of grass-roots accountability. While these projects may be to the benefit of some communities, they are often in direct contradiction to the interests of others, particularly rural *campesino* and indigenous communities that suffer the immediate consequences of extractive industries.

The current communicative strategies of social movements are often poorly aligned with this new, emerging reality. Community media processes are often positioned within the logic of economic development for regional autonomy being advanced by the likes of ALBA and Telesur. The membership of these networks is aligned around their desire for social-democratic economic development, or in other words, the capitalization of national resources to finance social spending. This means that community radio networks often find themselves in simpatico with the logic of economic development for regional autonomy being advanced by left-wing governments in the region. This form of class-consciousness has sometimes come at the cost of a decline in the critical capacity of media (see, for example, Urribarrí 2007).[3] Of particular concern, community media may lack the critical capacity to analyse the linkages between regional development patterns, national distributive policies and autonomous cultural production.

Regional alternative media networks are also poorly aligned with regional indigenous communications networks such as CLACPI or Abya Yala (personal interviews). In these latter cases, media is seen as a right to be exercised autonomously in order to advance multiculturalism, cultural preservation and identity formation. But communicative practices *also* form part of a strategic battle for territory, dignity and integrity.[4] In particular, for indigenous communities, the fight for cultural autonomy depends on the fight for territorial autonomy, especially given the close links that exist between land and culture in many cases, and this means that extractive industries work to *reverse* the autonomy of these groups, regardless of their access to the media.

In any case, neither community radio nor indigenous communication networks are well positioned to leverage media to deal with regional integration processes. Neither of them constitute, for example, part of a South American civil society's counterweight to regional governance. There is, in fact, a Citizen Participation Forum for UNASUR, but in a recent letter[5], this group outlined a series of considerations necessary to ensure the integrity of the space, including the autonomy of the civil society organization representatives, guaranteed indigenous participation and 'making a commitment to real institutionalization, formalization and legitimization of participation through the creation of consensual mechanisms for civil society participation in UNASUR and COSIPLAN' (*translation mine*). This points to a vacuum in civil society accountability mechanisms with regards to regional integration efforts.

Recently, however, regional communications networks have begun to re-think their focus on grass-roots autonomy and to move more in the direction of strategic integration. For example, Radio Mundo Real (RMR), which emerged in 2003 as a response to the World Trade Organization's Fifth Ministerial Conference, has become an important expression of 'communication in resistance' in Latin America. Drawing on ten years of experience, in a recent retrospective, RMR journalist Ignacio Cirio observed that:

> The current era is evolving and is characterized by the need for a methodological shift that can account for the challenges of the moment. We see this new methodological growth in terms of *convergence*.... Given that the methodology of dispersion, which was characteristic of the cycle of World Social Forums and their corresponding approach to communications, is exhausted, we believe that complementarization and collaboration between communications collectives are essential to confront the singular and inescapable discourse of capital as a the guiding principle for the co-evolution of humanity and the planet. And we have discovered that in order to achieve this, communicators should take on the roll of political actor, and enter into debate on the political plain in order to create agreements and join forces.
>
> (Cirio 2013)

Agencia Latinoamerica de Información (ALAI) has also signalled a movement in this direction, as is evidenced by a recent publication entitled *Democratizing the Word: Movements Converging in Communication* (Leon 2013). But which themes and topics will these media-oriented groups converge around as they begin to consider their response to regional integration, capitalist insertion and the processes that take place at the borders between the state system and domestic comparative politics? There seems to be an emerging consensus about the need to move past 'legacy community media' as alternative media (interviews), which suggests that careful thinking needs to be done about the meaning of alternative media.

Meanwhile, the analysis presented here suggests that alternative media needs to be built on a foundation of regional analytical capacity, development of greater capacity for reporting, and upgrading of social movement communications abilities. Just as it isn't enough to have spectrum reform without concrete processes of economic redistribution, it also isn't enough to have community media without concrete processes of local critical analysis of the conditions of economic production, both nationally and regionally. It will be interesting to see how this agenda develops. For academics, these shifts push us to reconsider our approaches to studying media reform in the region.

Conclusions: Shifting the focus of media reform research

South America has moved into a post-global and post-democratic moment. But just because states have become more (or perhaps differently) active in processes of capitalist formation does not mean that we should become state bound in our analysis of media reform. Indeed, if the full arc of thinking about globalization taught us anything, it is that many different spaces inhere and shift in the layered production, reproduction and transformation of the social, cultural, economic and political. The post-neoliberal moment has given rise to new institutional arrangements driven forward by new social forces. For critical political economy, these processes do not take place in a container, but rather are driven forward by actors that play significant roles in shaping processes of capitalist insertion at the border between the state system and comparative politics. In this chapter, I have suggested that communications scholars need to pay much more attention to these processes, because the nature of capitalist insertion will condition the constitution of justice and democracy. The types of media reforms pursued, and also the implications, sustainability and impact of those reforms, will depend on these larger questions.

To the extent that academics can support the search for answers to such questions (Santos 2011), it would be helpful to imagine new approaches that can address the shifting balance between post-democratic processes directed at localized processes of media reform and new regionalized processes of convergence. This is a tricky proposition. If left-leaning governments have gone to the regional level to pursue policies that are against the interests of local actors, can it still be argued (as is suggested by the work of Otero 2004) that the best strategy for communities is to use community media to mobilize their local class interests in ways that place democratic constraints on the integration policies of the state? The analysis presented in this chapter would suggest that localized efforts are insufficient. But, then, where should energies be directed? While regional integration is positioned as a means to create regional economic and political autonomy, in truth the spaces of transnational capitalist accumulation and the spaces of regional political integration do not map onto each other. Just look at the role of Canadian mining corporations in natural resource extraction throughout the Americas, or the influence of Asian resource markets on South American regional political processes.

I do not pretend to have a good answer, but by way of a closing thought, perhaps one possible response would be to approach media formulations as themselves variegated processes of capitalist formation within a combined capitalist system. This, in turn, begs the question of what frameworks would be appropriate for academic work in this area. I think that this formulation pushes as to re-think the idea of media environments. That is, rather than thinking of media environments as contexts that structure human experience (see, for example, Mattoni 2009 as cited in Della Porta 2011), they should be thought of as the products of uneven capitalist processes. Using this kind of metaphor, we can ask questions such as whether and how different kinds of media interact in the formation of spaces and processes; how private, public and citizen media constitute changing media publics in the region; whether media publics can be conceived of at a regional level; and how media publics interact with processes of class formation (Hesketh 2012; Wolfson and Funke 2013) within either political or economic contexts (which as I mentioned above, are not necessarily overlapping). These types of processes need to be studied vis-à-vis Brazilian neoimperialism; Chinese economic influences; the fate of ALBA, given Chavez' death; and the emerging Pacific Rim Alliance between the more conservative countries along the Pacific coast of the Americas, given how these different processes are reshaping the regional context. Finally, work needs to be done to better understand the alignment of different spaces: spaces of accumulation, spaces of discursive circulation and spaces of political articulation. This kind of geopolitical analysis, it seems to me, can provide an effective foundation for reflection and change.

Notes

1. The word 'peripheral' in this context is meant to indicate a contextually dependent and relative power differential between states when they enter into negotiations over economic or political issues. In this sense, it is important to always attribute relativity to the word 'dependent' and avoid any temptation to make dependency an absolute condition.
2. Original text is as follows: '... *una política de desarrollo basada en los sectores de menor valor agregado de la industria es una política de corto plazo que no puede ser sustentable en el largo plazo. Lo que nos enseña el capitalismo cognitivo es la inversión del hombre para el hombre... En este sentido, el capitalismo cognitivo señala la necesidad de desarrollar las instituciones y los servicios colectivos que permitan, al mismo tiempo, satisfacer las*

necesidades esenciales y que corresponden a una inversión en estas capacidades humanas que serán la condición esencial para un desarrollo a largo plazo'. (Miguez 2012)

3. Though efforts have proceeded apace to counteract these tendencies. See, for example: http://www.aporrea.org/medios/a22656.html.
4. See, for example, the Declaration from the Abya Yala Continental Summit on Indigenous Communication available at: http://ayi-noticias.blogspot.ca/p/declaracion-de-la-cumbre-continental-de.html
5. Which is available here: http://www.redextractivas.org/es/novedades/203-carta-a-unasur.html

10
Towards a Critical IPE of Media, Power and Regionalism

Ernesto Vivares and Cheryl Martens

We began our introduction questioning the extent to which the current clash over media reform and power in South America is related to questions concerning freedom of speech and structural change that are at work between media, power and new paths of development. The first issue is generally led by corporate media with regional and transnational influence, and the latter often voiced by neopopulist governments, following not dissimilar political paths of capitalism management and international insertion, but undeniably bound up in conflict. The authors in this collection have considered these fraught relations; however, we have sought to move beyond the discursive trap of siding with either media corporate powers in their attacks on government or governments as they confront corporate media power, reforming their role in democracies.

The chapters of this book have advanced the idea that we are witnessing a dialectical process of conflict associated with structural change, of regional and national nature in response to a changing world order in the aftermath of neoliberal development in South America. Through this process, and as a result of different strategies of global insertion, national governments have put a great deal of energy into focusing on media power distribution and democratization, viewing corporate media, in many cases, as political actors. Corporate media, however have equally sought to delegitimize governments which they view as dangerous neopopulist and left-wing actors who are leading nations on false paths of development. In summary, as governments seek to politicize media in relation to political projects, corporate media have stood by discourses concerning the freedom of speech in order to negate official views (Cerbino et al., Chapter 4).

It has become apparent to many observers that this conflict has contours that allow us to escape the simple logic of conflict between one and the other. Therefore, it is possible to begin to build our general theory of international political economy (IPE) considering its complexity and diversity to its common features. In the first component of this construction, struggle flows along with the structural changes and international insertion that go beyond national frontiers and where certain media corporations, of regional and transnational level, have turned into quasi-political actors (Follari Chapter 8, Martens and Vivares 2013). Media corporations have come to play the role of oppositional forces in the politics of new structural changes and international insertion, pursuing and fighting for their interests and political projects at stake as all-important actors (ibid).

As the chapters of this collection make clear, these conflicts are located in countries with new democracies, orientating their strategies of development and governmental efforts towards restructuring the conditions of financial and political crises, and of inequality left by decades of failed neoliberal political recipes in the region (ibid). This trial and error in development terms has taken place across different regional lines defined by the management of South American capitalisms and international insertion (Reilly, Chapter 9).

A key element observable here is that the conflicts surrounding media reform are taking place principally in countries characterized by left-wing, neopopulist and regionalist paths of transformation. These include Venezuela, Argentina, Ecuador, Brazil and Bolivia. The conflicts taking place between corporate media versus government are not taking place to the same extent in countries that currently embrace neoliberal approaches to development, such as Chile, Peru and Colombia. Thus, if the struggle around media and power is mainly taking place in countries following paths of development oriented towards overcoming and dismantling the structures of the unequal development, which have brought about financial crises and inequality at unprecedented levels, it is evident that structural change precedes such conflict. In this sense, if the structural change and conflict are brought about due to the differing political approaches to development, it is important to take this into consideration with regard to approaches used to theorize the relations between media and power.

To apply this approach and fully grasp the issues at stake, a critical and international political economy enables us to with the dynamics in different settings of development, making it possible to unravel the complex relations between media and power. This represents an uneasy academic challenge, as media and power have often been conceived as separate components of study, with much work in the area of media studies focused on media discourses and audiences, public opinion in relation to politics and democracy, the digital revolution and the digital divide. Over the years, much emphasis has been placed on the terrain of media discourses and audience analyses in relation to power. The issue of power has also been analysed extensively in the field of Political Science and in terms of capacities. Media power, however, remains insufficiently discussed within the framework of development. This is first line of tension that a critical and IPE of media and power needs to resolve both theoretically and methodologically: How might we best design approaches to media power, which bridge the gap between discursive approaches and the political realities in different contexts of development? To what extent can we apply such these approaches to neopopulist and left-wing scenarios?

We've broached this question by introducing the need of critical and pluralist perspectives, which unavoidably include the concept of development in different national and regional settings (McChesney, Chapter 1, Martens and Vivares). The work has thus reviewed the role of corporate media with a focus particularly on news media and its relation with power in different political configurations and settings in order to open the door for the examination of case studies of different neopopulist and left-wing South American configurations (Cerbino et al.; Follari, Sel and Gasloli; Gonzalez; Matos).

Between Part 1 and Part 2, it is possible to observe the tensions and gaps between the formal and institutional relations of media and power in liberal democracies and in the new substantive democracies of the South. Therefore, it is possible to conclude that the relation between media and power within democracy cannot be ahistorically predefined, universalized or applied across the board, a central premise for an IPE of media and power. Instead, this relation needs to be critically explored in context and in relation to changes in development, politics and society, by which media is intimately connected to the struggles pertaining to development and dimensions of power. A comparative study of these relations between different regional configurations such as the Pacific Alliance and the Mercosur, for example, could easily demonstrate this.

The next point concerning the IPE of media and power is that if media cannot be analytically separated from power and the struggle over paths of development, then, methodologically, media and power cannot be explored, reducing the study of media to discursive analysis and the study of development to a philosophical phenomenon. As demonstrated here, we need to combine, in a pluralist, pragmatic and coherent methodological way, approaches to examining discourses in relation to historical processes in context in order to construct a critical political economy of media and power in South America (Cerbino et al.; Follari, Sel and Gasloli; Gonzalez; Matos). The South American experiences, in this sense, constitute outstanding case studies that can be contrasted with other regional experiences in order to explore the outcomes and interrelationships between discourses, agency and changing historical structures of development. The study of the relation between neopopulism and media, in the context of a developmental rupture, is thus related to the management of capitalism and international insertion in a changing world order, representing an analytical as well as dynamic unit, key to unravelling the power dynamics involved in the politization of media.

Bibliography

Abreu, A. D. et al. 2006. *Elas ocupam as redacoes.* Rio: FGV.

Acosta-Belen, E. and C. Bose. 1993. *Researching Women in Latin American and the Caribbean.* Boulder: Westview Press.

Aguirre Alvis, A., Torrico Villanueva, E. and B. Poma. 2009. Bolivia. *The Invisible Gags: New and Old Barriers to Diversity in Radio Broadcasting,* Buenos Aires: AMARC, Available at: http://legislaciones.amarc.org/mordazas/eng_indice2.htm

Al Jazeera. 2012. France's Left Front Hopes to 'Reinvent' Left, April 30, Available at: http://www.aljazeera.com/indepth/features/2012/04/2012424191716534108.html

AMARC. 2007. Community Radio Impact Evaluation: Removing Barriers, Increasing Effectiveness, Available at: http://evaluation.amarc.org/evaluation.php?p=CRSIA_Chapter_01

AMARC. 2008. Principles on Democratic Regulation of Community Broadcasting, Available at: http://legislaciones.amarc.org/Principios/Principles%20on%20Democratic%20Regulation%20of%20Community%20Broadcasting%20(eng).pdf

AMARC. 2010. AMARC Link, 13(1), January–March, Available at: http://www.amarc.org/amarclink/amarc_link_AVRIL_2010_EN_final.pdf

Aronowitz, S. 2012. *Taking It Big: C. Wright Mills and the Making of Political Intellectuals.* New York: Columbia University Press.

Asamblea Constituyente. 2008. Constitución del Ecuador, Available at: http://www.asambleanacional.gov.ec/documentos/constitucion_de_bolsillo.pdf

Baccaro, A., Maglieri, A. and N. Manchini. 2012. Proceso de implementación de la TDT en Brasil. ¿Globo está? In *Siete Debates Nacionales en Políticas de Comunicación,* edited by G. Mastrini and O. Carboni. Argentina: Universidad Nacional de Quilmes Editorial, 227–254.

Bailey, O., Cammearts, B. and N. Carpentier. 2008. *Understanding Alternative Media.* New York: Open University Press.

Baker, C. E. 2006. *Media Concentration and Democracy: Why Ownership Matters,* Cambridge University Press.

Baker, C. E. 2007. *Media Concentration and Democracy.* Cambridge: Cambridge University Press.

Balvé, B. and C. Suárez. 2001. *La estrategia neocolonial del imperio. Los Documentos de Santa Fé.* Argentina: Gentesur.

Barros Filho, C. et al. 2007. Os usos das novas midias na campanha presidencial de 2006. In *A Mídia nas eleicoes de 2006,* edited by V. A. D. Lima. SP: Fundação Perseu Abramo, 89–113.

Barros, F., Fernandes, P., Gosula, V. and D. Swift. 2012. Rio Rising: Leveraging Digital Marking Opportunities in Brazil, iConsumer Series, McKinsey& Company White Paper, Available at: http://www.mckinsey.com/~/media/mckinsey/dotcom/client_service/high%20tech/pdfs/rio%20rising.ashx

Barthes, R. 2002. *El Susurro del Lenguaje. Más allá de la palabra y de la escritura.* Barcelona: Paidós.

Baudrillard, J. 1988. *El otro por sí mismo.* Barcelona: Anagrama.

BBC. 2012. Defying the Double Dip Down in the Valleys, May 2, Available at: http://www.bbc.co.uk/news/uk-scotland-17932383

Becerra, M. and G. Mastrini. 2001. 50 años de concentración de medios en América Latina: del patriarcado artesanal a la valorización en escala. In *Globalización, comunicación y democracia. Crítica de la economía política de la comunicación y la cultura*, edited by F. Quirós Fernández and F. Sierra Caballero. Sevilla: Comunicación Social Ediciones y Publicaciones, 179–208.

Becker, M. 2011. Correa, Indigenous Movements, and the Writing of a New Constitution in Ecuador. *Latin American Perspectives*, January 38, 1: 47–62.

Beigel, F. 2006. Vida, Muerte y Resurrección de las 'Teorías de la Dependencia'. In *Crítica y teoría en el pensamiento social latinoamericano*, edited by F. Beigel et al. Buenos Aires: CLACSO, 287–326.

Bennett, W. L. 2003. New Media Power: The Internet and Global Activism. In *Contesting Media Power*, edited by N. Couldry and J. Curran. London: Rowman and Littlefield, 17–38.

Bennett, W. (forthcoming) Press-Government Relations in a Changing Media Environment. In *The Oxford Handbook of Political Communication*, edited by K. Kenski and K. Hall Jamieson. New York: Oxford University Press.

Bennett, W., Lawrence, R. and S. Livingston. 2007. *When the Press Fails: Political Power and the News Media from Iraq to Katrina*. New York: Cambridge University Press.

Bernier, A. 2012. Ecuador's Plan Falters. *Le Monde Diplomatique*, July, Available at: http://mondediplo.com/2012/07/12ecuador

Biglieri, P. 2012. Popular Governments, Post Democracy and the Media. Paper presented at the *Media, Power and Citizenship Conference*, May 16th. Quito, Ecuador.

Blumenthal, S. 1982. *The Permanent Campaign*. New York: Simon and Schuster.

Bourdieu, P. 1997. *Sobre la televisión*. Barcelona: Anagrama.

Braman, S. 2006. *Change of State. Information, Policy, and Power*. Cambridge: MIT Press.

Britto García, L. 2006. *Dictadura mediática en Venezuela. Investigación de unos medios por encima de toda sospecha*. Caracas: Ministry of Communication and Information.

Burbach, R. 2013. A Cuban Spring? *Counterpunch*, April 23th, Available at: http://www.counterpunch.org/2013/04/23/a-cuban-spring/

Buvinic, M. and V. Roza. 2004. Women, Politics and Democratic Prospects in Latin America. In *Sustainable Development Department Technical Paper Series*. Washington, DC: Inter-American Development Bank, Available at: http://publications.iadb.org/bitstream/handle/11319/5212/Women,%20Politics%20and%20Democratic%20Prospects%20in%20Latin%20America.pdf?sequence=1

Buzan, B. 2004. *From International to World Society? English School Theory and the Social Structure of Globalization*. Cambridge: Cambridge University Press.

Cabral, A. 2011. Social Participation and Decision-Making Process in Communications in Brazil: The 1 National Conference on Communications. *Journal of Latin American Communication Research*, 1(2): 100–115.

Cameron, M. A. 2009. Latin America's Left Turns: Beyond Good and Bad. *Third World Quarterly*, 30(2): 331–348.

Cardoso, G. 2010. Da comunicacao em massa a comunicacao em rede: modelos comunicacionais e a sociedade de informacao. In *Mutacoes do visivel – da comunicacao de massa a comunicacao em rede*, edited by D. Moraes. RJ: Pao e Rosas Editora, 23–53.

Carpentier, N. 2011. *Media and Participation: A Site of Ideological-Democratic Struggle*. Bristol: Intellect.

Castells, M. 1998. Information Technology, Globalization and Social Development, Presented at the UNRISD Conference on Information Technologies and Social Development, Geneva. *United Nations Research Institute for Social Development*, June,

Available at: http://www.unrisd.org/80256B3C005BCCF9/%28httpAuxPages%29/F270E0C066F3DE7780256B67005B728C?OpenDocument

Castells, M. 2003. Internet e sociedade em rede. In *Por uma outra comunicacao – midia, mundializacao cultural e poder*, edited by D. Moraes. RJ: Editora Record, 255–289.

Castells, M. 2009. *Communication Power*. Oxford: Oxford University Press.

Castells, M. 2010. The New Economy: Informationalism, Globalization, Networking. In *The Rise of the Network Society*, West Sussex: Wiley-Blackwell, 77–163.

Castells, M. 2011. A Network Theory of Power. *International Journal of Communication*, 4: 773–787.

Checchini, D. and J. Mancinelli. 2010. *Silencio por Sangre. La verdadera historia de Papel Prensa*. Buenos Aires: Miradas al Sur.

Cerbino, M. 2012. Postmarxismo, discurso y populismo, un diálogo con Ernesto Laclau. *Revista Iconos*, 44.

Cerbino, M. and I. Ramos. 2009a. Medios de comunicación y despolitización de la política en Ecuador. In *Tiempos de Cambio. Política y Comunicación en América Latina*, edited by A. Cañizález. Caracas: Universidad Católica Andrés Bello–ALAIC, 47–62.

Cerbino, M. and I. Ramos. 2009b. La Comunicación de masas en tiempos de la revolución ciudadana. Apuntes para la democratización del espacio mediático en Ecuador. *Revista Comunicación*, 145.

Cerbino, M. and A. Rodríguez. 2005. Movimientos y máquinas de guerra juveniles. *Nómadas*, 23: 112–121.

Cervo, A. L. 2008. *Inserção internacional: formação dos conceitos brasileiros*. São Paulo: Saraiva.

Chakravartty, P. and Z. Yuezhi. 2008. *Global Communications: Towards a Transcultural Political Economy*. Lanham: Rowman & Littlefield.

Chomsky, N. 2003. *Los guardianes de la libertad: propaganda, desinformación y consenso en los medios de comunicación de masas*. Barcelona: Crítica.

Chomsky, N. 2012. Noam Chomsky on WikiLeaks, Obama's Targeted Assassinations and Latin America's Break from the U.S., interviewed by Amy Goodman. *Democracy Now*, Available at: http://www.democracynow.org/2012/5/14/noam_chomsky_on_wikileaks_obamas_targeted

Christians, C., Glasser, T., McQuail, D., Nordenstreng, K. and R. A. White. 2009. *Normative Theories of the Media: Journalism in Democratic Societies*. Urbana: University of Illinois Press.

Ciespal. 2010. La influencia del discurso presidencial en la agenda de los periódicos ecuatorianos, Available at: http://www.ciespal.net/mediaciones/images/discurso%20presidencial-medios%20v3.pdf

Cirio, I. 2013. Convergencia estratégica: Radio Mundo Real: Una década de comunicación ambientalista orgánica desde los movimientos sociales. *La Jornada* del Campo, September 21, no. 72, Available at: http://www.jornada.unam.mx/2013/09/21/cam-agua.html

Clark, J. and P. Aufderheide. 2009. *Public Media 2.0: Dynamic, Engaged Publics*. Washington: Centre for Social Media – School of Communication of the American University. Available at: http://www.cmsimpact.org/future-public-media/documents/articles/public-media-20-dynamic-engaged-publics

Coffey, G. 2004. How the British Media Covers Latin America. *Red Pepper*, December, Available at: http://www.redpepper.org.uk/How-the-British-media-covers-Latin/

Cohen, H. 2011. In the Midst of a Media War in Argentina, the Birth of a More Critical Audience. *Media Policy*, Available at: http://www.mediapolicy.org/argentina-broadcasting-law

Colciencias. 2013. Colciencias en cumbre de Ciencia, Tecnología e Innovación de Unasur, Colciencias.gov.co, May, Available at: http://www.colciencias.gov.co/noticias/colciencias-en-cumbre-de-cienciatecnolog-e-innovaci-n-de-unasur

Collins, R. 1992. *Dictating Content: How Advertising Pressure Can Corrupt a Free Press.* Washington, DC: Center for the Study of Commercialism.

Committee to Protect Journalists. 2009. *Attacks on the Press 2009*: Ecuador, Available at: http://cpj.org/2010/02/attacks-on-the-press-2009-ecuador.php

Committee to Protect Journalists. 2011. Confrontation, Repression in Correa's Ecuador, Available at: http://cpj.org/reports/2011/09/confrontation-repression-correa-ecuador.php

Comor, E. (ed). 1994. *The Global Political Economy of Communication: Hegemony, Telecommunication and the Information Economy.* Basingstoke: Palgrave MacMillan.

Comunicación y Ciudadanía. 2009. Informe Comisión para la Auditoría de las concesiones de las frecuencias de radio y televisión, Ecuador, Available at: http://www.movimientos.org/foro_comunicacion/show_text.php3?key=15153

Coleman, G. 2009. Code is Speech: Legal Tinkering, Expeertise, and Protest Among Free and Open Source Software Developers. *Cultural Anthropology* 3: 420-454.

Cooke, J. W. 2011. *Peronismo y revolución.* 2nd edn. Buenos Aires: Colihue, Bs.Aires.

Cornego, D. 2012. Interview with Author. Quito, Ecuador, May 16.

Correa, R. 2011a. Informe a la Nación. Quito, Ecuador, agosto.

Correa, R. 2011b. Sociedades Vulnerables: Medios y Democracia en América Latina. Academic Conference in Columbia University. New York, September 23.

Correa, R. 2012. The Julian Assange Show: Interview with President Rafael Correa, Available at: http://www.youtube.com/watch?v=ZvUwC5JTAJY.

COSECCTI-UNASUR. 2012. *Informe de Industrias Culturales de UNASUR,* Available at: http://www.ipanc.org/es/31-noticias/151-industrias-culturales-unasur-2.html

Council of Europe. 2009. Declaration of the Committee of Ministers on the Role of Community Media in Promoting Social Cohesion and Intercultural Dialogue, Available at: http://www.cmfe.eu/docs/_Declaration_Community_media_adopted_CM-11-02-09E1.pdf

Cox, R. 1981. Social Forces, States and World Orders: Beyond International Relations Theory. *Millennium: Journal of International Studies,* 10 (2): 162–175.

Cox, R. 1983. Gramsci, Hegemony and International Relations: An Essay in Method. *Millennium: Journal of International Studies,* 12 (2): 162–175.

Coyer, K. and A. Hintz. 2010. Developing the 'Third Sector': Community Media Policies in Europe. In *Media Freedom and Pluralism: Media Policy Changes in the Enlarged Europe,* edited by B. Klimkiewicz. Budapest: CEU Press, 275–298.

Coyer, K. and P. Tridish. 2005. A Radio Station in Your Hands is Worth 500 Channels of Mush! The Role of Community Radio in the Struggle Against Corporate Domination of Media. In *News Incorporated: Corporate Media Ownership and Its Threat to Democracy,* edited by E. D. Cohen. Amherst: Prometheus Books, 287–314.

Coyer, K., Dowmunt, T. and A. Fountain (eds). 2007. *Alternative Media Handbook.* London: Routledge.

Crespi, I. 1997. *The Public Opinion Process: How the People Speak.* New Jersey: Routledge.

Curran, J. 2012. James Curran's Speech to the TUV Conference on Media Regulation. *Coordinating Committee for Media Reform,* Available at: http://www.mediareform.org.uk/leveson/james-currans-speech-to-the-tuc-conference-on-media-regulation

Dangl, B. 2010. Ecuador's Challenge: Rafael Correa and the Indigenous Movements. *Upsidedown World,* Available at: http://upsidedownworld.org/main/ecuador-archives-49/2743-ecuadors-challenge-rafael-correa-and-the-indigenous-movements-

De Certeau, M. 1999. *La cultura en plural*. Buenos Aires: Nueva Visión.
Decreto Ejecutivo N° 1661. 1969. Registro Oficial 252, agosto.
Decreto Supremo N° 26. 1935. Registro Oficial 58, diciembre.
Decreto Supremo N° 256. 1971. Registro Oficial 165, agosto.
Decreto Supremo N° 533. 1965. Registro Oficial 405, abril.
Decreto Supremo N° 1852. 1965. Registro Oficial 570, agosto.
Della Porta, D. 2011. Communication in Movement. *Information, Communication and Society*, 14(6): 800–819.
De Moraes, D. 2011. *La cruzada de los medios en América Latina*. Buenos Aires: Paidós.
De Nardis, L. 2009. *Protocol Politics: The Globalization of Internet Governance*. Cambridge: MIT Press.
Diamond, L. 2010. Liberation Technology. *Journal of Democracy*, 21(3): 69–83.
Diario Co Latino. 2013. Proyecto de Ley de Medios Públicos busca crear el marco jurídico para medios al servicio de la ciudadanía. *DiarioCoLatino.com*, September 20, Available at: http://www.diariocolatino.com/es/20130920/nacionales/120247/Proyecto-de-Ley-de-Medios-P%C3%BAblicos-busca-crear-el-marco-jur%C3%ADdico-para-medios-al-servicio-de-la-ciudadan%C3%ADa.htm
Disposición transitoria 5°. 1995. Ley Reformatoria a Ley de Radiodifusión y Televisión, R.O. 691, septiembre.
Dosh, P. and N. Kligerman. 2010. Correa vs. Social Movements: Showdown in Ecuador. *North American Congress on Latin America (NACLA)*, Available at: https://nacla.org/node/6094
Downing, J. 2001. *Radical Media: Rebellious Communication and Social Movements*. London: Sage.
Downing, J. (ed). 2010. *Encyclopedia of Social Movement Media*. Thousand Oaks: Sage.
Durán Magliardi, C. 2013. Neopopulismo: la imposibilidad del nombre. In *Vox populi: populismo y democracia en Latinoamérica*, edited by J. Aibar Gaete. Buenos Aires: FLACSO-Univ. de Gral. Sarmiento-Univ. de Avellaneda, 83–139.
Eagleton, T. 2001. *La idea de cultura*. Barcelona: Paidós.
Economist Intelligence Unit. 2010. Democracy Index 2010: Democracy in Retreat. *The Economist*, Available at: http://graphics.eiu.com/PDF/Democracy_Index_2010_web.pdf
Edelman, M. 2005. When Networks Don't Work: The Rise and Fall and Rise of Civil Society Initiative in Central America. In *Social Movements: An Anthropological Reader*, edited by J. Nash. Malden, MA: Blackwell, 29–45.
El Ciudadano. 2011. Presidente insta a que los medios demuestren si el Gobierno miente en cadenas nacionales (AUDIO), Available at: http://www.elciudadano.gob.ec/index.php?option=com_content&view=article&id=28604%3Apresidente-insta-a-que-medios-demuestren-si-el-gobierno-miente-en-cadena-nacional-sobre-libertad-de-expresion&catid=2%3Apolitica&Itemid=43
El Comercio. 2012. Proyecto de Ley Orgánica de Comunicación, Available at: http://www.elcomercio.com/politica/Ley-Comunicacion-debate-Asamblea-Nacional_ECMFIL20120719_0001.pdf
El Nuevo Herald. 2013. Gobierno de El Salvador propone ley de medios de comunicación públicos. *El Nuevo Herald*, September 18, Available at: http://www.elnuevoherald.com/2013/09/18/1569849/gobierno-de-el-salvador-presento.html
El Universo. 2011a. Los cobardes y los asesinos no están en la revolución ciudadana, Available at: http://www.eluniverso.com/2011/08/11/1/1355/los-cobardes-asesinos-estan-revolucion-ciudadana.html
El Universo. 2011b. No a las Mentiras, www.eluniverso.com/2011/02/06/1/1363/mentiras.html

Escribano, Escribano, J. 2003: Treinta y seis horas de un carnaval decadente, *La Nación*, May 15
Escudé, C. 1995. *El realismo de los estados débiles*. Buenos Aires: GEL.
European Parliament. 2008. Report on Community Media in Europe, 2008/2011 (INI), Approved, Available at: http://www.europarl.europa.eu/sides/getDoc.do?language=EN&reference=A6-0263/2008
Exeni, J. L. 2005. Gobernabilidad Mediática. Mass media y grado de gobierno: difícil (des) encuentro. *Organicom*, 4: 90–105.
Fancher, M. 2011. Seattle: A New Media Case Study. *Pew Research Center's Project for Excellence in Journalism*, Available at: http://stateofthemedia.org/2011/mobile-survey/seattle-a-new-media-case-study/
Feinmann, J. 2011. *El Flaco (diálogos irreverentes con Nestor Kirchner)*. Buenos Aires: Planeta, Avellaneda.
Financial Times. 2012. Brazil Becomes World's Sixth Biggest Economy. *The Financial Times*, Available at: http://www.ft.com/cms/s/0/e23a2b34-678e-11e1-b4a1-00144feabdc0.html#axzz2Z34DWW4e
Fiorentini, F. 2012a. Argentina: Que se Vayan Todos! – They all Must Go! *Red Pepper*, Available at: http://www.redpepper.org.uk/argentina-que-se-vayan-todos-they-all-must-go/
Fiorentini, F. 2012b. The Paraguayan Coup: How Agribusiness, Landowning and Media Elite, and the U.S. are Paving a Way for Regional Destabilization. *War Times*, July 4, Available at: http://war-times.org/node/463
Fiss, O. 2008. Las dos caras del Estado. Conferencia dictada en la Universidad de Palermo, Buenos Aires.
Fiss, O. 2010. *Democracia y disenso. Una teoría de la libertad de expresión*. Buenos Aires: Ad-Hoc.
Follari, R. 2010. *La alternativa neopopulista. El reto latinoamericano al republicanismo liberal*. Rosario: Homo Sapiens.
Follari, R. 2011. Los medios como oposición encubierta. In *Los medios y la política: relación aviesa*, edited by M. Salazar. Buenos Aires: El Aleph, 23–38.
Fortique, J. 2013. Alianza del Pacífico: ¿El nuevo club neoliberal? *ALAI América Latina*, Mayo, Available at: http://www.alainet.org/active/64285
Fox, E. and S. Waisbord. (eds). 2002. *Latin Politics, Global Media*. Austin, TX: University of Texas Press.
Freedman, D. 2008. *The Politics of Media Reform*. London: Polity.
Freedom House. 2009. Undermining Democracy: 21st Century Authoritarians, Washington: F. House, Available at: http://www.freedomhouse.org/sites/default/files/UnderminingDemocracy_Full.pdf
Friel, H. and R. Falk. 2004. *The Paper of Record: How the New York Times Misreports U.S. Foreign Policy*. New York: Verso.
Gallagher, K. P. and R. Porzecanski. 2010. *The Dragon in the Room: China & The Future of Latin American Industrialization*. Stanford: Stanford University Press.
García de Madariaga, J. M. and C. S. Domínguez. 2006. La construcción de la realidad desde los medios venezolanos. Censura, autocensura y militancia política en los profesionales de la información. *Revista de Estudios para el desarrollo social de la comunicación*, 3: 319–334.
Garnham, N. 1980. *Structures of Television*, rev. edn. London: British Film Institute.
Garnham, N. 1990. *Capitalism and Communication*. London: Sage.
Gasloli, P. 2012. Perspectivas de la comunicación audiovisual entre el éxtasis y la fatalidad. *Revista Sociedad*, Universidad de Buenos Aires.

Geary, D. 2009. *Radical Ambition: C. Wright Mills, the Left, and American Social Thought.* Berkeley: University of California Press.

Gibbon, R. K. and S. J. Ward. 1999. Party Democracy Online: UK Parties and New ICTs. *Information Communication and Society*, 2(3): 340–367.

Girard, B. (ed). 2003. *The One to Watch: Radio, New ICTs and Interactivity*. Rome: Food and Agriculture Organization of the United Nations.

Girard, B., Camacho, C., Vannini, P. and R. Roemersma. 2010. *El bit de la cuestión: Radio popular y comunitaria en la era digital*. Buenos Aires: AMARC ALC.

Gomez, G. and C. Aguerre. 2009. The Regulation of Broadcasting Concessions in Latin America. In *The Invisible Gags: New and Old Barriers to Diversity in Radio Broadcasting*, edited by AMARC ALC, Buenos Aires: AMARC, Available at: http://legislaciones.amarc.org/mordazas/eng_indice2.htm

Gomez Garcia, R. 2013. Media Reform in Latin America: Experiences and Debates of Communication Public Policies. *The Political Economy of Communication*, May 1, Available at: http://academic.wwwss2.a2hosting.com/ojs/index.php/polecom/article/view/16/146

González Prada, M. 1985. *Nuestro Periodismo. Páginas Libres/Horas de Lucha*. España: Biblioteca Ayacucho.

Gramsci, A. 1986. *Cuadernos de la Cárcel*. México: Juan Pablos Ed.

Greenwald, G. 2012. What NPR Means by 'Reporting'. *Salon*, March 27, Available at: http://www.salon.com/2012/03/27/what_npr_means_by_reporting/

Groppo, A. 2009. *Los dos príncipes (Juan D. Peron y G.Vargas), un estudio comparativo del populismo latinoamericano*. Cordoba: Universidad de Villa María.

Grossi, G. 2004. *L'opinione pubblica. Teoria del campo demoscopico*. Roma: Editori Laterza.

Habermas, J. 1981. *Historia y crítica de la opinión pública: la transformación estructural de la vida pública*. México Barcelona: Gustavo Gili.

Habermas, J. 1989. *The Structural Transformation of the Public Sphere*. Cambridge, MA: MIT Press.

Hadl, G. 2010. Alternative Media: Policy Issues. In *Encyclopedia of Social Movement Media*, edited by J. Downing. Thousand Oaks: Sage, 33–35.

Hallin, D. and S. Papathanassopoulos. 2002. Political Clientelism and the Media: Southern Europe and Latin America in Comparative Perspective. *Media, Culture and Society*, 24(2): 175–195.

Hallin, D. and P. Mancini. 2004. *Comparing Media Systems: Three Models of Media and Politics*. Cambridge: Cambridge University Press.

Hallin, D. and P. Mancini. 2008. *Sistemas mediáticos comparados. Tres modelos de relación entre los medios de comunicación y la política*. Barcelona: Hacer.

Hastings, M. 2012. *The Operators: The Wild and Terrifying Inside Story of America's War in Afghanistan*. New York: Blue Rider Press.

Hedges, C. 2009. *Empire of Illusion*. New York: Nation Books.

Held, D. and A. McGrew. 2003. The Great Globalization Debate. In *The Global Transformations Reader*, edited by D. Held and A. McGrew. Cambridge: Polity Press, 1–50.

Herman, E. S. and N. Chomsky. 1989. *Manufacturing Consent*. New York: Pantheon.

Herman, E. and R. McChesney. 1997. *The Global Media: The New Missionaries of Global Capitalism*. London/Washington: Cassel.

Herman, E. S. and R. W. McChesney. 1999. *Los medios globales. Los nuevos misioneros del capitalismo corporativo*. Madrid: Ed. Cátedra, Col. Signo e imagen.

Hernández, D. 2005. *La libertad de expresión: ¿voces diversas y conciencias críticas o hegemonía mediática?* Caracas: Ministry of Communication and Information.

Hernández, D. and O. Reina. 2010. Elementos para la definición de una política de información y comunicación de Estado. In *Políticas de comunicación en el capitalismo contemporáneo. América Latina y sus encrucijadas*, edited by S. Sel. Buenos Aires: CLACSO: 17–38.

Herrera, E. 2007. *Lo que se robó el periodismo que lo devuelva*. Caracas: Fundación Editorial el perro y la rana.

Hesketh, C. 2012. The Clash of Spatializations: Geopolitics and Class Struggles in Southern Mexico. *Latin American Perspectives*, 40(4): 70–87.

Hintz, A. 2009. *Civil Society Media and Global Governance: Intervening into the World Summit on the Information Society*. Münster: Lit.

Hintz, A. 2011. From Media Niche to Policy Spotlight: Mapping Community-Media Policy Change in Latin America. *Canadian Journal of Communication*, 36: 147–159.

Hintz, A. 2013. Dimensions of Modern Freedom of Expression: WikiLeaks, Policy Hacking, and Digital Freedoms. In *Beyond WikiLeaks: Implications for the Future of Communications, Journalism and Society*, edited by B. Brevini et al. Basingstoke: Palgrave MacMillan, 146–165.

Hobsbawn, E. 1989. *The Age of Empire*. London: Brown Book Group.

Howley, K. 2005. *Community Media: People, Places and Communication Technologies*. Cambridge: Cambridge University Press.

How News Happens: A Study of the News Ecosystem of One American City. 2010. *Pew Research Center's Project for Excellence in Journalism*, January 11, Available at: http://www.journalism.org/analysis_report/how_news_happens

Hudson, R. 2004. Conceptualizing Economies and Their Geographies: Spaces, Flows and Circuits. *Progress in Human Geography*, 28(4): 447–471.

Human Rights Watch. 2009. Ecuador: Amend Draft Communications Law. Human Rights Watch, Available at: http://www.hrw.org/news/2009/12/15/ecuador-amend-draft-communications-law

Human Rights Watch. 2011. World Report 2011: Ecuador. Human Rights Watch, Available at: http://www.hrw.org/world-report-2011/ecuador

Hutchinson, D. 2009. The European Union and the Press. In *Media in the Enlarged Europe. Politics, Policy and Industry*, edited by Charles, Alec. Bristol-Chicago:Intellect, 53-60.

Ianni, O. 1996. *A ideia de Brasil Modern*. San Pablo: Editora Brasiliense.

IAPA. 2011. IAPA Reviews State of Press Freedom in 2011, Available at: http://www.sipiapa.org/v4/comunicados_de_prensa.php?seccion=detalles&id=4662&idioma=us

Infodev and M. Jensen. 2011. Broadband in Brazil: A Multipronged Public Sector Approach to Digital Inclusion. Washington: The International Bank for Reconstruction and Development/the World Bank, Available at: http://broadbandtoolkit.org/Custom/Core/Documents/br.pdf

Institute of Development Studies. 2012. The British Media in the Global Sout, Available at: http://www.ids.ac.uk/news/ids-film-examines-how-british-media-portray-global-south

Inter-American Commission on Human Rights. 2000. Declaration of Principles on Freedom of Expression, Available at: http://www.oas.org/en/iachr/mandate/Basics/19.FREEDOM%20EXPRESSION.pdf

Inter-American Commission on Human Rights. 2009. Annual Report of the Inter-American Commission on Human Rights 2009, Report of the Special Rapporteur of Freedom of Expression, Available at: http://www.cidh.org/pdf%20files/Annual%20Report%202009.pdf

International Federation of Journalists. 2014. IFJ List of Journalists and Media Staff Killed in 2013, Available at: http://www.ifj.org/assets/docs/192/093/7c0fac0-6d91e5d.pdf

Izaguirre, I. 2003. Algunos ejes teórico-metodológicos en el estudio del conflicto social. In *Movimientos sociales y conflicto en América Latina*, Buenos Aires: CLACSO, Available at: http://biblioteca.clacso.edu.ar/clacso/formacion-virtual/20100724072158/16izagui.pdf

Jaguaribe, H. 1979. Autonomía periférica y hegemonía céntrica. *Estudios Internacionales*, 46: 91–130.

Jameson, F. 2001. *Ensayos sobre el postmodernism*. Buenos Aires: Imago Mundi.

Jones, T. 2012. Latin America's Past Offers Lessons on Debt, But Are EU Ministers Bothered? *The Guardian*, February 24, Available at: http://www.guardian.co.uk/global-development/poverty-matters/2012/feb/24/latin-america-past-lessons-debt-eurozone

Kaitatzi-Whitlock, S. 2008. The Political Economy of the Media at the Root of the EU's Democracy Deficit. In *Media, Democracy and European Culture*, edited by I. Bondebjerg and P. Madsen. Intellect: Bristol, 25–48.

Kaplan, R. 2002. *Politics and the American Press: The Rise of Objectivity, 1865–1920*. New York: Cambridge University Press.

Keck, M. and K. Sikkink. 1998. *Activists Beyond Borders. Advocacy Networks in International Politics*. Ithaca: Cornell University Press.

Keohane, R. O. and J. S. Nye. 1977. *Power and Interdependence: World Politics in Transition*. Boston: Little, Brown.

Khagram, S., Riker, J. and K. Sikkink. 2002. From Santiago to Seattle: Transnational Advocacy Groups Restructuring World Politics. In *Restructuring World Politics: Transnational Social Movements, Networks, and Norms*, edited by S. Khagram et al. Minneapolis: University of Minnesota Press, 3–23.

Kidd, D. et al. (eds). 2009. *Making Our Media: Global Initiatives Toward a Democratic Public Sphere*. Cresskill: Hampton Press.

King, G., Mattos, J. C., Mulder, N. and O. Rosales. 2012. *The Changing Nature of Asian-Latin American Economic Relations*. Santiago, Chile: ECLAC.

Kingdon, J. 1984. *Agendas, Alternatives, and Public Policy*. Boston: Little Brown.

Klinger, U. 2011. Democratizing Media Policy: Community Radios in Mexico and Latin America. *Journal of Latin American Communication Research*, 1(2): 4–22.

Kuhn, T. 1980. *La estructura de las revoluciones científicas*. México: F.C.E.

Laclau, E. 2005. *La Razón Populista*. México: FCE.

Laclau, E. 2006. La deriva populista y la centroizquierda latinoamericana. *Revista Nueva Sociedad*, 205: 56–61.

Laclau, E. 2008a. *La razón populista*. Buenos Aires: Fondo de Cultura Económica.

Laclau, E. 2008b. *Debates y Combates (por un nuevo horizonte de la política)*. Buenos Aires: Fondo de Cultura Económica.

Lafer, C. 2001. *A identidade internacional do Brasil e a política externa brasileira*. São Paulo: Perspectiva.

La Follette, R. M. 1920. *The Political Philosophy of Robert M. La Follette*. Compiled by Ellen Torelle, Madison, WI: Robert M. La Follette Co.

La Hora. 2007. Vandalismo Oficial, Available at: http://www.lahora.com.ec/index.php/noticias/show/543753/-1/Vandalismo_oficial.html

La Morada Women's Development Corporation. 2009. Chile. In *The Invisible Gags: New and Old Barriers to Diversity in Radio Broadcasting*, edited by AMARC ALC. Buenos Aires: AMARC, Available at: http://legislaciones.amarc.org/mordazas/eng_indice2.htm

Lanza, E. and O. Lopez-Goldaracena. 2009. Uruguay. In *The Invisible Gags: New and Old Barriers to Diversity in Radio Broadcasting*, edited by AMARC ALC. Buenos Aires: AMARC, Available at: http://legislaciones.amarc.org/mordazas/eng_indice2.htm

La Rue, F. 2009. Es lo más avanzado que he visto en el continente. *Página 12*, Available at: http://www.pagina12.com.ar/diario/elpais/1-128260-2009-07-15.html

Lasch, C. 1995. *The Revolt of the Elite and the Betrayal of Democracy*. New York: W. W. Norton.

Lavin, A. 2013. Ecuador's Communications Law: With a View Toward a More Democratic Law. In *Digital Rights: Latin America and the Caribbean*, no. 1, Available at: http://www.digitalrightslac.net/en/ley-de-comunicacion-en-ecuador-de-cara-a-una-ley-mas-democratica/

Lazarsfeld, P. F. 1957. Public Opinion and the Classical Tradition. *Public Opinion Quarterly*: 39–53.

Leiva, F. I. 2008. *Latin American Neostructuralism: The Contradictions of Post-Neoliberal Development*. Minneapolis: University of Minnesota Press.

Leon, O., Burch, S. and F. Tamayo. 2001. *Movimientos Sociales en la Red*. Quito, Ecuador: ALAI/IDRC.

Leon, O., Burch, S. and E. Tamayo. 2005. *Comunicación en Movimiento*. Quito, Ecuador: ALAI.

Leon, O., Burch, S. and E. Tamayo. 2005. *Communication in Movement*. Quito: Agencia Latinoamericana de Informacion.

Leon, O. 2013. *Democratizar la palabra: Movimientos convergentes en comunicación*. Quito, Ecuador: ALAI.

Leveson Inquiry. 2012. The Leveson Inquiry, Available at: http://www.levesoninquiry.org.uk/

Levy, P. 2003. Pela ciberdemocracia. In *Por uma outra comunicacao – midia, mundializacao cultural e poder*, edited by D. Moraes. RJ: Editora Record, 367–385.

Ley Reformatoria a Ley de Radiodifusión y Televisión. 1995. *Registro Oficial 691*, Mayo.

Light, E. 2011. From Pirates to Partners: The Legalization of Community Radio in Uruguay. *Canadian Journal of Communication*, 36: 51–67.

Lima, V. A. 2007. *A Midia nas eleicoes de 2006*. Sao Paulo: Editora Fundacao Perseu Abramo.

Lippmann, W. 1946. *Public opinion*. New Jersey: Transaction Publishers.

Lippmann, W. 2008. *Liberty and the News*. Princeton: Princeton University Press.

Lippmann, W. and C. Merz. 1920. A Test of the News, Supplement. In *The New Republic*, August 4, Available at: http://archive.org/stream/LippmannMerzATestoftheNews/Lippmann_Merz_ATestoftheNews#page/n5/mode/1up

López, A. (ed). 1993. *Inventario de Medios de Comunicación en América Latina*. Quito: CIESPAL.

Loreti, D. 2011. Research interview by Arne Hintz, Montreal, February 11.

Lovenduski, J. 1993. Introduction: The Dynamics of Gender and Party. In *Gender and Party Politics*, edited by J. Lovenduski and P. Norris. London: Sage Publications.

Lovink, G. and M. Rasch (eds). 2013. *Unlike Us Reader: Social Media Monopolies and Their Alternatives*. Amsterdam: Institute of Network Cultures.

Lugo-Ocando, J. 2008. An Introduction to the Maquilas of Power: Media and Political Transition in Latin America. In *Media in Latin America*, Buckingham: Open University Press, 1–12.

Lugo-Ocando, J. 2008. *The Media in Latin America*. Berkshire: Open University Press.

Lugones, M. C. and E. V. Spelman. 2005. Have We Got Theory for You! Feminist Theory, Cultural Imperialism and the Demand for the Woman's Voice. In *Feminist*

Theory: A Reader, edited by W. Kolmar and F. Bartkowski. New York: McGraw Hill, 16–27.

Lukacs, G. 1969. *Historia y conciencia de clase.* México: Grijalbo.

MacBride, S., et al. 1980. *Many Voices, One World. Communication and Society Today and Tomorrow. Towards a New More Just and More Efficient Information and Communication Order.* Ibandan and Paris: Ibandan University Press and UNESCO Press.

Major, J. 2012. Submission to Leveson Inquiry, Available at: http://www.levesoninquiry.org.uk/evidence/?witness=sir-john-major

Manin, B. 2006. *Los principios del gobierno representativo.* Madrid: Alianza Editorial.

Mansell, R. 2013a. Comments, Panel 10: Measuring Progress and Global Review, eLAC2015, presented at the Fourth Ministerial Conference on the Information Society in Latin America and the Caribbean, April 3–5.

Mansellh, R. 2013b. Open Development: Exploring the Future of the Information Society in Latin America and the Caribbean. Conference sponsored by Fundación Comunica and the International Development Research Centre (IDRC), April 2–3.

Margolis, M., Resnick and J. Levy. 2003. Major Parties Dominate, Minor Parties Struggle. In *Political Parties and the Internet: Net Gain?*, edited by R. Gibson, P. Nixon and S. Ward. London: Routledge, 53–68.

Marino, S. 2009. Argentina. In *The Invisible Gags: New and Old Barriers to Diversity in Radio Broadcasting*, edited by AMARC ALC, Buenos Aires: AMARC, Available at: http://legislaciones.amarc.org/mordazas/eng_indice2.htm

Mastrini, G. and C. Aguerre. 2009. Telecommunications Regulation and Broadband Development: Implications for the Andean region. Report for the Association for Progressive Communication, Available at: http://www.apc.org/en/system/files/CILACInvestigacionesIntroduccion_EN_20090630.pdf

Mastrini, G. and M. Becerra. 2005. *Periodistas y Magnates. Estructura y concentración de las industrias culturales en América Latina.* Buenos Aires: Prometeo.

Matos, C. 2008. *Journalism and Political Democracy in Brazil.* Maryland: Lexington Books.

Mattoni, A. 2009. *Multiple Media Practices in Italian Mobilizations Against Precarity of Work*, PhD Thesis. Florence: European University Institute.

Mauersberger, C. 2011. Whose Voice Gets on Air? The Role of Community Radio and Recent Reforms to Democratize Media Markets in Uruguay, Chile and Argentina. *Journal of Latin American Communication Research*, 1(2): 23–47.

McAdam, D., Tilly, C. and S. Tarrow. 2005. *Dinámica de la contienda política*. Barcelona: Hacer.

McChesney, R. 1998. The Political Economy of Global Communication. In *Capitalism and the Information Age: The Political Economy of the Global Communication Revolution*, edited by R. McChesney et al. New York: Monthly Review Press, 1–26.

McChesney, R. 2008. *The Political Economy of Media: Enduring Issues, Emerging Dilemmas.* New York: Monthly Review Press.

McChesney, R. 2013. *Digital Disconnect: How Capitalism Is Turning the Internet Against Democracy.* New York: New Press.

McChesney, R. W. and J. Nichols. 2010. *The Death and Life of American Journalism: The Media Revolution That Will Begin the World Again.* New York: Nation Books.

Merke, F. 2011. Bifurcaciones (en las Relaciones) Internacionales o el Estado de la Disciplina. *Espacios Politicos*, 7(12): 4, Available at: http://www.espaciospoliticos.com.ar/actualidad-por-academicos/bifurcaciones-en-las-relaciones-internacionales-o-el-estado-de-la-disciplina

Mermin, J. 1999. *Debating War and Peace: Media Coverage of U.S. Intervention in the Post-Vietnam Era*. Princeton: Princeton University Press.

Meyer, D. 2005. Social Movements and Public Policy: Eggs, Chicken, and Theory. In *Routing the Opposition. Social Movements, Public Policy, and Democracy*, edited by D. Meyer et al. Minneapolis: University of Minnesota Press, 1–26.

Miguez, P. 2012. Capitalismo y conocimiento: 'Existe una contradicción sustancial entre la lógica del capitalismo cognitivo y las condiciones para una economía basada en el conocimiento'. *Revista Herramienta*, entrevista a Carlo Vercellone, 50, Available at: http://www.herramienta.com.ar/revista-herramienta-n-50/capitalismo-y-conocimiento-existe-una-contradiccion-sustancial-entre-la-log

Mihr, C. 2005. Über die Gleichzeitigkeit der Ungleichzeitigkeit: Der Medienwandel in Lateinamerika im Lichte neuerer soziologischer und postkolonialer Theorieperspektiven. In *Alte Medien – Neue Medien. Theorien, Beispiele, Prognosen*, edited by K. Arnold and C. Neuberger. Wiesbaden, 291–331.

Milan, S. 2010. Community Media Activists in Transnational Policy Arenas. In *Understanding Community Media*, edited by K. Howley. Thousand Oaks: Sage, 308–317.

Milan, S. 2013. *Social Movements and Their Technologies. Wiring Social Change*. Basingstoke: Palgrave Macmillan.

Miliband, E. 2012. Submission to Leveson Inquiry, Available at: *http://www.levesoninquiry.org.uk/evidence/?witness=ed-miliband-mp*

Mills, C. W. 2008. *The Politics of Truth*. Oxford: Oxford University Press.

Ministry of Communication and Information. 2007. *Libro Blanco de RCTV*. Caracas: Ministry of Communication and Information.

Miralles, A. 2011. *El miedo al disenso. El disenso periodístico como expresión democrática de las diferencias y no como provocación de violencia*. Barcelona: Gedisa.

Morris, T. and S. Goldsworthy. 2008. *PR – A Persuasive Industry? Spin, Public Relations and the Shaping of the Modern Media*. Basingstoke: Palgrave Macmillan.

Mouchon, J. 2002. La resistible decadencia del debate público en televisión. In *Designis. La Comunicación política. Transformaciones del espacio público*. Barcelona: Gedisa, 219-229.

Morley, D. (1996): Televisión, audiencias y estudios culturales. Buenos Aires: Amorrortu.

Mowlana, H. 1996. *Global Communication in Transition*. London: Sage.

Moyses, D. and G. Gindre. 2009. Brasil. In *The Invisible Gags: New and Old Barriers to Diversity in Radio Broadcasting*, edited by AMARC ALC, Buenos Aires: AMARC, Available at: http://legislaciones.amarc.org/mordazas/eng_indice2.htm

Narváez, A. 2005. Cultura política y cultura mediática. Esfera pública, intereses y códigos. In *Economía política, comunicación y conocimiento: una perspectiva crítica latinoamericana*, edited by C. Bolaño, G. Mastrini and F. Sierra. Buenos Aires: Ediciones La Crujía, 201-227.

Nederveen Pieterse Nixon, J. 2010. *Development Theory*. London: Sage.

Newscorp. 2011. Newscorp Annual Report 2011, Available at: http://www.newscorp.com/Report2011/2011AR.pdf

Newsosaur. 2012. Philly Papers Sold at 10% of 2006 Value. *Reflections of a Newsosaur*, April 2, Available at: http://newsosaur.blogspot.com/2012/04/philly-papers-sold-at-10-of-2006-value.html

Nichols, J. and R. McChesney. 2005. Bush's War on the Press. *The Nation*, December 5, 9–10, Available at: http://www.thenation.com/article/bushs-war-press-0

Nietzsche, F. 2003. *Así hablaba Zaratustra*. Madrid: Alianza.

Noelle-Neumann, E. 1995. *La espiral del silencio: opinión pública: nuestra piel social.* Madrid: Paidós Ibérica.
Norris, P. 2001. *Digital Divide: Civic Engagement, Information Poverty and the Internet Worldwide.* Cambridge: Cambridge University Press.
Orlando, R. 2012. *Discursividades mediáticas contra hegemónicas: nuevas leyes de comunicación y radiodifusión en Argentina y Ecuador.* Quito: Flacso/Abya-Yala.
O'Shea, J. 2011. *The Deal from Hell: How Moguls and Wall Street Plundered Great American Newspapers.* New York: Public Affairs.
Ó Siochrú, S. and B. Girard. 2002. *Global Media Governance.* New York/Oxford: Rowman & Littlefield.
Otero, G. 2004. Global Economy, Local Politics: Indigenous Struggles, Civil Society and Democracy. *Canadian Journal of Political Science,* 37(2): 325–346.
Parisi, A. 1979. *Filosofía y dialéctica.* México: Edicol.
Pasquali, A. 1995. Reinventar los servicios públicos. *Nueva Sociedad,* 140: 70–89.
Pasquali, A. 2004. Es una ley totalitaria, militarista, generadora de censuras y autocensuras. *Diario El Nacional,* October 28, Caracas, B10.
Peck, J. and N. Theodore. 2007. Variegated Capitalism. *Progress in Human Geography,* 31(6): 731–772.
Perón, J. D. and J. W. Cooke. 2007. *Correspondencia Perón-Cooke.* Buenos Aires: Colihue.
Porto, M and Hallin, D., 2009. Media and Democratization in Latin America. The International Journal of Press/Politics. 14 (3): 291–295.
Poster, M. 2003. Cidadania, midia digital e globalizacao. In *Por uma outra comunicacao – midia, mundializacao cultural e poder,* edited by D. Moraes. RJ: Editora Record, 317–339.
Prensa Latina. 2012. Venezuela pidió en la Unasur soberanía en contenidos mediáticos, CanTV, March 11, Available at: http://www.cantv.net/servicios/resena.asp?id=209143&cat=2&Fresena=TRUE
Prometheus Radio Project. 2010. We Won! Senate Joins House in the Passing Local Community Media Act!, Available at: http://www.prometheusradio.org/we_won
Puig, J. C. 1980. *Doctrinas internacionales y autonomía latinoamericana.* Caracas: Instituto de Altos Estudios de América Latina, Universidad Simón Bolívar.
Raboy, M. 2002. *Global Media Policy in the New Millennium.* Luton: University of Luton Press.
Raboy, M. and C. Padovani. 2010. Mapping Global Media Policy: Concepts, Frameworks, Methods, Available at: http:www.globalmediapolicy.net
Ramos, I. 2012. Interview with Author. Quito, Ecuador, May 17.
Real News Network. 2013. Ecuador's President Attacks US over Press Freedomn Critique, May 21, Available at: http://therealnews.com/t2/index.php?option=com_content&task=view&id=31&Itemid=74&jumival=10225
Regalado, R. 2007. *Latin America at the Crossroads: Domination, Crisis, Popular Movements, & Political Alternatives.* New York: Ocean Press.
Reglamento a la Ley Orgánica de Elecciones. 1998. Registro Oficial 370, julio.
Reguero, N. and S. Scifo. 2010. Community Media in the Context of European Media Policies. *Telematics and Informatics,* 27(2): 131–140.
Reilly, K. 2012. Is Media Reform Enough? Latin America's Post-Neoliberal Democratic Reforms in Perspective. *Media Development: Journal of the World Association for Christian Communication,* Available at: http://www.globethics.net/web/media-development/journal-articles?p_auth=2Eeu3V0C&p_p_id=read_panel_portlet_WAR_digitallibraryspring25portlet&p_p_lifecycle=1&p_p_state=maximized&p_p_mode=view&p_p_col_id=column-3&p_p_col_count=1&preSelectedDocUrl=%2FFedoraAccessServlet%3FfedoraGetUrl%3Dhttp%3A%2F%2Fglobethics05

.colo.iway.ch%3A8082%2Ffedora%2Fget%2Fglobethics%3A5139758%2Freilly .pdf%26contentType%3Dapplication%2Fpdf

Rennie, E. 2006. *Community Media: A Global Introduction.* Lanham: Rowman & Littlefield.

Reuters. 2010. Unrest Rocks Ecuador, Correa Blames Coup Attempt. *Reuters,* Available at: http://www.reuters.com/article/2010/09/30/us-ecuador-correa -idUSTRE68T40I20100930

Robinson, W. I. 2011. Global Capitalism Theory and the Emergence of Transnational Elites. *Critical Sociology*, 38(3): 349–363.

Rodriguez, C. 2001. *Fissures in the Mediascape: An International Study of Citizens' Media.* Cresskill: Hampton Press.

Russell, R. and J. G. Tokatlian. 2003. From Antagonistic Autonomy to Relational Autonomy: A Theoretical Reflection from the Southern Cone. *Latin American Politics and Society,* 45(1): 1–24.

Salter, L. and D. Weltman, 2012. Class, Nationalism and News: the BBC's Reporting of Hugo Chavez and the Bolivarian Revolution. Paper presented at *Journalism Research Group Presentation,* Bournemouth University, February 8.

Santiso, J. 2006. *Latin America's Political Economy of the Possible.* Cambridge, MA: MIT Press.

Santos, B. 2011. Why and How to Take a Distance from the Western Critical Tradition. *The Epistemologies of the South: Reinventing Social Emancipation.* Madison, WI: Lecture given at the Havens Centre, Department of Sociology, University of Wisconsin-Madison, Available at: http://www.havenscenter.org/audio/boaventura -de-sousa-santos-why-and-how-take-distance-western-critical-tradition

Schiller, D. 1969. *Mass Communications and American Empire.* Boston: Beacon Press.

Scott, B. 2009. Labor's New Deal for Journalism: The Newspaper Guild in the 1930s. PhD dissertation. University of Illinois at Urbana-Champaign.

Secretaría Nacional de Planificación y Desarrollo. 2013. Reseña histórica, SENPLADES, Available at: http://www.planificacion.gob.ec/resena-historica

Sel, S. 2011. Actores sociales y espacio público. Disputas por la Ley de Servicios de Comunicación Audiovisual en Argentina. *Políticas de Comunicación en el Capitalismo Contemporáneo. América Latina y sus encrucijadas,* Argentina: CLACSO.

Senado de la Nación Argentina. 2010. Preocupación por las trabas a la implementación de la Ley de Servicios de Comunicación Audiovisual, Available at: http://www .senado.gob.ar/prensa/8352/noticias

Sheinin, D. 2006. *Argentina and the United States: An Alliance Contained.* Athens: University of Georgia Press.

Sieff, J. 2012. It Could Be Worse – You Could Be a Lumberjack. *Niles Star,* April 18, Available at: http://dev.nilesstar.com/2012/04/18/jessica-sieff-it-could-be -worse-%E2%80%94-you-could-be-a-lumberjack/

Silverstone, Roger. 2000. The sociology of mediation and communication. In *The Sage Handbook of Sociology*, edited by Calhoun, Craig, Rojek, Chris and Turner, Bryan. London: Sage, 188-207.

Sinclair, U. 2003. *The Brass Check.* Urbana: University of Illinois Press.

Sklair, L. 2000. *The Transnational Capitalist Class.* Oxford: Blackwell.

Smith, R. D. 2004. *Strategic Planning for Public Relations.* Mahwah, NJ: Lawrence Erlbaum Associates.

Solomon, N. 1992. *Unreliable Sources: A Guide to Detecting Bias in News Media.* New York: Carol Publishing Group.

Stoltzfus, D. C. S. 2007. *Freedom from Advertising: E. W. Scripps's Chicago Experiment.* Urbana: University of Illinois Press.

Stone, I. F. 1964. What Few Know About the Tonkin Bay Incidents. *I. F. Stone's Weekly*, August 4: 1–4.
Stoneman, R. 2008. *Chávez: The Revolution Will Not Be Televised*. London and New York: Wallflower Press.
Strange, S. 1994. *States and Markets*, 2nd edn. London/Washington: Pinter.
Tambini, D. 2012. Market Fundamentalism and New Communications Regulation. *MECCSA Three-D. Issue 18*, Available at: http://www.meccsa.org.uk/news/three-d-issue-18-market-fundamentalism-and-new-communications-regulation/
Tarrow, S. 2005. *The New Transnational Activism*. New York: Cambridge University Press.
The Editors. 2012. The Future of News. *New York Observer*, March 21, Available at: http://observer.com/2012/03/opinion-the-future-of-news/
The Guardian. 2012. Greek Leftist Leader Alexis Tsipras: It's a War Between People and Capitalism. *The Guardian*, Available at: http://www.guardian.co.uk/world/2012/May/18/greek-leftist-leader-alexis-tsipras?fb=native&CMP=FBCNETTXT9038
The Official Gazette. 2000. Ley Orgánica de Telecomunicaciones, no. 36.970.
The Official Gazette. 2002. Reglamento de Radiodifusión Sonora y Televisión Abierta comunitaria de Servicio Público, sin fines de lucro, no. 37.359.
The Official Gazette. 2005. Ley de Responsabilidad en Radio y Televisión, no. 38.333.
The Official Gazette. 2011. Nueva Ley de Responsabilidad Social en Radio, Televisión y Medios Electrónicos, no. 39.610.
The Reporters without Borders. 2012. Press Freedom Index 2011–12, Available at: http://en.rsf.org/press-freedom-index-2011-2012,1043.html
The World Bank. 2001. Global Economic Prospects and Developing Countries, December.
Thompson, E. P. 1959. The New Left. *The New Reasoner*, 9: 1–17, Available at: http://marxists.org/archive/thompson-ep/1959/newleft.htm
Thompson, J. 1995. *The Media and Modernity: A Social Theory of the Media*. Cambridge: Polity Press.
Thussu, D. 1996. *International Communication*. London: Arnold Publishers.
Thussu, D. 2006. *International Communication – Continuity and Change*. London: Arnold.
Tickner, A. B. 2003. Hearing Latin American Voices in International Relations Studies. *International Studies Perspectives*, 4: 325–330.
Tickner, A. B. 2008. Latin American IR and the Primacy of lo práctico. *International Studies Review*, 10(4): 735–748.
Tilly, C. 2007. *Contienda política y democracia en Europa, 1650–2000*. Barcelona: Hacer.
Tilly, C. 2008. *Contienda política y democracia en Europa, 1650–2000*. Barcelona: Hacer.
Trigona, M. 2009. Argentina's Community Media Fights for Access and Legal Reform. *Americas Policy Program*, Available at: http://dspace.cigilibrary.org/jspui/bitstream/123456789/26340/1/Argentinas%20Community%20Media%20Fights%20for%20Access.pdf?1
Turney, M. 2002. Working with the Media. *On-line Readings in Public Relations* by Michael Turney, Available at: http://www.nku.edu/~turney/prclass/readings/media_rel.html
UNESCO. 2000. *Informe mundial sobre la Comunicación y la Información*. Madrid: Ediciones UNESCO
UNESCO. 2001. African Charter on Broadcasting. Windhoek May 3–5, Available at: http://portal.unesco.org/ci/en/files/5628/10343523830african_charter.pdf/african%2Bcharter.pdf

UNESCO. 2011. Assessment of media development in Ecuador – 2011, Available at: http://www.unesco.org/new/fileadmin/MULTIMEDIA/HQ/CI/CI/pdf/IPDC/ecuador_mdi_report_eng.pdf

Urbina Serjant, J. 2009. Venezuela. In *The Invisible Gags: New and Old Barriers to Diversity in Radio Broadcasting*, edited by AMARC ALC, Buenos Aires: AMARC, Available at: http://legislaciones.amarc.org/mordazas/eng_indice2.htm

Urribarrí, R. 2007. Medios comunitarios: el reto de formar (se) para la inclusión. *Revista Comunicación del centro Gumilla*, 137(1), Available at: http://www.saber.ula.ve/bitstream/123456789/16610/1/comunitaria.pdf

U.S. Congress. 1960. *Congressional Record: Proceedings and Debates of the 86th Congress.* 106(14). Washington, DC: USGPO.

Verón, E. 1987. La Palabra Adversativa. Observaciones sobre la enunciación política. In *El discurso político. Lenguaje y acontecimientos*. Buenos Aires: Hachette, 11–26.

Verón, E. 1998. Mediatización de lo político. Estrategias, actores y construcción de los colectivos. In *Comunicación y Política*, edited by G. De Gilles, A. Gosselin and J. Mouchon. Barcelona: Gedisa, 220–236.

Verón, E. 2001. *El Cuerpo de la Imágenes*. Buenos Aires: Norma.

Vialey, P., Belinche, M. and C. Tovar. 2008. The Media in Argentina: Democracy, Crisis and the Reconfiguration of Media Groups. In *Media in Latin America*, edited by J. Lugo-Ocando, Open University Press: Buckingham, 13–28.

Vidigal, C. 2010. Brazil: A Cordial Power? Brazilian Diplomacy in the early 21st Century. *RECIIS: R. Eletr. de Com. Inf. Inov. Saúde. Rio de Janeiro*, 4(1): 33–41.

Vocus. 2011. State of the Media Report 2011: Adapting, Surviving and Reviving, Available at: http://www.vocus.com/resources/the-guides/

Waisbord, S. 2000. Between the Rock of the State and the Hard Place of the Market. In *De-Westernizing Media Studies*, edited by J. Curran and M. Park. London: Routledge, 50–62.

Waisbord, S. 2009a. Bridging the Divide Between the Press and Civic Society: Civic Media Advocacy as 'Media Movement' in Latin America. *Nordicom Review: Nordic Research on Media & Communication*, 30: 30.

Waisbord, S. 2009b. Research Directions for Global Journalism Studies: Ideas from Latin America. *Journalism*, 10: 393.

Waisbord, S. 2010a. All-Out Media War: It's *Clarín* vs. the Kirchners, and Journalism Will Be the Loser. *Columbia Journalism Review*, Available at: http://www.cjr.org/reports/allout_media_war.php?page=all

Waisbord, S. 2010b. The Pragmatic Politics of Media Reform: Media Movements and Coalition-Building in Latin America. *Global Media and Communication* , 6(2): 133–153.

Waisbord, S. 2013. Media Policies and the Blindspots of Media Globalization: Insights from Latin America. *Media, Culture and Society*, 35(1): 132–138.

Waldman, S. and The Working Group on Information Needs of Communities. 2011. *The Information Needs of Communities: The Changing Media Landscape in a Broadband Age*, Washington, DC: Federal Communications Commission, Available at: http://transition.fcc.gov/osp/inc-report/The_Information_Needs_of_Communities.pdf

Ward, S., Gibson, R. and P. Nixon. 2003. Parties and the Internet: An Overview. In *Political Parties and the Internet: Net Gain*, edited by R. Gibson, P. Nixon and S. Ward. London: Routledge, 11–33.

Weisbrot, M. 2009. Why Latin America's Left Keeps Winning. *The Guardian*, May 1, Available at: http://www.guardian.co.uk/commentisfree/cifamerica/2009/apr/30/ecuador-election-economy

Weisbrot, M. 2010. Power versus the Press. *The Guardian*, January 8, Available at: http://www.theguardian.com/commentisfree/cifamerica/2010/jan/08/ecuador-press-freedom-media

Weisbrot, M. 2011. Honduras: America's Great Foreign Policy Disgrace. *The Guardian*, November 18, Available at: http://www.guardian.co.uk/commentisfree/cifamerica/2011/nov/18/honduras-america-foreign-policy-disgrace?INTCMP=SRCH

Williams, G. 2004. Media Industry in EU Lobbying Offensive. *Spinwatch*, Available at: http://www.spinwatch.org/index.php/issues/science/item/188-media-industry-in-eu-lobbying-offensive

Williams, R. 1960. Class and Voting in Britain. *Monthly Review*, 11(9): 327–333.

Williams, R. 1961. *The Long Revolution*. London: Chatto and Windus.

Williams, R. 1962a. *Britain in the Sixties: Communications*. Harmondsworth: Penguin.

Williams, R. 1962b. *The Existing Alternatives in Communications*. London: Fabian Society.

Williams, R. 1966. *Communications*, rev. edn. London, Chatto & Windus.

Williams, R. 1976. *Communications*, 3rd edn. London: Penguin.

Williams, R. 1980. *Marxismo y Literatura*. Barcelona: Península.

Williams, R. 1983. *Culture and Society, 1780–1950*. New York: Columbia University Press.

Wolfson, T. and P. N. Funke. 2013. Communication, Class and Concentric Media Practices: Developing a Contemporary Rubric. *New Media Society*, doi: 10.1177/1461444813481199.

World Movement for Democracy. 2011. Statement on Violations of Freedom of Expression in Ecuador, Available at: http://www.wmd.org/about/statements/statement-violations-freedom-expression-ecuador

Zibechi, R. 2012a. South American Fiber Optic Ring. Center for International Policy America's Program, April 12, Available at: http://www.cipamericas.org/archives/6734

Zibechi, R. 2012b. *Brasil Potencia: Entre la Integración Regional y Un Nuevo Imperialismo*. Chile: Quimantú.

Zuluaga, J. and M. Martínez. 2012. *Mapping Digital Media. Colombia*. London, UK: Open Society Foundations-Media Program.

Index

Note: The letter 'n' following locators refers to notes.